Planen und Lebensqualität

Planning and the Quality of Life

Colloquium Geographicum

ISSN 0588 – 3253

Herausgegeben von H. Hahn, W. Kuls und W. Lauer

Schriftleitung: H. - J. Ruckert

Band 15

Planen und Lebensqualität
Verhandlungen des 3. deutsch−britischen Symposiums
zur Angewandten Geographie

Planning and the Quality of Life
Proceedings of the 3rd Anglo−German Symposium
on Applied Geography

herausgegeben von

Gerhard Aymans, Hanns J. Buchholz und Günter Thieme

1982

In Kommission bei
FERD. DÜMMLERS VERLAG · BONN
—Dümmlerbuch 7415—

Planen und Lebensqualität / Planning and the Quality of Life

herausgegeben von

Gerhard Aymans, Hanns J. Buchholz und Günter Thieme

mit 44 Figuren, 9 Bildern, 5 Abbildungen, 2 Fotos,
1 Karte und 24 Tabellen im Text und 1 Figur,
1 Bild und 4 Karten als Beilagen

In Kommission bei

FERD. DÜMMLERS VERLAG · BONN

Dümmlerbuch 7415

Gedruckt mit Unterstützung der Deutsch-Britischen Stiftung
für das Studium der Industriegesellschaft

Printed with financial support of the Anglo-German Foundation
for the Study of Industrial Society

Alle Rechte vorbehalten

ISBN 3-427-74151-6

© **1982 Ferd. Dümmlers Verlag, 5300 Bonn 1**
Herstellung: Richard Schwarzbold, Witterschlick b. Bonn

Vorwort

P l a n e n u n d L e b e n s q u a l i t ä t war das Leitthema des Dritten Deutsch-Britischen Symposiums zur Angewandten Geographie, das vom 15.-20. Mai 1978 in Bonn und Bochum stattfand. Wie die beiden vorausgegangenen Symposien in Gießen, Würzburg und München (1973) sowie in Aberdeen und Newcastle upon Tyne (1975) suchte auch das dritte in Bonn und Bochum den Gedankenaustausch über Fragen der Landesentwicklung in Großbritannien und der Bundesrepublik Deutschland zu intensivieren. Das Leitthema P l a n e n u n d L e b e n s q u a l i t ä t sollte das Gespräch vor allem auf jene Fragen lenken, die sich aus den Bemühungen beider Staaten um eine V e r b e s s e r u n g d e r L e b e n s q u a l i t ä t ergeben.

Der vorliegende Verhandlungsband entspricht in besonderer Weise den Zielen des "Colloquium Geographicum", einer wissenschaftlichen Schriftenreihe, die sich ausdrücklich als internationales Diskussionsforum der Geographie versteht. Für die Aufnahme der Beiträge in diese Reihe sei daher den Herausgebern des Colloquium Geographicum recht herzlich gedankt.

Bei der Vorbereitung und Durchführung des Symposiums haben Veranstalter und Teilnehmer viel freundliche Unterstützung erfahren, für die auch an dieser Stelle herzlich gedankt sei. Dieser Dank gilt vor allem der Deutsch-Britischen Stiftung für das Studium der Industriegesellschaft (London), die die Veranstaltung selbst und die Drucklegung der dort gehaltenen Vorträge in diesem Band aus ihren Mitteln tatkräftig unterstützt hat, sowie dem Projektdirektor der Stiftung, Herrn Dr. Hans Wiener, der uns schon in der Vorbereitungsphase manche Last abgenommen und an allen Veranstaltungen des Symposiums mit großem Interesse teilgenommen hat. Unser Dank gilt aber auch den Institutionen und Personen, die uns im Rahmen des Exkursionsprogramms empfangen und mit uns über Probleme ihres Zuständigkeitsbereiches gesprochen haben. Bei dem auf der Burg Altena vom Oberkreisdirektor des Märkischen Kreises, Herrn Dr. Albath, veranlaßten Empfang sind dies vor allem der Landrat, Herr Dr. Horstert, und der Kreisplaner, Herr Dr. von Borcke, gewesen, im Rathaus von Lüdenscheid der Baudirektor der Stadt, Herr Dipl. Ing. Hering, und Herr Dipl. Ing. Droste, im Rathaus von Herne der Leiter des Planungsamtes der Stadt, Herr Dipl. Ing. Leyh, sowie Herr Holtkamp, im Rathaus von Marl der Leiter des Amtes für Wirtschaftsförderung, Herr Dr. Marquard, bei der Bootsfahrt auf der Rheinachse zwischen Duisburg und Wesel der Geschäftsführer der Niederrheinischen Industrie- und Handelskammer, Herr Dipl. Volksw. Ewers, sowie Herr Martin und auf Haus Schmidthausen der Oberkreisdirektor des Kreises Kleve, Herr Dr. Schneider, dessen Empfang zugleich die Schlußveranstaltung des Symposiums gewesen ist. Aus dem Kreis der Teilnehmer haben Prof. Dr. K.A. Sinnhuber und Dr. J.A. Hellen dafür gesorgt, daß es auf keiner Gesprächsebene auch nur die geringsten Verständigungsschwierigkeiten gab. Ihnen allen, aber auch den vielen nicht einzeln genannten Helferinnen und Helfern danken wir herzlich.

Preface

"P l a n n i n g a n d t h e Q u a l i t y o f L i f e" was the main theme of the third German-British Symposium on Applied Geography held in Bonn and Bochum from the 15th to the 20th May, 1978. Like the two previous ones in Giessen, Würzburg and Munich (1973) and Aberdeen and Newcastle upon Tyne (1975), the third symposium set out to intensify the exchange of views concerning questions of regional development in Great Britain and the Federal Republic of Germany. With "P l a n n i n g t h e Q u a l i t y o f L i f e" as its leitmotiv, the objective was to concentrate the discussions upon questions arising from attempts at i m p r o v i n g t h e q u a l i t y o f l i f e in both countries.

The present volume fulfils in a special way the objectives of "Colloquium Geographicum", a scientific series primarily devoted to the publication of international discussions in geography. We are grateful to the editors of this series for accepting the papers for publication in Colloquium Geographicum.

During the preparations for and the course of the symposium the organizers and the participants received a great deal of friendly support, for which we would like to express our deep appreciation. Our especial thanks are due to the Anglo-German Foundation for the Study of Industrial Society in London, which contributed substantially through the donation of a grant both for the symposium itself and for the publication of the papers presented in this volume. We are also greatly obligated to Dr. Hans Wiener, the Project Director of the Foundation, for his encouraging help during the symposium's preparatory phase, and for his keen interest and participation in all the events involved in it. We would also place on record our gratitude to those institutions and persons whom we visited during the excursions and with whom we discussed problems falling within their areas of responsibility. Our thanks and appreciation are therefore due to the following persons: Dr. Albath, Oberkreisdirektor of the Märkische Kreis, for arranging the reception at Burg Altena, as also to Dr. Horstert, Landrat, and to the Kreis planner Dr. von Borcke and to Herr Dipl. Ing. Leyh and Herr Holtkamp; both of the planning department of the Herne town hall; Herr Dipl. Ing. Hering, head of the surveyor's office, and to Herr Dipl. Ing. Droste, both of the Lüdenscheid town hall; Dr. Marquard, director of the office for economic development at the town hall in Marl; Herr Dipl. Volksw. Ewers, manager of the Lower Rhineland Chamber of Industry and Commerce, and to Herr Martin who accompanied the party on the boat trip on the Rhine between Duisburg and Wesel; and, lastly, to Dr. Schneider, Oberkreisdirektor of the Kreis Kleve, whose reception at the Haus Schmidthausen provided the closing event of the Symposium. From the circle of participants Prof. Dr. K.A. Sinnhuber and Dr. J.A. Hellen made sure that none of the conversational levels involved even the smallest difficulty in comprehension. To all those mentioned above, as well as to the many helpers not included here, we extend our deepest expressions of appreciation.

Inhalt

	Seite
AYMANS, GERHARD: Einleitung	7
Teilnehmer am Deutsch-Britischen Symposium zur Angewandten Geographie in Bonn und Bochum	11
PRINGLE, DAVID G.: Measuring the quality of life: Some fundamental methodological problems	15
GATZWEILER, HANS-PETER: Situation and tendencies of the regional distribution in the quality of life in the Federal Republic of Germany	27
WHITELEGG, JOHN: Who perceives the problem and who prescribes the solution: A critique of contemporary regional planning philosophy	45
KLUCZKA, GEORG: Zur Planungssituation ländlicher Problemgebiete	61
THIEME, GÜNTER / HANS-DIETER LAUX: Regional disparities in West German agriculture	73
PACIONE, MICHAEL: Planning the quality of life in rural communities	89
PAESLER, REINHARD: Strukturschwache Gebiete am Rande der Region München - Die Problematik von Strukturverbesserungsmaßnahmen am Beispiel des Landkreises Landsberg/Lech	101
WILD, M. TREVOR: The textile regions of Western Europe as problem regions	113
DAWSON, ANDREW H.: Putting back the land - The adaption of environment and settlement in Fife, Scotland, to the closure of coal mining	127
JONES, PHILIP N.: Bro and Blaenau in industrial South Wales: Reconciling the irreconcileable?	149
BLOWERS, ANDREW: Industry versus environment in the metropolitan fringe	161
CHALKLEY, BRIAN: Uran renewal and industry	185
HUSAIN, M. SOHAIL: The role of the local authority and the interaction of policy determinants in urban housing strategy: the example of Nottingham	193
WADE, ALLAN J.R.: Problems of renewal and redevelopment in a medium sized town	209
DUFFIELD, BRIAN: Leisure as a tool for social development in oil-affected areas of the Highlands and Islands of Scotland	221
BUCHHOLZ, HANNS JÜRGEN: Exkursion Ruhrgebiet	239
AYMANS, GERHARD / GÜNTER THIEME: Exkursion Niederrhein	259

Einführung

Raumordnungspolitik wird in Großbritannien wie in der Bundesrepublik Deutschland grundsätzlich als Teil einer übergeordneten Sozialpolitik verstanden, die interregionale Ausgleichsziele zu verfolgen oder — in der Sprache des Bundesraumordnungsprogramms — gleichwertige Lebensverhältnisse in allen Regionen zu schaffen hat. In britischen Programmen, beispielsweise im White Paper on Northeastern England (Hailsham White Paper) ist schon sehr früh von einem verbesserten Lebensumfeld (improved living environment) als vorrangigem Ziel die Rede, desgleichen in vielen späteren Weißbüchern, Programmen und Plänen. In der Bundesrepublik Deutschland schlagen sich, nicht zuletzt aus verfassungsrechtlichen Gründen, erst später ausgleichspolitische Auffassungen auch in der Raumordnungspolitik des Bundes mit ähnlichen Formulierungen nieder. So spricht das Bundesraumordnungsprogramm von 1974 schon in seinem ersten Satz die Ziele der Raumordnungspolitik als Teil des übergeordneten sozialpolitischen Zieles der V e r b e s s e r u n g d e r L e b e n s q u a l i t ä t an.

Begriff und Inhalt dessen, was V e r b e s s e r u n g d e r L e b e n s q u a l i t ä t umschreibt, sind indessen weder in Großbritannien noch in der Bundesrepublik Deutschland unumstritten. Die Kritiker sprechen von einer Leerformel, die auch bei einer inhaltlichen Anreicherung auf der Ebene konkreter Maßnahmen keine wirksame Raumordnungspolitik begründen könne, da sie von einheitlichen Normen ausgehe, die komparativen Vorteile der unterschiedlich ausgestatteten Regionen jedoch außer acht lasse. Auf die komparativen Vorteile der Regionen aber zielen die zahlreichen privaten Investoren wie auch jene Teile der öffentlichen Hand, die aufgrund ihrer Aufgabe dem Wachstumsziel der Gesamtwirtschaft verpflichtet sind und so zum Abbau interregionaler Disparitäten nicht herangezogen werden können. Treibt man die durch Normen bestimmte Gleichstellung regionaler Ungleichheiten auf die Spitze, so die Kritiker, so kann zu der einen Gefahr, daß die angestrebten Ziele regional nicht erreicht werden, leicht die andere hinzukommen, daß die regional erreichbaren Ziele nicht einmal mehr angestrebt werden.

Diese wenigen Bemerkungen zur Raumordnungspolitik in Großbritannien und der Bundesrepublik Deutschland einerseits und der sich mit ihr auseinandersetzenden Kritik andererseits zeigen zur Genüge, daß es durchaus sinnvoll ist, die jüngere regionale Entwicklung in beiden Ländern auf der Grundlage der Ergebnisse konkreter, problembezogener Untersuchungen im Rahmen eines Symposiums P l a n e n u n d L e b e n s q u a l i t ä t zur Erörterung zu stellen. Die wesentlichste Grundlage dieser Diskussion waren die während des Symposiums gehaltenen Vorträge, die in ihrer Spannweite von allgemeinen und regional begrenzten Themen, Studien aus ländlichen Räumen wie auch aus Ballungsgebieten, teils stärker analytisch, teils eher planungsorientiert, die vielfältigen Interessen der beteiligten Geographen aus Wissenschaft und Planung widerspiegeln.

Diese Vorträge werden hier in einer von thematischen Zusammenhängen bestimmten Reihenfolge schriftlich vorgelegt. Auf eine Veröffentlichung der sich jeweils anschließenden Diskussionen mußte verzichtet werden, da hierzu nur persönliche Aufzeichnungen der Herausgeber vorlagen, die den tatsächlichen Verlauf der Auseinandersetzungen notwendigerweise nur unvollständig hätten wiedergeben können. In den Anhang dieses Bandes aufgenommen wurde jedoch, dem Wunsche verschiedener Teilnehmer und des Sponsors der Veranstaltung folgend, eine zusammenfassende Darstellung der Exkursionsprogramme der Veranstaltung. Diese gibt nicht den Verlauf der Exkursionen im einzelnen wieder, doch richtet sie noch einmal den Blick auf Tatbestände, die den Veranstaltern im Rahmen des Leitthemas P l a n e n u n d L e b e n s q u a l i t ä t damals wichtig erschienen.

Tagungen wie diese — so war eingangs ausgeführt worden — dienen dem Gedankenaustausch der Beteiligten. In der Tat gibt es für die mit den Problemen des jeweils anderen Landes befaßten Geographen kaum eine bessere Möglichkeit zur aktuellen und authentischen Information als ein solches durch Feldstudien ergänztes Symposium. Nimmt man die wechselseitigen Forschungsaufenthalte britischer und deutscher Geographen allein zwischen dieser Tagung und der Publikation ihrer Ergebnisse zum Maßstab für den Erfolg, so ist dies ein überaus erfreulicher Beweis dafür, daß auf der Grundlage solcher Treffen sowohl bestehende Kontakte intensiviert als auch neue Verbindungen angeknüpft werden können. Schon dieses Ergebnis rechtfertigt den Wunsch nach einer Fortsetzung des nun fast schon zu einer Institution gewordenen Deutsch-Britischen Symposiums der Geographen.

Introduction

In both Great Britain and the Federal Republic regional planning policy is basically understood to be part of a higher level social policy aimed at the reduction of inter-regional disparities, or — in the words of the Federal Regional Planning Programme — to create equal living conditions within all regions. In British programmes the pre-eminent goal of an improved living environment was mentioned quite early, as for example in the Hailsham White Paper on North-East England or later white papers, programmes and plans. Lastly, it is due to constitutional reasons that such points of view were formulated somewhat later within the regional planning policy in the Federal Republic. Accordingly the Federal Regional Planning Programme of 1974 stated in its opening sentence, that the aims of the regional planning policy are part of an overall socio-political goal of i m p r o v i n g l i v i n g q u a l i t y.

In neither Great Britain nor the Federal Republic of Germany do the concept and content of what is embraced by the term "i m p r o v e m e n t o f t h e q u a l i t y o f l i f e" go wholly undisputed. The critics speak of an empty formula incapable of establishing an effective regional policy even if strengthened through the application of concrete measures. This, the critics would say, is due to the fact that these concepts are derived from unified norms which disregard the comparative advantanges of the differently equipped regions. The aim of numerous private investors, as also that of certain sectors of those government bodies whose objective and task it is to increase overall economic growth, is directed towards these very same comparative advantages and their help could scarcely be enlisted in attempts to reduce inter-regional disparities. If the levelling-out of regional inequalities in accordance with certain norms is over-emphasized, some critics predict that in addition to the one danger — that the aims aspired to cannot be attained regionally — another one can easily be added, namely that the attainable regional aims will not even be striven for. These few remarks on the regional planning policies in Great Britain and the Federal Republic of Germany on the one hand, and its pertinent criticism on the other, provide sufficient reason to place the more recent regional developments in both countries under discussion, basing them on the results of concrete problem-oriented research within the framework of the "P l a n n i n g a n d t h e Q u a l i t y o f L i f e" symposium.

The quintessential basis of this discussion were the papers presented during the symposium, which encompassed themes from the general to the regional, studies from the rural areas to the agglomerations, in part analytic, in part planning-oriented. These mirror the multifarious interests of the geographers, working in research and planning, who participated. Their papers are presented here in a thematically coherent order. The idea of publishing the discussions had to be abandoned because only the personal notes taken by the editors were available and these would have provided only an incomplete record of what was said. However, in accordance with the request of several participants as well as the sponsor, the symposium's excursion programme is presented in a comprehensive form as a supplement to this volume. Here the idea is not to describe the excursions in complete detail but rather to point out once again what seemed relevant to the organizers with regard to the leitmotiv P l a n n i n g a n d t h e Q u a l i t y o f L i f e.

As explained at the outset, conferences such as this make possible the exchange of views and ideas between the participants. There is scarcely a better opportunity than through participation in a symposium supplemented by such field studies for geographers working on the problems of their reciprocal countries to meet, discuss and exchange the most recent and authentic information. If one regards the reciprocal research visits of British and German geographers that have taken place between the date of the conference and the publication of its results as a measure of success, then it is a pleasant affirmation that on the basis of such meetings existing contacts can not only be intensified but new ones can also be initiated. Already this result justifies the wish for the continuation of the British-German Symposia, which are already well on the way to becoming an established custom.

Teilnehmer am Deutsch-Britischen Symposium
zur Angewandten Geographie in Bonn und Bochum

AYMANS, Prof. Dr. G.: Geographische Institute
der Universität Bonn
Franziskanerstraße 2
5300 Bonn 1

BLOWERS, Dr. A.: Faculty of Social Sciences
The Open University
Waltan Hall
Milton Keynes MK7 6AA / England

BUCHHOLZ, Prof. Dr. H.J.: Geographisches Institut
Ruhr-Universität Bochum
Universitätsstraße 150
4630 Bochum-Querenburg

CHALKLEY, B.A. Ph.D.: Geography Department
Plymouth Politechnic
Drakes Circus
Plymouth, Devon / England

DAWSON, Dr. A.: Department of Geography
University of St. Andrews
St. Andrews, Fife KY16 9AL
Scotland

DEITERS, Prof. Dr. J.: Universität Osnabrück
Fachbereich 2
Postfach 44 69
4500 Osnabrück

DODT, Dr. J.: Geographisches Institut
Ruhr-Universität Bochum
Universitätsstraße 150
4630 Bochum-Querenburg

DUFFIELD, Dr. B.S.: Tourism and Recreation Research Unit.
Department of Geography
Edinburgh University
Edinburgh 4SS / Scotland

ELKINS, Prof. T.H.: Arts Building
University of Sussex
Brighton BN1 9QN / England

FLÜCHTER, Dr. W.: Geographisches Institut
Ruhr-Universität Bochum

FULLERTON, Dr. B.:
Universitätsstraße 150
4630 Bochum-Querenburg
Department of Geography
University of Newcastle
Newcastle upon Tyne NE1 7RU
England

GAEBE, Priv. Doz. Dr. W.:
Auf dem Steppenberg 4a
5330 Königswinter

GATZWEILER, Dr. H.P.:
Bundesforschungsanstalt für
Landeskunde und Raumordnung
Postfach 130
5300 Bonn 2

GREENWOOD, Prof. R.:
Department of Geography
University College
Swansea SA2 8PP / England

HALL, Dr. J.M.:
Department of Geography
Queen Mary College
University of London
Mile End Road, London E1 4NS
England

HAUTH, Studiendirektor P.:
Am Rödelstein 4
5427 Bad Ems

HEINEBERG, Prof. Dr. H.:
Westf. Wilhelms-Universität Münster
Robert-Koch-Straße 26
4400 Münster / Westfalen

HELLEN, Dr. A.J.:
Department of Geography
University of Newcastle
Newcastle upon Tyne NE1 7RU
England

HOMMEL, Dr. M.:
Geographisches Institut
Ruhr-Universität Bochum
Universitätsstraße 150
4630 Bochum-Querenburg

HOTTES, Prof. Dr. K.H.:
Geographisches Institut
Ruhr-Universität Bochum
Universitätsstraße 150
4630 Bochum-Querenburg

HUSAIN, Dr. S.:
Department of Geography
University of Southampton
Southampton SO9 5NH / England

JONES, Dr. P. N.:	Geography Department The University of Hull Cottingham Road Hull HU6 7RX / England
KLUCZKA, Prof. Dr. G.:	Institut für Anthropogeographie Angew. Geogr. und Kartogr. der Freien Universität Berlin Grunewaldstraße 35 1000 Berlin 41
KRONER, Studienrat B.:	Im Auel 44c 5350 Euskirchen
KULS, Prof. Dr. W.:	Geographische Institute der Universität Bonn Franziskanerstraße 2 5300 Bonn 1
LAUX, Dr. H.-D.:	Geographische Institute der Universität Bonn Franziskanerstraße 2 5300 Bonn 1
LEISTER, Prof. Dr. I.:	Geographische Institute der Universität Marburg/Lahn Deutsches Haus Deutschhausstraße 10 3550 Marburg/Lahn
LIENAU, Prof. Dr. C.:	Westf. Wilhelms-Universität Münster Robert-Koch-Straße 26 4400 Münster/Westfalen
NIEDERBÖSTER, Dr. H.:	Margeritenweg 7 2121 Vögelsen b. Lüneburg
PACIONE, Dr. M.:	Department of Geography University of Strathclyde Glasgow Glasgow/Scotland
PAESLER, Dr. R.:	Institut für Wirtschaftsgeographie der Universität München Ludwigstraße 28 8000 München 22
PRINGLE, Dr. D.:	Geography Department St. Patricks College Maynooth, Co Kildare / Ireland

SCHÖLLER, Prof. Dr. P.:	Geographisches Institut Ruhr-Universität Bochum Universitätsstraße 150 4630 Bochum-Querenburg
SINNHUBER, Prof. Dr. K.A.:	Geographisches Institut der Wirtschaftsuniversität Franz-Klein-Gasse A 1190 Wien / Österreich
SPORBECK, Dr. O.:	Geographisches Institut Ruhr-Universität Bochum Universitätsstraße 150 4630 Bochum-Querenburg
THIEME, Dr. G.:	Geographische Institute der Universität Bonn Franziskanerstraße 2 5300 Bonn 1
TIETZE, Dr. W.:	Einsteinstraße 5 3180 Wolfsburg
UHLIG, Prof. Dr. H.:	Geographisches Institut der Universität Gießen Landgraf Philipp-Platz 2 6300 Gießen
WADE, Allan J.R.:	Borough Planning Office Summerfields, Bohemia Road Hastings, East Sussex / England
WHITELEGG, John, B.A. PhD.:	Geography Department University of Lancaster Bailrigg / Lancaster / England
WIENER, Dr. H.B.:	Anglo German Foundation for the Study of Industrial Society St. Stephen's House Victoria Embankment Westminster, London SW1A 2LA England
WILD, Dr. T.:	Geography Department The University of Hull Cottingham Road Hull HU6 7RX / England
WOODRUFFE, Dr. B.J.:	Department of Geography University of Southampton Southampton SO9 5NH / England

MEASURING THE QUALITY OF LIFE: SOME FUNDAMENTAL METHODOLOGICAL PROBLEMS

with 4 figures and 2 tables

DAVID G. PRINGLE

Introduction

The quality of life is a subjective concept which means different things to different individuals. To some people the quality of life is largely determined by aspects of their material well-being (e.g. income, housing standards), whereas less tangible criteria (e.g. friends, peace of mind) may be more important to others. In short, the features which constitute the quality of life vary considerably from one individual to the next.

Nevertheless, despite the difficulty of defining exactly what is meant by the 'quality of life', it is obvious that it varies over space. People living in certain areas generally have a higher quality of life than those living in other areas. This fact makes the quality of life a legitimate and highly pertinent subject for geographical enquiry.

To facilitate objectively in this enquiry, a number of attempts have been made to derive quantitative measures of the quality of life. This, however, causes a number of problems. The major difficulty is that the quality of life cannot be measured directly, but may only be quantified using surrogate measures. The approach adopted in geography is often the same. First, the study area is subdivided into a number of spatial units for which data are available. Second, a number of measurable features which either contribute to the quality of life, or which may be regarded as a suitable surrogate for the quality of life, are identified. These are referred to in this paper as the 'constituent elements'. Third, data are collected for each constituent element for each spatial unit. Variations in the size of the spatial units are typically controlled for by expressing the data as percentages. Finally, the measures of each of the constituent elements are aggregated to form a composite index of the quality of life for each spatial unit.

Individual studies vary considerably in detail, but the overall approach is generally as outlined above. D.M. SMITH (1973), for example, in a study of social well-being in the United States measured 47 features of social well-being (classified under the headings: 'income, wealth and employment'; 'environment'; 'health'; 'education'; 'social disorganization'; and 'alienation and participation') for each of 48 states (Alaska and Hawaii were omitted). These measures were then aggregated to form a composite index using principal components analysis. Likewise, P.L. KNOX (1974) measured 53 features for 145 local authorities in England and Wales. These were aggregated using principal components analysis to form a composite index of the 'level of living'. Similar approaches have also been adopted by numerous local authorities (e.g. see AMOS, 1970; TITTERINGTON, NORMINGTON, 1970; DOE, 1977; Project Team, 1977).

The approach is illustrated here using data on social problems in the Belfast Urban Area in 1971. (The results of this analysis are reported in more detail elsewhere (BOAL, DOHERTY and PRINGLE, 1974; 1978)). The urban area was first divided into 97 relatively homogeneous social areas, for each of which data were collected on six types of social problem (viz. male unemployment; children in care; juvenile delinquency; illegitimate births; infant mortality; and deaths from bronchitis). The percentage incidence of each type of problem was calculated for each area, and then correlated to yield a correlation matrix (table 1). This matrix was analysed using principal components analysis. The scores on the first compo-

Table 1: Correlation matrix.

		U	C	J	I	M	B
male unemployment	U	1.00	0.50	0.56	0.32	0.35	0.50
children in care	C	0.50	1.00	0.47	0.33	0.18	0.53
juvenile delinquency	J	0.56	0.47	1.00	0.19	0.24	0.37
illegitimacy	I	0.32	0.33	0.19	1.00	0.13	0.34
infant mortality	M	0.35	0.18	0.24	0.13	1.00	0.16
bronchitis deaths	B	0.50	0.53	0.37	0.34	0.16	1.00

nent (which explains 47 per cent of the total variance) may be treated as a composite index of 'social malaise'. When mapped (figure 1) the first component quite clearly highlights the inner city. It might also be noted that it cuts across the religious divide (i.e. both Protestant and Catholic areas are identified as 'bad').

It might be argued that 'social malaise' is not quite the same as the 'quality of life'. This is true, but both concepts are similar in that they are both rather nebulous, and can only be precisely defined relative to their constituent elements. Both require a similar aggregative measurement methodology. It is this aggregative methodology which is the subject of this paper.

It might be noted that a similar methodology is required to quantify other related concepts such as 'social well-being', 'multiple need', 'level of living', 'multiple deprivation' etc.

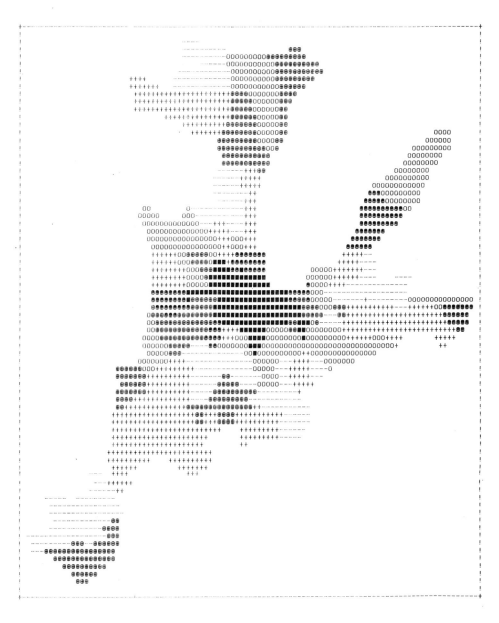

Fig 1: Map of scores on the first principle component

Objectives when measuring the quality of life

In order to assess the effectiveness of a composite index, and its methodological problems, it is useful to consider the reasons for quantifying. At least four alternative objectives may be identified:
1. To identify the areas with the lowest quality of life, in order that they might receive priority attention.
2. To monitor changes over time. This would be useful if one wished to evaluate the cost effectiveness of a particular social policy.
3. To help develop theories to explain the causes of regional disparities in the quality of life.
4. To develop a sampling frame for questionnaire or field research. For example, the scores on the first two components might be used to devise a regional typology. Different types of areas could then be compared using more detailed research techniques.

For simplicity, this paper only discusses the effectiveness of the composite social malaise index relative to the first objective (i.e. to identify the areas with the lowest quality of life). The other objectives are mentioned briefly at the end of the paper.

Identification of the areas with the lowest quality of life has obvious practical implications. Government thinking in many fields currently favours a policy of positive territorial discrimination, whereby the most deprived areas are designated to receive priority attention. This policy has been widely adopted, but it is often arguable whether the areas designated for assistance are actually the worst. Some writers even suggest that there may be an 'inverse care law', whereby the amount of ameliorative assistance received by each area is inversely related to its need for assistance (e.g. DUNCAN, 1974). An objective quantitative measure of the quality of life would obviously prove invaluable for identifying which areas actually are most in need.

It is argued, however, that an *objective* measure of the quality of life is not possible due to the fact that the researcher must, in the absence of a definition of 'quality of life', make a number of arbitrary decisions in the course of an empirical study. Three such decisions are considered:
1. The choice of the *number* of constituent elements to be aggregated to form the composite index.
2. The choice of *which* constituent elements to include.
3. The choice of *weights* to be given to each element when aggregating.

These are now illustrated using the empirical data for Belfast.

1. The number of constituent elements:

The social malaise index depicted in figure 1 is an aggregate measure of six different types of social problem, but what would happen if we only used five types of problem?

To test, the study reported above was replicated using five social problems. (Infant mortality was omitted). The map of the scores on the first component was found to be very similar to that of the scores for the original study. In fact, the map of the scores in the replicated study is almost identical to that shown in figure 1. This is reflected by the high correlation coefficient between the two indices (r = 0.76). One might be tempted to conclude that the two indices are more or less the same and that it makes very little difference if infant mortality is included or not.

This conclusion requires closer investigation. If the objective is to identify the worst areas, both indices should identify the same areas. This is not the case. The degree of overlap between the n worst areas as identified by each index is

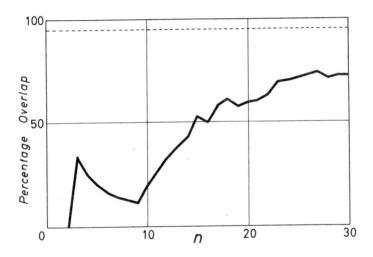

Fig. 2: Percentage overlap between the original study and replication 1

graphed in figure 2. For example, if the 10 worst areas are to be identified (i.e. n = 10), only 2 (i.e. 20 per cent) are amongst the 10 worst areas identified by each index. The percentage overlap generally increases as the number of areas to be 'designated' is increased, but even if 30 areas are designated (i.e. almost one third of the city) the percentage overlap is still only 73 per cent. The implication is that using either of these two indices we cannot be sure of identifying the worst areas with a 95 per cent confidence. This would only be the case if the percentage overlap was consistently higher than 95 per cent.

By reducing the number of constituent elements from 6 to 5, we make a relatively large reduction in the amount of information used in the construction of the composite index. One would expect that the addition of one extra element would make proportionately less impact as the total number of constituent ele-

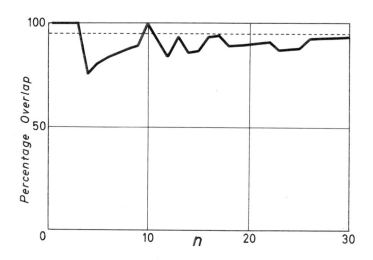

Fig. 3: Percentage overlap between replication 2 and replication 3

ments is increased. This hypothesis was tested by replicating the study two more times using 10 and 11 constituent elements respectively (see table 2). The percentage overlap between these two replications is depicted in figure 3. Although still generally short of our desired 95 per cent, the overlaps show a marked improvement relative to figure 2.

Table 2: Summary of constituent elements used in each replication.

original study (6)	male unemployment; children in care; juvenile court convictions; illegitimate births; infant mortality; deaths from bronchitis.
replication 1 (5)	male unemployment; children in care; juvenile court convictions; illegitimate births; deaths from bronchitis
replication 2 (10)	male unemployment; children in care; juvenile court convictions; illegitimate births; infant mortality; deaths from bronchitis; overcrowding; female unemployment; juvenile unemployment; deaths from pneumonia.
replication 3 (11)	male unemployment; children in care; juvenile court convictions; illegitimate births; infant mortality; deaths from bronchitis; overcrowding; female unemployment; juvenile unemployment; deaths from pneumonia; illegitimacy (measure 2).
replication 4 (5)	children in care; juvenile court convictions; illegitimate births; infant mortality; deaths from bronchitis.

The evidence therefore suggests that the composite indices only become sufficiently stable to satisfy normal standards of objectivity if they are based upon a large number of constituent elements (possibly 15 or more). Composite indices based upon smaller numbers of constituent elements are, in the absence of a fully defined concept, too arbitrary to be considered objective.

2. The choice of constituent elements:

The second arbitrary decision which the researcher must make is the choice of which constituent elements to include. The first replication was based upon 5 elements, infant mortality having been omitted. The study was replicated a fourth time using 5 elements, but this time male unemployment was omitted to see how the choice of elements affected the empirical results.

The resulting index shows a dramatic improvement upon that in which infant mortality was omitted (see figure 4). The percentage overlap with the areas

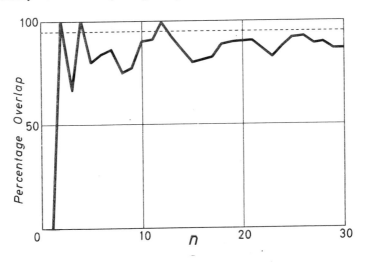

Fig. 4: Percentage overlap between the original study and replication 4

identified as worst by the original index is generally much higher than in figure 2, although it settles down in the 80 to 90 per cent range - still much lower than the desired 95 per cent.

The reasons for the difference between omitting infant mortality and omitting male unemployment may be understood if one re-examines the correlation matrix (table 1). The correlations involving male unemployment are much higher than those involving infant mortality. In fact, infant mortality has its highest correlation with male unemployment, whereas male unemployment's lowest correlation is with infant mortality. Because male unemployment is reflected to a much greater extent by the other types of problem, its omission makes relatively little difference to the component scores. Infant mortality, on the other hand, is more unique, therefore it is not reflected by the other types of problem to the same extent and its omission consequently has a proportionately greater impact upon the component scores.

This finding highlights an odd paradox. Male unemployment, by virtue of its high correlations with the other types of problems, might be regarded as more typical of social malaise as a whole, than infant mortality which has lower correlations. However, the decision to include or omit male unemployment has much less bearing upon the composite index than the decision to include or omit infant mortality. In other words, the more typical an element is of the concept to be measured, the less impact it appears to make upon the values of the composite index.

This in turn introduces a contradiction. It was argued in the previous section that stability in the composite index required a relatively large number of constituent elements. But, as we increase the number of constituent elements, we are more likely to have to introduce elements which are less central to the concept to be measured. Increasing the number of elements may therefore lead to a decrease in the stability of the composite index.

3. The weighting of elements:

The third arbitrary decision to be made is the choice of the weight to be given to each element when constructing the composite index. This may be regarded as an extension of the choice of elements dilemma. If an element is omitted it is equivalent to giving it a weight of zero. Variations in the weights given to a specific set of constituent elements result in variations in the composite index which may be as large as those described in the previous two sections. There is little to be gained by empirically demonstrating this fact. Rather, discussion is confined to some of the less obvious aspects of weighting.

In practice the researcher may not make an explicit decision regarding weights, but the weights may be determined by his choice of method of aggregation. For example, using principal components analysis each element is weighted in proportion to its component loading. The component loadings in turn reflect the extent to which each element is correlated with each other element. Elements with high correlations with the other elements (e.g. male unemployment) are given a large weight, whereas those with low correlations are given a small weight. The method is objective in the sense that the researcher does not need to assign weights based upon subjective value judgements, but it is also arbitrary because the weights do not necessarily reflect the true importance of the elements to the quality of life. One element might be a very important facet of the quality of life, but may not be highly correlated with the other elements!

One alternative might be to decide in advance what weight is to be given to each element based upon an a priori notion of relative importance. The subjective nature of this approach is obvious, but it may be preferable to feigning objectivity by feeding the data into a computer and letting the computer 'make the decision'. At least the limitations would be obvious to everyone and not obscured by the use of pseudoscientific jargon.

A refinement upon this approach might be to conduct a sample survey to find out how various people evaluate the importance of each of the constituent elements of the quality of life. This information could then be used to assign an average set of weights to be used in the construction of a composite index. This approach has considerable appeal, given the alternatives, but it tends to obscure the fact that each individual has a different set of values. Except for individuals whose values correspond fairly closely with the average, the composite index will not be a reliable measure of the quality of life at the individual level. Further, there is reason to believe that values vary systematically over space. For example, people living in advanced countries will tend to place more emphasis upon aesthetics, whereas those living in underdeveloped regions will tend to place more value upon the essentials (food and shelter). A composite index of the quality of life may therefore incorporate huge distortions even at a spatial or aggregate scale.

Discussion

The three decisions discussed above each introduce an arbitrary element into the composite index. This problem is probably recognised to some extent by most researchers who construct composite indices, but it is suggested that many researchers may not be fully aware of the degree of subjectivity which may be introduced. As illustrated above, the areas which are identified as the worst, using slightly different indices, vary to such an extent that one could not be 95 per cent confident of having identified the areas which actually are the worst. In other words, we fall short of minimal statistical standards of reliability.

The degree of variability is largely caused by the relatively small number of elements considered. If the empirical examples had been based upon 50 constituent elements, the results would not have been so spectacular. Nevertheless the arbitrary element would still be present. Also, as the number of elements is increased it becomes increasingly more difficult to understand exactly what the index actually measures.

Although not discussed in this paper, the degree of subjectivity introduced by these three arbitrary decisions is often sufficiently large to thwart the other three objectives for quantifying, as identified in the second section above. This can be illustrated by replicating an empirical study in a manner analogous to that described above, except that the results are assessed relative to different objectives.

The fundamental problem is that we are trying to quantify something which is at best only loosely defined. Composite indices of this type may be very useful in the initial stages of a research project, when one merely wants to gain a general overall impression of the spatial distribution of the quality of life or its major dimensions. This paper should not be construed as an attack upon such studies. However, if one wishes to proceed to a more incisive analysis of the quality of life, the concept must be defined explicitly and more precisely. This would necessitate specifying the constituent elements and the weights to be given to each, in order to remove the need for each researcher to make his own arbitrary decisions. However, given that each individual has a different perception of what constitutes the quality of life, it is very unlikely that any one definition would gain a concensus of support.

Some other fundamental difficulties would also have to be faced. For example, many constituent elements of the quality of life are themselves unquantifiable (e.g. satisfaction). Also it may not always make sense to add the effects of constituent elements together. For example, areas with a high cost of living might be regarded as 'bad' in terms of the quality of life. Areas with high incomes might be regarded as 'good', yet these areas tend to be those with the highest cost of living. It does not make much sense to try to add the effects of these two elements together, even with weighting. Rather, it is more reasonable to divide income by cost of living to create a new element: spending power.

The point about this simple example is that it is not sufficient to simply add the effects of constituent elements together. We require a theory of how each element is related to the others. For example, outmigration might be regarded as a symptom of a low quality of life, but if the area is overpopulated it may lead to a higher quality of life for those who remain. On the other hand, if it is underpopulated, migration might lead to an even lower quality of life for those who remain. Each region needs to be considered on its own merits. The region must also be considered in the context of a larger system - changes in any one region tend to have ramifications for other regions.

Simple composite indices have a role to play, but only in the initial stages of research. To continue measuring the quality of life using such crude indices is, in the terminology of HARVEY (1973, p. 144), 'counter-revolutionary':

> 'Mapping even more evidence of man's patent inhumanity to
> man is counter-revolutionary in the sense that it allows the
> bleeding-heart liberal in us to pretend we are contributing to a
> solution when in fact we are not.'

A more plausible alternative, although not particularly radical, might be to accept that the quality of life is an arbitrary concept which means different things to different people. Rather than attempt to quantify the unquantifiable, it may be better to focus research upon each of the constituent elements of the quality of life in an attempt to understand their inter-relationships, as opposed to aggregating them to form what must become a meaningless composite.

For example, in the case of social problems in Belfast, it is only by treating each type of problem separately that one can even begin to understand the causal processes. The composite index depicted in figure 1 highlights the areas of both religious groups equally, yet examination of each type of problem separately reveals that some tend to be found mainly in Catholic areas (e.g. unemployment) whereas others tend to be found mainly in Protestant areas (e.g. illegitimacy). This suggests that different causal factors are involved. The use of a composite index only tends to obfuscate the issue.

Likewise, if the objective is to provide ameliorative assistance, even if one was able to identify the worst areas with confidence (which one cannot do), one must disaggregate the composite index to find out what problems do actually need to be solved because each problem requires a different solution. The composite index is therefore redundant.

Summary

It is argued that composite indices, as frequently used in research in the quality of life or related concepts, introduce subjectivity. This defeats the objectives for quantifying which are to increase objectivity. Also, and perhaps more serious, composite indices encourage sloppy thinking as they tend to be regarded as objective measures of well defined phenomena, whereas in fact they are really statistical artefacts. There is nothing wrong with dealing with nebulous concepts, but one should not try hide the fact that they are nebulous by quantifying. One cannot measure something which cannot be defined.

Zusammenfassung

Messung der Lebensqualität: einige grundlegende methodische Probleme

Offensichtlich weist Lebensqualität regionale Unterschiede auf und ist somit ein angemessener Gegenstand geographischer Untersuchungen. Andererseits ist Lebensqualität ein recht vager Begriff und kann, ebensowenig wie "multiple Deprivation" oder "soziales Wohlbefinden", direkt gemessen werden. Eine Quantifizierung ist vielmehr nur möglich, indem man eine Anzahl von Indikatoren (z.B. Einkommen oder Gesundheitsverhältnisse) mißt und diese Werte zu einem einzigen komplexen Index aggregiert. Trotz Verwendung hoch komplexer Berechnungsverfahren, wie z.B. der Hauptkomponentenanalyse, muß angemerkt werden, daß derartige Indizes grundsätzlich subjektiv sind und durch eine Reihe willkürlicher Entscheidungen bezüglich der Anzahl, Auswahl und Gewichtung der beteiligten Variablen erheblich beeinflußt werden, unabhängig davon ob diese Entscheidungen vom vermeintlich objektiven Computer getroffen werden. Diese These wird anhand eines Beispiels mit Daten aus Belfast belegt. Es zeigt sich, daß derartige Indizes selbst für verhältnismäßig einfache Aufgaben, wie z.B. die Identifizierung der am meisten benachteiligten Bezirke einer Stadt, nur bedingt geeignet sind.

In Anbetracht der fehlenden begrifflichen Präzision solcher Begriffe wie

"Lebensqualität" sowie der unzureichenden Kenntnis der Beziehungen ihrer konstituierenden Elemente wird empfohlen, komplexe statistische Verfahren nicht zu nutzen, um auf undurchsichtige Weise zusammengesetzte Indizes abzuleiten, die durch wahllose Kombinationen vielfach widersprüchlicher Elemente entstanden sind. Die Komplexität solcher Verfahren erweckt den falschen Eindruck wissenschaftlicher Objektivität, verdeckt aber dabei den in Wahrheit hohen Anteil subjektiver Entscheidungen.

References

AMOS, F.J.C. (1970): "Social malaise in Liverpool", Liverpool City Planning Department

BOAL, F.W., P. DOHERTY & D.G. PRINGLE (1974): "The spatial distribution of some social problems in the Belfast urban area", Northern Ireland Community Relations Commission, Belfast

BOAL, F.W., P. DOHERTY & D.G. PRINGLE (1978): Social problems in the Belfast urban area: an exploratory analysis", Occasional Papers no. 12, Queen Mary College, University of London

Department of the Environment (1977): "Inner area studies", London HMSO

DUNCAN, S.S. (1974): "Cosmetic planning or social engineering? Improvement grants and improvement areas in Huddersfield", Area, 6, pp. 259-71

HARVEY, D. (1973): "Social justice and the city", London

KNOX, P.L. (1974): "Spatial variations in the level of living in England and Wales in 1961", Transactions of the Institute of British Geographers, no. 62, pp. 1-24

Project Team (1977): "Belfast: areas of social need", London HMSO

SMITH, D.M. (1973): "The geography of social well-being in the United States", New York et al.

TITTERINGTON, P.M. & R. NORMINGTON (1970): "Identification of areas of multiple deprivation in Leeds", Leeds

SITUATION AND TENDENCIES OF THE REGIONAL DISTRIBUTION IN THE QUALITY OF LIFE IN THE FEDERAL REPUBLIC OF GERMANY

with 10 figures

Hans-Peter Gatzweiler

It is Friday the 28th of April 1978, 3 o'clock p.m.. In Untertürkheim near Stuttgart, Robert S. is looking forward to the weekend. Robert S. works for a big car manufacturer, the Mercedes-Benz company in Untertürkheim. He earns a lot of money. He is the owner of a house with a large well cared foregarden. In the present economical crisis he needs not worry about his job. There is a very great demand for Mercedes Benz products. The unemployment rate of 2,8% in the Stuttgart area is far below the federal average.

200 km away in Bärnau, a little town in the Upper Palatinate, in Eastern Bavaria, Paul A. is worrying about his occupational future. He has been out of work since the first of October 1977, well over half a year. He has little hope of finding a permanent job during this time of economic crisis. Paul A. is living in a region that ranks among the poorest in the Federal Republic. The unemployment rate in the Upper Palatinate is far above 10%. Therefore Paul A. is considering moving to a region with better economical perspectives, to a region that might offer a secure job.

What can be demonstrated by using the examples of Robert S. and Paul A? These cases show that economical prosperity or poverty today is not only dependent on the qualifications and motivations of the individual blue or white collar worker but primarily on the region in which he is living. Robert S. is living in a centrally located and highly agglomerated region with a sturdy economy, he lives in a metropolitan area. Paul A. lives in a peripherally located and sparsely populated region with structural deficiencies; in other words a rural area.

Ever since the sixties the imbalance between these two types of areas, namely the metropolitan and the rural areas has grown. We can monitor a growing disparity of the regional distribution in the quality of life. This development has mainly been caused by market orientated processes.

The selective agglomeration of jobs, infrastructure and population in the Federal Republic will continue if there is no intervention to control this process.

Measured by the standards of private enterprise it will always be of greater interest to invest more capital in metropolitan areas. Decisions by entrepreneurs as to where to allocate their facilities will primarily be orientated towards gaining as many agglomeration advantages as possible. The negative consequences due to this agglomeration play a less role for most entrepreneurs and the standard of living of their qualified employees and well to do classes. As to the rest of the population, it is only the retired who react to the disadvantages of the agglomeration process by moving out of the metropolitan areas.

Accompanying the agglomeration process is an increased movement out of the rural areas. Here the supply of jobs is insufficient and little differentiated; people looking for work have only a small job selection. There is also a lack of high quality infrastructure due to the rising per capita costs of these facilities in sparsely populated areas. The mobile parts of the population react to this poor infrastructure and minimal offer of attractive jobs by moving into the metropolitan areas.

In the Federal Republic nobody questions the fact that there are regional differences in the quality of life. However there is much dispute about how to measure and assess these regional disparities.

One common opinion is that the Federal Republic, compared to Italy, France or Great Britain, has a comparatively balanced spatial structure. In fact, the differences in the Federal Republic are not as dramatic as those between Sicily and Northern Italy or between the French Central Massif and the Parisian area, or between the Scottish Highlands and Southeast England for example.

However, there are considerable disparities between Emsland and Hamburg or between the Eifel mountains and the Cologne area or between the Upper Palatinate and the Stuttgart area. However the general statement that there are regional disparities is insufficient to instigate regional development programs. It is necessary to develop a reliable information system that measures the regional distribution in the quality of life.

For the last two years the Federal Institute for Regional Geography and Regional Planning (BfLR) has been working on a project to solve this problem. The information system that is being developed has the objective of monitoring developments in the various regions of the Federal Republic, in a systematic and comprehensive manner at regular intervals through the use of indicators. The system will also reflect the effects of political decisions on the regional development. The information system has been named "Monitoring System of Regional Development", it measures the regional distribution in the quality of life through indicators.

The monitoring of regional development supports an active Federal Regional Policy. The monitoring system-produces better information for all stages of planning, namely the discussion of goals, the design of programs and the transformation of goals into specific measures. The system also helps in controlling and assessing the realization of aims and measures of the Federal Regional policy.

The logical structure of the Monitoring System of Regional Development is based on an analytical definition of the phenomenon "regional development process". It is thought that impulses for regional development come from private capital investments and public investments of the basic type. So, initially, we have to consider the fields of employment, education, energy, community facilities and transportation. Investments in these fields mainly control the overall distribution of population, mainly of the gainfully employed persons, who also generate a demand for housing. Consequently the fields of population and housing will be considered next. Finally subsequent processes in regional development can be seen in the fields of health services, social services, leisure and recreation, land use and environment. Development in these fields influences the spatial distribution of population, in particular of the retired. The spatial structure is therefore a result of this regional development process. On the other hand, the historically grown spatial structures have also partly influenced the regional development process (figure 1).

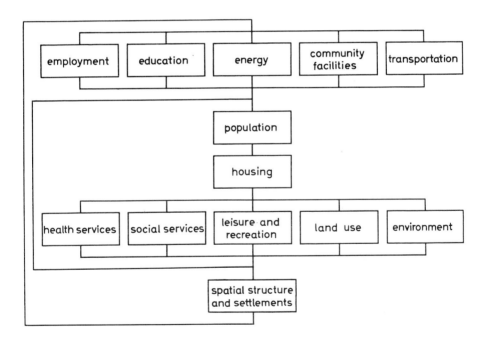

Fig. 1: Indicator system for monitoring the regional distribution in the quality of life, general structure

The following chapter demonstrates how indicators of the monitoring system can reveal the current state of the regional distribution and the probable future trends of the quality of life in the Federal Republic. I will stress a few of the important points here.

First it must be noted that quality of life is to be measured in functional regions. These are special subdivisions of the Federal Republic, altogether 58 regions. A subdivision is based on the accessibility of high level central places (measured in minutes needed to reach the point of destination).

Regional disparities are in most cases the consequence of deficiencies in spatial structure. Agglomeration disadvantages in the sparsely populated areas exist and the central place structure is underdeveloped. Not only is the economical structure weak, but the labour market is limited in both quantity and quality and these areas are lacking a higher quality infrastructure.

In analysing our regions according to the attributes "agglomeration" and "centrality" we found four types of agglomeration areas. These can be devided in two major groups: highly agglomerated areas and less agglomerated areas (figure 2).

Highly agglomerated areas usually are urban areas with a dense population and with the advantages of metropolitan facilities. The less agglomerated areas are all situated peripherally, and are sparsely populated and underdeveloped.

A closer look at the indicators gives the following impression on the quality of life in the regions of the Federal Republic:

One of the essential conditions for equivalent quality of life is an adequate supply of jobs. Therefore the Federal Regional Policy is trying to obtain a regional distribution of jobs that guarantee a free choice of profession and occupation.

However, if we look at the indicator "percentage of gainfully employed persons relative to resident population" we find that jobs are concentrated in the highly agglomerated areas. The ratio in 1975 was 43.1% in the highly agglomerated areas compared to only 35.3% in the less agglomerated areas.

The vocational qualifications of young people graduating from the different schools has improved considerably in the last years, both in the fields of general and vocational education. Therefore we can expect a greater demand for high quality jobs. Thus the quality of jobs offered on the market will play an important role in the future.

An indicator of the quality of job opportunities are the income possibilities. This indicator varies considerably in the regions of the Federal Republic. The monthly total of salaries per capita in the manufacturing industries varied in 1976 between less than 1.700 DM and well over 2.600 DM. Between 1970 and 1976 these difference did not decrease (figure 3).

The security of employment opportunities are indicated by regional unemployment rates. Security is an important feature of the quality of the labour market. We can monitor considerable regional differences concerning this feature as well.

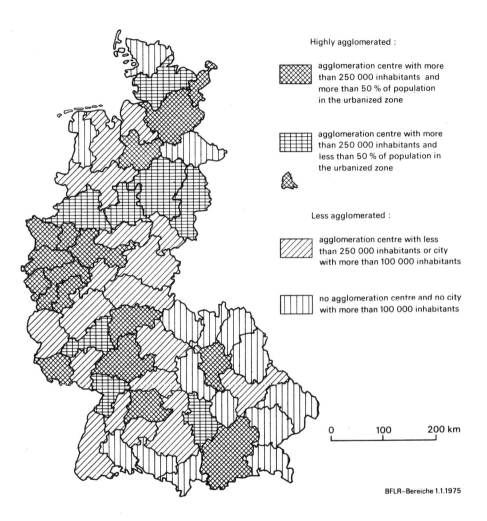

Fig. 2: Types of agglomeration

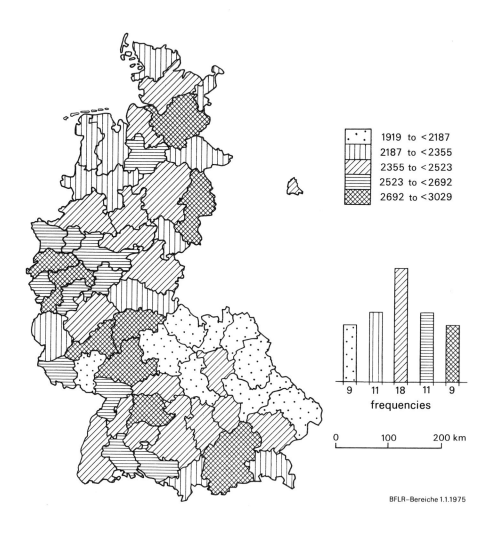

Fig. 3: Monthly total of salaries per capita in manufacturing (DM), 1978

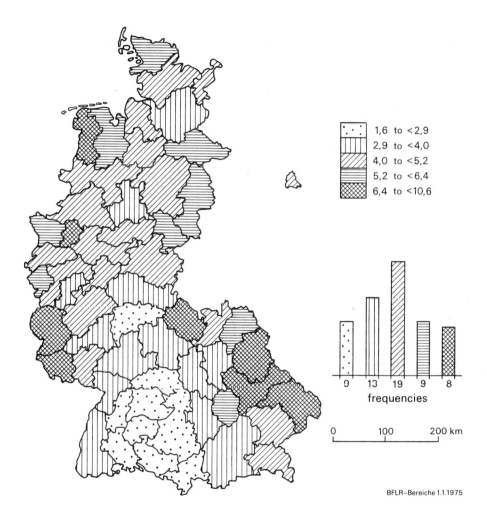

Fig. 4: Unemployment rate, 1979.

In the phase of economic recession it is mainly the monostructure problem in less agglomerated and older industrialized areas that can be felt. A major part of the less agglomerated regions can be counted among them. The unemployment rate in 1976 (6.4%) was about two percent higher in the monostructured areas than in the highly agglomerated regions (4.4%). In some regions it even surpassed the ten percent mark (figure 4).

Economic growth is a result of the presence and efficiency of two production factors, labour and capital. Regional differences in the presence and efficiency of both factors lead to a regionally unbalanced growth. The gross-inland-product is widely recognized as the indicator of economic potential and economic growth.

By using the indicator "gross-inland-product per capita" we can recognize the enormous span in economic capacity between highly and less agglomerated regions. In 1974 the variance amounted to 4.500 DM per capita. The region with the highest "gross-inland-product per capita" was Hamburg (with 21.350 DM). The region with the lowest "gross-inland-product per capita" was Passau (with 10.818 DM). Approximatedly 80% of the national gross-inland-product was produced in the agglomerated regions that cover only 20% of the Federal Republic.

The underdeveloped regions are characterized by a deficit in high quality job opportunities in growth orientated economical sectors and smaller chances for occupational promotion and selection. The younger working population, eighteen to twentynine years old, have only a small chance for occupational promotion and selection. Therefore they have a strong motive to move away from the less agglomerated regions (figure 5).

The age-specific selectivity of interregional migration in conjunction with the natural population development leads to a considerable age-specific segregation. The continuous migration of mainly younger people out of the less agglomerated areas increases the unfavourable age structure in these regions. The percentage of the dependent population, that is people not yet working or no longer working, in relation to the working population, is far above sixty percent. Whereas in the agglomerated regions the % of this group is only fifty three percent (figure 6).

A sufficiently large and varied supply of educational institutions within reasonable distances in all regions of the Federal Republic is a necessary prerogative in obtaining equivalent livingstandards. Therefore investments in educational facilities should be allocated primarily in those areas where lacking facilities and low participation rates are high. This is true of the less agglomerated regions. The possibility of university in academic education is far below the federal average here. In rural areas only fifty out if 1000 persons aged 20 to 25 are university students, whereas in the highly agglomerated regions there are 200 out of 1000 that are university students in this age group.

Serious problems have arisen during the last years in the combined education system of business practice and vocational schooling. Firms reduced the

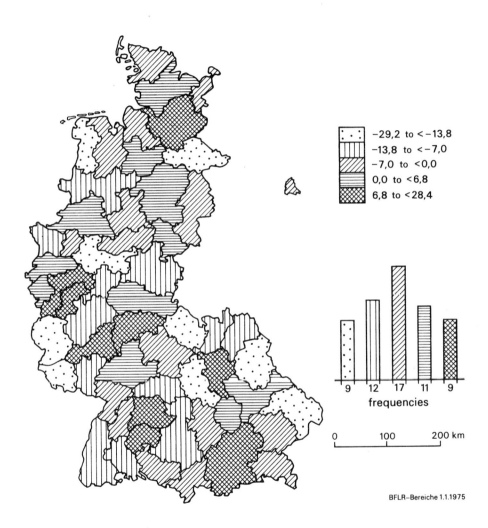

Fig. 5: Net migration, age group 18- ‹30, 1976/1977

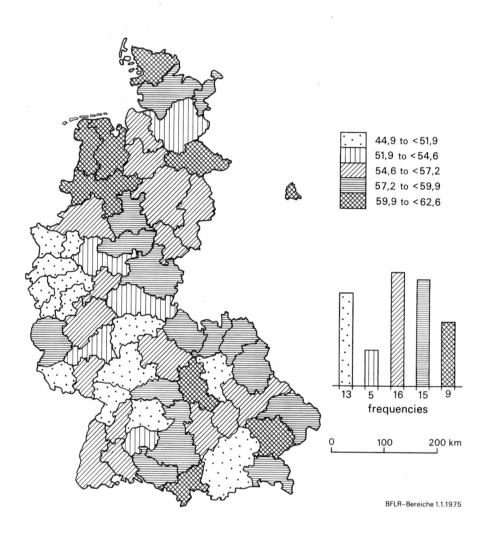

Fig. 6: Dependency ratio, 1977

number of apprenticeships while at the same time the respective age groups grew larger. Since 1976/77 the demand for apprenticeships has exceeded the supply.

In rural areas there is a much higher risk of young people not finding an apprenticeship than of those in the highly agglomerated areas. This can be demonstrated clearly through the indicator "percentage of unemployed under 20 years old, in relation to overall unemployment". In September 1976 the rate of young people without jobs was 4% higher in the lesser agglomerated regions in comparison to the metropolitan areas.

The insufficient supply of school and vocational education is a reinforcement to the migration of the younger groups of the population. The regional differences in educational infrastructure are reflected in the migrational behavior of the age group 18 to 24.

Year by year the less agglomerated regions loose up to approximately 20.000 persons in this age group through migration.

From region to region the relative differences are even greater. There are regions that loose over 30 out of 1000 of this age group. It is this selective migration that leads to a decrease in educational and occupational qualifications in the population of certain areas.

One of the permanent objectives of social and regional policy is an adequate supply of housing. There are still considerable interregional differences in this field. However, disparities seem to be, in this case, in favour of the less agglomerated areas. Even though the percentage of apartments with bath-rooms and central heating is much higher in metropolitan areas, the competition of the well to do for attractive housing forces the level of rents up here.

In the less agglomerated areas, on the other hand, there is a high percentage of privately owned homes. The especially low prices for building lots enabled many people to build their own homes. Approximately 45% of all persons live in their own homes, whereas in the highly agglomerated areas only 25 percent of all families live in their own homes.

A long period of job and high level infrastructure concentration and a constant population growth have lead to a deterioration of the environmental conditions and spatial narrowness in metropolitan areas. For example the amount of sulfurdioxyd in 1972 measured 118 kg per square km in the metropolitan areas. In the less agglomerated areas it was only 13 kg per square km. In the metropolitan areas there are only 1700 square meters of open land per capita compared to 8000 square meters in the rural areas (figure 7).

The quality of life in metropolitan areas has deteriorated due to air and noisepollution high costs of living, high rents and spatial narrowness, with little opportunity for recreation in the country side within reasonable distance. One of the consequences of these conditions is the (outward drift) migration of older people. They are mainly attracted to regions that can be described as rural, having a nice landscape and a healthier environment (figure 8).

Thus the regional development process in the Federal Republic has lead to

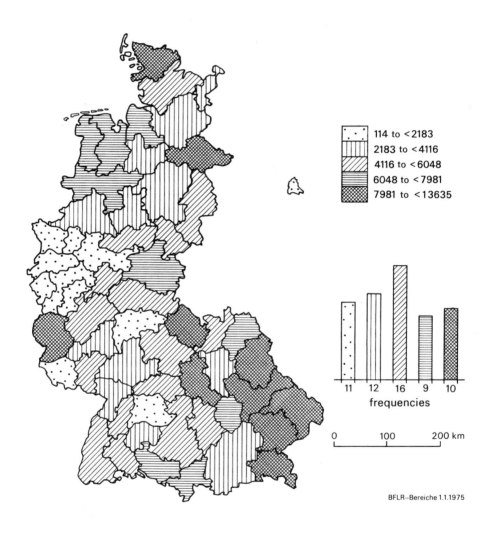

Fig. 7: Open land per capita in square meters, 1977

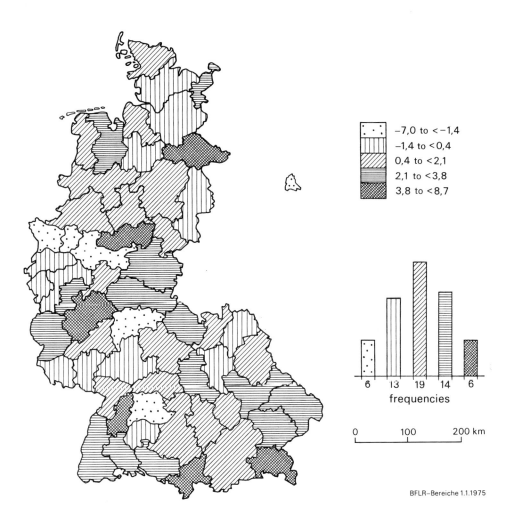

Fig. 8: Net migration, age group › 50, 1976/1977

twofold disparities in the quality of life between the types of highly agglomerated regions and less agglomerated regions. The process has not yet come to an end. The most evident proof for this is a selective migration flow between metropolitan and rural areas of specific age-groups that will also continue in the future. Let me demonstrate this for two age groups.

The migration of the age group 18 to 29 is an indicator for the disparity gradient between highly and less agglomerated regions. Due to status-quo conditions they will increasingly migrate out of the peripheral, less agglomerated areas into the metropolitan areas (figure 9).

The other indicator is the migration of people older than 49 years. In this case it is the difference in the conditions of the residential and natural environment between urban and rural areas that becomes evident. The flow of migrating older people is directed contrary to the gradient of the younger people. In the future we can expect an increase of this migration towards the peripheral rural regions, especially to the south of the Federal Republic, to Bavaria (figure 10).

From the examples presented above we can see that the chances for diminishing regional disparities in the Federal Republic of Germany are quite unfavourable. Apart from that, Federal Policy concerning regional development has not proven to be very successful in the last 15 years. There are people in research and decision-making who question the necessity or feasability of establishing equivalent conditions of living in rural and metropolitan regions. They advocate a "functional specialization" of areas. For example, rural regions should provide special services for the metropolitan areas like agricultural production, drinking water supplies, ecological regeneration or recreation.

There is no doubt that the functional specialization among the different types of regions in fact is growing in the Federal Republic. However, it must be questioned wether these tendencies should be adopted as principles of Federal Regional Policy in the 15 years to come. No one can estimate the possible consequences concerning public policy, ecology and regional economy. Also there is no proof that concentrating the industrial production function in the metropolitan areas increase the cost-effectivity of the national economic system.

The Federal Republic Policy will continue to maintain its present principles. Thus it aims at developing regions that are multifunctionally equipped and offer equal conditions of living.

The statements of the Federal Regional Development Program (Bundesraumordnungsprogramm) of 1975 are still valid today.

Its basic goals are:

— a more even distribution of the development potentials (inhabitants, occupations and infrastructure), mainly by limiting quantitative growth in the metropolitan areas;
— concentration of the resources that improve regional labour markets and infrastructure primarily in underdeveloped areas;

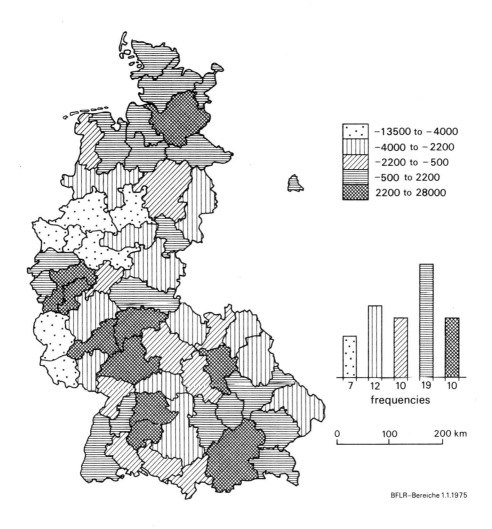

Fig. 9: Tendency of net migration, age group 18-<30, 1995

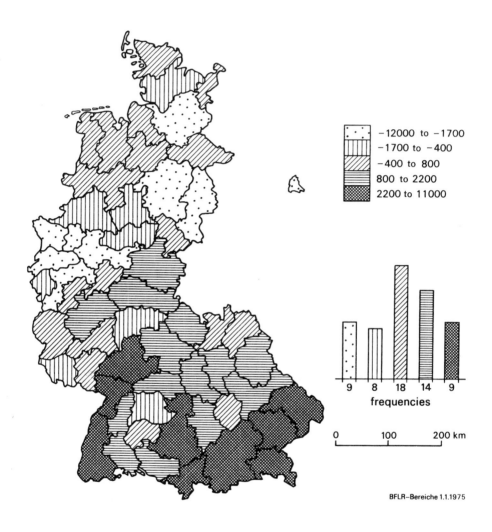

Fig. 10: Tendency of net migration, age group 50, 1995

— allocation of axes for development and centres for development in peripheral regions that presently lack interregional traffic links and high level central places.

In times of economic stagnation the decision makers will have to pay special attention to the structural and economic problems of rural areas.

An increased consciousness of these problems will be required of the politicians, planners and the public.

The indicators contained in the Monitoring System for Regional Development can reinforce this consciousness in describing and clarifying the specific problems of Federal Regional Planning. Thus the Monitoring System serves to put more efficiency into the Federal Regional Planning policy.

Zusammenfassung

Situation und Tendenzen der regionalen Verteilung der Lebensqualität in der Bundesrepublik Deutschland

Seit einiger Zeit ist in der Bundesforschungsanstalt für Landeskunde und Raumordnung ein Indikatorensystem zur Laufenden Raumbeobachtung eingerichtet. Es handelt sich dabei um eine Einrichtung zur regelmäßigen, systematischen, umfassenden und autonomen Beobachtung der großräumigen Entwicklungen im Bundesgebiet sowie der Wirkungen politischen Handelns auf die Raumentwicklung. Die umfassende Aufgabe der Laufenden Raumbeobachtung besteht in der laufenden Beobachtung regionaler Lebensbedingungen auf der Grundlage von Indikatoren.

Die Indikatoren belegen, daß der Prozeß der räumlichen Entwicklung im Bundesgebiet zu einem zweiseitigen Disparitätengefälle in den Lebensbedingungen zwischen den Gebietstypen "stärker verdichtete Regionen" und "weniger verdichtete Regionen" geführt hat. Zum einen besteht ein Disparitätengefälle in den Ausbildungs- und Erwerbsmöglichkeiten von den jeweils stärker verdichteten zu den weniger verdichteten Regionen. Zum anderen zeichnet sich ein Disparitätengefälle in den Wohnumfeld- und natürlichen Umweltbedingungen von den weniger zu den jeweils stärker verdichteten Regionen ab.

Der Prozeß der Raumentwicklung schreibt die derzeitige Raum- und Siedlungsstruktur fest. Das zeigt sich vor allem an einem auch in Zukunft altersgruppenspezifisch stark unterschiedlich ausgerichteten Wanderungsgefälle zwischen hoch verdichteten und ländlichen Regionen. Unzureichende und unattraktive Ausbildungs- und Arbeitsplatzangebote werden auch in Zukunft verstärkt zur Abwanderung jüngerer Personen aus den ländlichen in die hoch verdichteten Regionen führen. Dagegen führt die Beeinträchtigung der Lebensbedingungen durch Verschlechterung der Umweltqualität in verdichteten Regionen zunehmend zur Abwanderung in ländliche Regionen.

Das erste und wichtigste Ziel der Raumordnungspolitik ist die Schaffung gleichwertiger Lebensbedingungen in allen Teilräumen des Bundesgebietes. Die Laufende Raumbeobachtung ist ein Instrument zur Verwirklichung dieses Ziels. Im Rahmen eines umfassenden raumordungspolitischen Planungskonzepts wird die Laufende Raumbeobachtung der Aufgabe gerecht, aus der Analyse der räumlichen Situation und der bisherigen Raumentwicklung unerwünschte Zukunftsperspektiven, die sich aus Status-quo-Prognosen abzeichnen, durch geeignete Maßnahmen in raumordnungspolitisch zielgerechte Bahnen zu lenken.

References

Bundesminister f. Raumordnung, Bauwesen u. Städtebau (1975): "Raumordnungsprogramm für die großräumige Entwicklung des Bundesgebietes (Bundesraumordnungsprogramm)", Raumordnung, Schriftenreihe d. Bundesministers f. Raumordnung, Bauwesen u. Städtebau, 06.002, S. 4 ff., Bonn

Bundesminister f. Raumordnung, Bauwesen u. Städtebau (1979): "Raumordnungsbericht 1978 und Materialien", Raumordnung, Schriftenreihe d. Bundesministers f. Raumordnung, Bauwesen u. Städtebau, 06.040, S. 75 ff., Bonn

GATZWEILER, H.P. (1978): "Laufende Raumbeobachtung - ein planungspraktisches Informationssystem", Informationen zur Raumentwicklung, S. 599-615

GATZWEILER, H.P. & L. RUNGE (1978): "Regionale Disparitäten im Bundesgebiet", Informationen zur Raumentwicklung, S. 669-95

ZAPF, W. (1976): "Sozialberichterstattung - Möglichkeiten und Probleme", Schriftenreihe der Kommission f. wirtschaftlichen u. sozialen Wandel 125, S. 3 ff., Göttingen

WHO PERCEIVES THE PROBLEM AND WHO PRESCRIBES THE SOLUTION: A CRITIQUE OF CONTEMPORARY REGIONAL PLANNING PHILOSOPHY

with 3 figures and 2 tables

JOHN WHITELEGG

Geographers are in a good position to contribute to the debate on the 'quality of life' in that the core of their professional concern has been to account for differences between areas and places in the sort of variables which collectively describe a 'quality of life'. This concern neatly sidesteps the issue of collapsing a number of variables into some composite index of quality of life, though this difficult problem has been assessed in the opening address to this symposium.[1] It is more than likely that a search for some generally acceptable index will continue for some time and in the end prove unproductive and the reason for this is that a 'quality of life' assessment springs directly from the domain of experience and perception to be subsequently filtered by the agencies within a democratic society which control public expenditure and the nature of ameliorative activities. This, to my mind, reinforces the traditional concern of the geographer who has the experience and ability to make comparisons in 'quality of life' or 'levels of living' between different areas and places at one point in time and comparisons through time for one or more areas and places. However such an ability is insufficient in itself and if the geographer wishes to achieve more than description, collation and cataloging he or she must understand the many ways in which such differences can come about in the first place, how they may be perpetuated and rationalised within the prevailing value system and ideology of the state and how they may be realistically altered by means which do not threaten this prevailing ideology. These are difficult issues which many geographers are not accustomed to dealing with but are nevertheless crucial to any understanding of 'quality of life'. Recent academic studies which have focused on the European Economic Community as a basic unit have underlined the necessity for such an eclectic treatment of contemporary issues.[2]

The significance of 'quality of life' as a topic is in its capacity to stimulate new approaches and solutions within geography and in its great relevance to a Western Europe Society which has largely failed to transmit the benefits of economic growth (when such a thing existed) to all groups within society, and which now compounds these inequalities with the evils of unemployment and deprivation in a period of recession. These themes are well developed in PEET[3] which opens with the statement 'Radical Geography is a study of the quality of life'.

This paper is concerned with one facet of the quality of life and that is public (i.e. state) intervention in regional planning and the economic and social condition of regions within a nation state. It is further concerned with the way in which regional 'problems' are perceived and identified and how this influences the nature and scale of subsequent intervention and expenditure. It is however particularly concerned with the consumer of such interventions. What place does the consumer who, let us remember, is the same person who is unemployed, under-employed, deprived, 'enjoys' below average income, etc., have in the regional planning process?

Regional planning varies in detail throughout Europe but there are some common features. These include an acceptance by the state of some failing in the market mechanism of liberal capitalism which precipitates the need for state intervention. The state will, for example, become involved in running the railways, coal or steel and other basic sectors of the economy whilst leaving other sectors of manufacturing activity to private enterprise. The reasons for this are discussed in HOLLAND.[4] The state also takes on an explicit regional concern so that in every country some areas are designated as eligible for financial assistance for industry and job creation. This principle has now received approval at the supranational level with the creation of the European Regional Development Fund. Also in common is the subject of such aid and assistance. Usually regional policies are conceived in terms of influencing firms to expand production in the designated areas or to move production and jobs from 'congested' or 'developed' areas to the designated areas. The agent of regional development is thus the firm or similar entrepreneurial unit and regional development policies evolve around that focus in terms of fiscal incentives, i.e. company taxation relief, accelerated depreciation allowances, free factories or rent free periods and so on. Similarly infrastructure development reflects this focus. Serviced sites, i.e. with electricity, water, roads and effluent disposal capabilities may be constructed in anticipation of demand and regional transportation networks upgraded. A large number of regional policy measures are directly contingent on the identification of the firm as the primary agent. There is not scope in this presentation for a detailed critique of such a focus but suffice it to say that in spite of the identification of several major drawbacks[5] this central focus is still maintained.

Regional planning in the democracies of W. Europe is by no means the only or even most important agent of 'regional compensation'. In terms of expenditure (depending on country), health services, transport, education and subvention of local authority expenditure accounts for a far greater share of public expenditure than do regional planning aids. In addition, the problems which regional planning attempts to alleviate are no more than the spatial dimension of inequality in a market economy. The usual response in W. Europe is to regard regional problems as distinct say from educational deprivation in inner cities or housing and social problems generally. This separation, academic and policy, is responsible for much muddled thinking and ineffective attacks on problems.

Finally in terms of common elements and the scale of direct public investment is the state subsidy of the private sector within and without designated areas. BARRATT—BROWN[6] has estimated that in the U.K., the cumulative affect of capital grants, investment allowances, and employment premia since the early 1960's has been equal to one-half of company taxation. The total figure which includes indirect subsidies on raw materials and services from the British Steel Corporation, Post Office Corporation etc., where price restraint has been exercised, is estimated to be between £2,100 m. and £2,300 m.

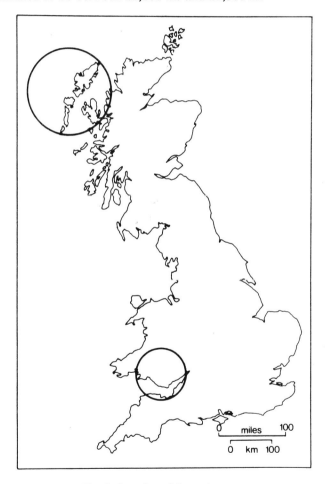

Fig. 1: Location of the study areas

There is therefore a massive state involvement in the economies of W. Europe which is usually if not always directed towards the improvement of quality of life, conceived in terms of jobs and jobs created by private enterprise.[7] Our main purpose now is to examine the record of such a policy in two very distinct and distinctive regions of the U.K. paying particular attention to the interest of the consumer. One is rural and remote and the other largely urban with a legacy of early industrialisation and subsequent decline. The urban is the older industrialised area of South Wales known as the Valleys (figure 2). The history of regional planning in Wales particularly with respect to South Wales is not one which dem-

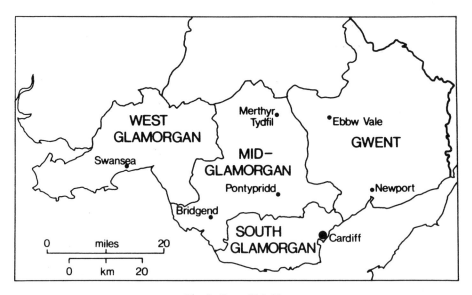

Fig. 2: Outer Hebrides

onstrates a clear understanding of the regional distinctions within the principality and of the cultural identity or tenacity of Valley communities. This history is outlined in ALDEN.[8] It would seem, from official documents, that this area, primarily based on coal mining, has been abandoned to fend for itself and depend on the development of industry and jobs in the region of Cardiff or along the M4 and the Newport-Cwmbran axis. The commuting and community implications of this 'marginal shift' strategy have been extensively examined by a group of interested and involved individuals in the Valleys to produce a new strategy of renewal and development for the Valleys.[9a] and [9b]

In common with the Ruhr and many other older industrial regions throughout Europe the problem of the Valleys can be characterised as lack of social and economic investment, deteriorating infrastructure, consistently high (until recently) rates of outmigration and close-knit communities of high resolve and independence with the capacity to redress the imbalance. Unfortunately regions with a declining industrial base tend to repel those entrepreneurs which are the agents of regional planning. It is also salutory to reflect that these 'agents' are in substance the same as the ones who originally took their profits from the Valleys and left them scarred and derelict. It is clear that regional policy measures based on the firm have not worked in the Valleys. It is not that aids and incentives are insufficient but that the area is simply unattractive to the entrepreneur who can gain the same advantages in a more accessible industrial estate or on the M4 axis. This may well turn out to be an advantage to the Valleys in the search for self determination, rather than replacing one set of unaccountable entrepreneurs for another. That regional policies have not worked is evidenced by simple population indices. From 1961 to 1971 the population of the Central and Eastern Valleys fell by 21,000 despite a natural increase of 23,000.[10] The population of the Valleys in 1971 stood at 822,112 and is broken down by constituent areas in table 1. Analysis of unpublished 1971 census data on migration shows that all but four valley local authorities lost population through net migration losses between 1966 and 1971. The migrants themselves tended to be younger and more economically active than the rest of the population. Population projections have been prepared for the Valleys and these can be seen in table 2. Such projections whilst closely adhering to demographic information and conventions can in no way account for the possible large scale renewal and revitalisation of the Valleys, or indeed its converse, and general demographic uncertainty coupled with the actual facts of outmigration provide an impetus and a stimulus for those in the Valleys to attempt to influence their own future.

The situation in the Valleys reflects the traditional impotence of the consumer of regional policies. Committed individuals and groups who see beyond the blind phrases of official documents towards a different future for themselves and their area find themselves in a weak situation. Regional policy is decided at national level in such a way that Co. Durham may be in competition with South Wales for new jobs and because of this areas such as South Wales have to behave like a microcosm of the national economy. In other words just as nationally there is a division into core and periphery, within a development area there will emerge more and less favoured areas. Within Wales and within South Wales the Valleys have emerged as a less-favoured area with all the implications of such a status. This is another consequence of a firm-oriented regional policy which neglects social goals, communities, and community selfdetermination. The consumer interest is better served by 'more' local concentration of decision making powers but within the framework of regional planning as currently conceived this is really irrelevant as it would only produce more authorities competing with one another in order to attract the same few jobs. This would force up the rate of public subvention of private enterprise and that loss of resources would not be compensated for by any real increase in stability or long term jobs. The quality of jobs, scale of industry, etc. is a pertinent regional policy variable and has been discussed by this author elsewhere.[11] Devolution is seen by some as a partial answer to the problem of locally based planning,

Table 1: Population of the Valleys: 1971 Census

				1971 Pop.
GWENT				
	Blaenau Gwent			85,559
	Islwyn			66,037
	Torfaen			88,308
MID GLAMORGAN				
	Cynon Valley			69,583
	Merthyr Tydfil			63,170
	Rhondda			88,990
	Rhymney Valley			101,950
	Taff Ely:	Pontypridd UD		34,608
		Llantrisant and Llantwit Fardre RD		37,117
		1 ward of Caerphilly UD: Taffswell		2,910
		1 parish of Cowbridge RD: Llanharan		2,015
	Ogwr:	Maesteg UD		20,835
		Ogmore and Garw UD		19,405
		5 parishes of Penybont RD:	Kenfig	4,940
			Pyle	8,070
			Ynysawdre	2,225
			Llangynwyd Middle	1,985
			Llangynwyd Lower	610
POWYS				
	Ystradgynlais RD			9,880
DYFED				
	Dinefwr:	Ammanford UD		5,795
		Cwmamman UD		3,947
		2 parishes of Llandeilo RD:	Betws	995
			Llandybie	7,645
	Llanelli:	3 parishes of Llanelli RD:	Pontyberem	2,765
			Llannon	5,475
			Llanedi	3,905
WEST GLAMORGAN				
	Afan:	Glyncorrwg UD		8,600
		1 ward of Port Talbot MB:	Cwmafan	4,995
	Lliw:	Pontardawe RD		29,448
		3 wards of Llwchwr UD:	Dulais	3,055
			Talybont	2,775
			Brynlliw	3,965
	Neath:	12 parishes of Neath RD:		
			Blaengwrach	1,335
			Resolfen	2,640
			Dulais Higher	5,555
			Dulais Lower	1,125
			Dyffryn Clydach	2,725
			Clyne	840
			Michaelstone Higher	1,150
			Tonna	2,195
			Blaenhonddan	7,260
			Neath Higher	5,055
			Neath Lower	305
			Baglan Higher	365

TOTAL: 822,112

Table 2: Population projections for the Valleys. Natural change only

		1971	1976	1981	1986	1991
GWENT:						
	Blaenau Gwent[1]	85,600	81,600	81,000	81,600	82,800
	Islwyn[1]	66,000	65,900	66,400	67,600	69,400
	Torfaen[1]	88,300	90,400	91,200	93,200	95,700
MID GLAMORGAN:				(1975)		
	Cynon[1]	69,580	69,600	70,500	71,700	73,300
	Merthyr[1]	63,170	60,600	60,800	61,500	62,900
	Rhondda[1]	88,990	86,400	85,400	86,200	87,200
	Rhymney[1]	101,950	105,700	111,200	116,300	121,900
				(1976)		
	Pontypridd UD[2]	34,610	34,250	34,070	34,020	34,040
	Llantrisant and Llantwit Fardre UD[2]	37,120	38,890	40,390	41,960	43,800
	Maesteg UD	20,840	20,930	21,070	21,330	21,690
	Ogmore and Garw UD[2]	19,410	19,290	19,260	19,380	19,630
	Llanharan[3]	2,020	2,060	2,110	2,150	2,190
	Taffswell[3]	2,910	2,950	3,000	3,000	3,040
	Penybont parishes[3]	17,830	17,750	17,850	17,980	18,190
POWYS:						
	Ystradgynlais RD[2]	9,880	9,610	9,330	9,100	8,900
WEST GLAMORGAN:						
	Glyncorrwg UD[2]	8,600	8,670	8,870	9,160	9,480
	Pontardawe Rd[2]	29,450	28,790	29,190	27,660	27,210
	Cwmafan[3]	5,000	5,010	5,020	5,070	5,090
	Llwchwr wards[3]	9,780	9,650	9,540	9,440	9,370
	Neath parishes[3]	30,550	30,320	30,020	29,680	29,320
DYFED:						
	Ammanford UD[2]	5,800	5,510	5,310	5,130	5,000
	Cwmamman UD[2]	3,950	3,800	3,650	3,510	3,400
	Llanelli parishes[3]	12,150	12,090	11,990	11,870	11,760
	Llandeilo parishes[3]	8,640	8,420	8,260	8,090	7,930
	TOTAL	822,130	818,190	825,330	836,670	853,240

Note: Figures have been rounded to the nearest unit of 10
Sources:
1) New District Projections by County Planning Departments.

2) Old local authorities - projected by Dr. I. BRACKEN, Department of Town Planning, UWIST, Cardiff.

3) Parishes and wards of old local authorities. Dr. I. BRACKEN, as above.

etc. Unless the structure and object of regional planning is altered the existence of an assembly in Cardiff or Edinburgh is unlikely to change the facts of life of private enterprise in a liberal capitalist system. The consumer interest demands more than this and it is not at all clear how rule from Cardiff or Edinburgh will be qualitatively different than that for London. (Quantitatively it will be nearer!).

It is now possible, probably for the first time in the U.K., to identify a clear consumer interest in a regional planning context. The publications referred to earlier have been produced by a group with a genuine mandate from as many of the public as wish to be involved and with a clear commitment to the preservation of community and culture within a buoyant economic framework. Lacking the resources or power to implement policies the group has prepared coherent and well-argued alternative strategies to planning in the South Wales Valleys in such a way that they could *not* be ignored by the relevant authorities. Through the medium of conferences and discussion groups and the willing participation of academics, local businessmen, churches, and others a genuine alternative machinery for collating information and generating choices and strategies has been created. It is difficult to exaggerate the significance of this achievement. Its significance lies not in its capacity to achieve the ends which have been identified, for this is clearly a governmental function, but in the potential of a community described as depressed and declining, abandoned by official regional planning agencies, to bounce back and, from within, produce its own analysis and solutions. The details of how this has been achieved can be found in the group's own publications. The group has issued a formidable challenge to the 'official' planners and we all await with interest to see their reply.

There can be no doubt that the Valleys have reacted positively to the failings of traditional regional policy and to their own fears for the future should this tradition continue unchallenged. Yet the definition and coalescence of a consumer interest is on its own, going to achieve very little. The last word of the Strategy[12] declares "we must produce a sustained tradition of initiating our own industries in the Valleys". There lies the clue for the next stage and the translation of consumer awareness into action designed to achieve a basic improvement in 'quality of life'.

In this the Valleys are in a position to capitalise on the experience of others particularly the co-operative movements of Ireland and Scotland (to be discussed later), the Mondragon experiment in Spain[13] and the Industrial Common Ownership movement in the U.K.[14] All the activities are linked by their concern for scale and community, that is activities which merge with and reinforce communities rather than overwhelm and dominate. They are activities which produce goods for consumption within the communities (import substitution) and for export and they are activities which are democratically run by the workers. The Industrial Common Ownership Movement in the U.K. is an umbrella organisation which provides advice and assistance to those interested in its aims and can advise on setting up enterprises under the terms of the Industrial Common Ownership Act of 1976, which provides grants and loans to common ownership enterprises. There is in addition a co-operative section of the Manpower Services Commission and a co-operative Development Agency, all of which point to growing state interest in this area. For the Valleys, co-operatives and common ownership offer the advantages of capitalising on one of their greatest assets in strength of community, and of achieving a degree of practical control of their own destiny which is not possible within the established regional planning framework even should the alternative strategies be adopted in some form.

The Western Isles of Scotland could not be more different from industrial South Wales but in spite of this difference exists under largely the same sort of re-

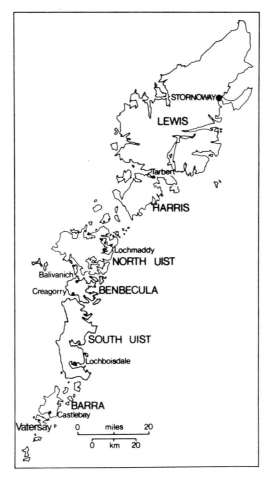

Fig. 3: The South Wales Valleys

gional planning policies and procedures. The Outer Hebrides of Scotland or the Western Isles lie off the N.W. coast of the United Kingdom and are approximately 200 km in length. (figure 3). The 1971 Census population of the Western Isles was 29,891 compared to a peak in 1911 of 46,732. In the twentieth century the overall trend has been one of decline. The population of the area as a whole declined by 8% in the period 1951/61 and by a further 8% in the period 1961/71, in contrast to the slight increase in the population of Scotland over both periods.

The Western Isles, on the N.W. periphery of Europe, have never experienced industrialisation nor indeed commercial agriculture as would be recognized in lowland Europe. The distinctive economy and society of this and similar areas on the mainland has been well described in HUNTER[15] and the society is still largely conditioned by custom and tradition as enshrined in the crofting legislation. Nevertheless it is not a fossilised peasant society within an advanced industrial economy but on the contrary an area of rapid change and development under the direction of a new regional authority - the Western Isles Islands Council or Comhairle nan Eilean, in Gaelic. 81.6% of the populaton aged three and over were registered as bilingual in 1971 - the highest rate of bilingualism (Gaelic and English) of any local authority area in Scotland. The region has an official bilingual policy and strong bilingual tradition in its schools. Both are indicative of a cultural integrity and singularity not in common with the remainder of Britain.

There is neither time nor space to discuss in detail the nature of the crofting system or the economy of the Islands area itself. In E.E.C. terms, crofting is not regarded as a viable agricultural activity, while in the Islands themselves it is regarded as the mainstay of that distinctive society and community. Official governmental agencies such as the Crofter Commission and the Highlands and Islands Development Board (H.I.D.B) seem to regard crofting as a part-time activity and a source of income which has to be supplemented by other forms of employment.

Before discussing these agencies and their role in national policy making and implementation a few words about regional planning in general. The situation in the South Wales Valleys is not repeated here. There is no indication of consumer involvement or awareness outside of the local authority administration itself - henceforth to be referred to as the Council. Unlike the South Wales Valleys which straddled many areas lacking the higher level functions of strategic planning the Western Isles are (since May 1975) a unitary or all-purpose authority responsible for planning and development, housing, education, social services, transport and so on. In other words effective power is concentrated in the hands of an elected Council from the whole of the Island chain. This Council in its Regional Report[16] has formulated a strategy which is directly parallel to that formulated by the non-official group in South Wales. The group in South Wales lacks the power base or authority to implement the solution as the Council lack the finance and possibly the degree of consent necessary from the Scottish Office. The latter may be particularly the case in a period of public expenditure cut backs which disproportionately damage those areas already relatively deprived.

The Islands raise many questions fundamental to any conception of regional planning. They are remote with corresponding poorly developed infrastructure. The cumulative cost of roads, bridges, causeways, ferry services and ordinary running expenses in a sparsely populated, extended area are much higher per capita than in many mainland areas. Together with a poorly developed resource base this calls for massive subvention by central funds and redistribution on a large scale from the core to the periphery. To what extent does a genuine concensus exist for this within the liberal democracies of W. Europe? In addition regional policies which were suspect in the context of the Welsh Valleys are woefully inappropriate in Islands off the N.W. coast of Scotland. Investment grants for firms and accelerated depreciation allowances have clearly no role to play and hold out no hope for any improvements in the quality of life of the Islands - if this is what the object of regional policies is really about. We may safely conclude, therefore, that the traditional regional planning approach, centred on the firm as noted earlier, is of no relevance in the Western Isles and in its turn the concept of an homogeneous set of regional policies applied nationally.

There is some evidence that this may have been tacitly understood and accepted by central government. The creation of the Highlands and Islands Development Board in 1965 responsible for the 'crofting counties' was an acknowledgement of the peculiar problems of remoteness and of the distinctiveness of the area it covered. The drafts of the Parliamentary Bill and subsequently the Board itself, failed to understand the basic problem of the area and accepted the prevailing status quo of regional planning ideology. Firms continued to be wooed and the only concessions made to the regional distinctiveness were in fishing, tourism and craft industries, which provide relatively few jobs and ensure that profits continue to leak out to the already established centres of finance and commerce at the core of the national economy. The performance of the H.I.D.B. is a worthwhile object of inquiry but cannot be pursued here. CARTER[17] has described at length this failure of the Board to make the impact which many expected of it.

It is possible to argue that through the Council of the Western Isles there is an expression of consumer preference in regional planning, yet it is weakly developed and the Council itself has not analysed its own situation in sufficient depth so as to produce a coherent strategy. National policies are clearly inappropriate and play practically no part in the life if the Islands, which leaves the writ of the H.I.D.B. The H.I.D.B. is not in any way accountable to the inhabitants of the Western Isles and is a case of a relatively non-remote body having little interaction with its consumers. Its accountability through the Secretary of State for Scotland is of no consequence to the daily lives of the Islanders and from a consumer point of view the Islands are as disenfranchised as the Valleys of South Wales.

Dating from approximately 1976 the Islands have been increasingly receptive to the 'do-it-yourself' strategy which has characterised the Valleys Movement. From many small beginnings there has emerged both within the Council and individual communities, a conviction that future development lies in local initiative rather than in a belief in the regional policies of the state or its agents. Once again this represents a not very well articulated, but nevertheless positive, rejection of traditional regional policies on the basis of their past performance.

Local initiative has taken many forms in these Islands and is still under active development. These initiatives include fishing co-operatives, horticultural co-operatives, multi-functional or general purpose co-operatives with developing interests in craft industries, weaving, spinning and dyeing etc. and so on. They all have in common elements of democratic control by the communities themselves, import substitution as a primary goal, the securing of better purchasing and market conditions in the case of activities such as fishing and possibly tourism. In economic terms they simply maximise the quantity and quality of local job opportunities, and constrain the flow of capital and profits which, instead of escaping the region, can be used to generate more activities. This has been the experience of the Mandragon co-operatives in the Basque area of Spain and of the co-operative movement in the Gaeltacht areas of the West of Irland, particularly Glencolumkille. There has indeed been a high degree of interchange of ideas between the latter and the Islands. Co-operatives also provide a framework for new initiatives and the careful exploitation of local resource such as peat and seaweed.

These two areas far removed from one another and very different in their geographical characteristics have both arrived at the same point. It is argued that this point is characterised by an implicit, and sometimes explicit, rejection of the prevailing philosophies of regional planning, based as they are on identifying large areas of the U.K. as development areas and relying on the firm as the agent of change and job creation. The rejection is based on its poor performance. Academic studies[18] of this performance, qualified consistently by tenuous assumptions, do not detract from this consumer reaction. It is unlikely, in any case, that an homogeneous set of policies could ever hope to cater for the needs of two areas as different as these.

In the 'celtic perphery' the rejection is possibly part of something much larger and more important. Both Scotland and Wales have a history of independence and a recent history of separatist and nationalist activity which has not been mollified by the devolution debate. The activity is undoubtedly fired by the cavalier activities of the colonising power towards the cultural and linguistic integrity of the Gaels and the Welsh[19] and economic domination was clearly a part of this. This is a theme behind much recent work on the 'Celtic Periphery' of the

U.K. in particular HECHTER[20] and in France, HOWARD[21] and PHLIPPONEAU.[22]

Remote control of distant regional economies is clearly seen as an extension of colonialism within the national territory and one which effectively syphons off profit and surplus value. HOLLAND[23] would go further than this and see regional problems at the periphery (and elsewhere) as a direct result of the operation of a capitalist society with its inbuilt tendencies to concentrate wealth both in space, i.e. at the core of the national economy - and amongst individuals - so as to create a priviledged elite who control finance, commerce and administration. In this context regional policies are seen as weak ameliorative responses to the failings of capitalism itself:

> "The regional problem is nothing less than the spatial dimension of inequality in a market economy. It is the social and economic problem writ wide."
> (STUART HOLLAND 'The Socialist Challenge' p. 95)

Those that exist at the periphery may not find themselves in agreement with HOLLAND's political and economic analysis but they have reached the same conclusion and gone beyond the analysis to construct an economy which, whilst within the capitalist system, is as effectively geared to small-scale, local needs and control as is feasible. If this attempt to assert the consumer interest in the operation of regional policies fails then more fuel will have been provided for both nationalist and separatist activity and the search for a new economic order.

Zusammenfassung

Wer erkennt das Problem, und wer verordnet die Therapie?
— Eine Kritik der gegenwärtigen Regionalplanungstheorie —

In dieser Arbeit wird das Problem staatlicher Eingriffe auf dem Sektor der Lebensqualität unter Betrachtung der Regionalplanungsmaßnahmen in Großbritannien untersucht. Die Hauptthese lautet, daß der Geograph aufgrund seiner Vertrautheit mit regionaler Differenzierung die Erfahrung und die Fähigkeit besitzt, Vergleiche zur 'Lebensqualität' anzustellen. Häufig gelingt es der Geographie aber nicht, Bezüge zwischen einer objektiven Realität - falls so etwas überhaupt definiert werden kann - und den Erfahrungen und Wahrnehmungen einzelner individueller Menschen in einer Region herzustellen, wo diese Grundzüge einer ihnen unzuträglichen Lebensqualität erleben. Darüber hinaus müßte der Geograph die Fähigkeit besitzen, diese individuellen Wahrnehmungen mit einer Erforschung der Problementstehung zu verknüpfen und mit dem maßgeblichen Wertesystem und der vorherrschenden Ideologie des Staates, die entscheidend ist für das Ausmaß, in dem die Probleme erkannt und entsprechend angepackt werden, in Beziehung zu setzen.

Der Verfasser beschreibt die maßgebliche Theorie, auf der basierend regionale Probleme identifiziert und in Angriff genommen werden, wobei die Erfahrung Großbritanniens mit der in anderen Ländern der Europäischen Gemeinschaft verglichen wird. Dies umfaßt die Analyse der wesentlichen Bereiche der Staatsausgaben sowie ihre Bedeutung für die Verbesserungen auf dem Sektor der 'Lebensqualität'.

Der empirische Teil dieser Arbeit besteht aus zwei Fallstudien. Die erste handelt von den regionalen Problemen und den Raumordnungsmaßnahmen in den 'Tälern' des Industriegebiets von Südwales, wo die Bevölkerungsabnahme mit einer Umverlagerung der industriellen Produktionsstätten aus den 'Tälern' in die Küstenebene einherging. Die 'Täler' haben eine beachtenswerte lokal verankerte Gemeindeorganisation hervorgebracht, die die regionale Raumordnungspolitik auswertet und die für spezifische Änderungen öffentlich eintritt. Ihre Aktivitäten werden als repräsentativer Ausdruck einer gemeinsamen Vorstellung von 'Lebensqualität' untersucht.

Die zweite Fallstudie handelt von einem recht andersartigen Gebiet. Die westlichen Inseln vor Schottland (die Äußeren Hebriden) sind ein klassisches Beispiel für die besonderen Probleme, die in entfernt gelegenen, dünn besiedelten ländlichen Räumen auftreten. Es gibt dort keine gemeinschaftliche Reaktion auf die regionale Raumordnungspolitik wie in den 'Tälern' von Südwales. Aber es existiert eine neue regionale Behörde, die die ihr zugewiesene Rolle als Entscheidungsträger als einen Auftrag ansieht, die Wirtschaftsentwicklung zu fördern und gegen die Wanderungen nach auswärts anzukämpfen. Die neue Regionalbehörde unterstützt eine Selbsthilfeorganisation und die Bildung von Gemeindekooperativen, was schlechthin den Trend anzeigt, mehr auf einheimisch entstandene Aktivitäten zu vertrauen als auf solche, die von außerhalb in das Gebiet hereingetragen werden.

Im folgenden werden diese zwei sehr verschiedenen Situationen miteinander verglichen, und es wird die Frage aufgeworfen, inwieweit sie einen Beweis für die Ablehnung der vorherrschenden Regionalplanungskonzepte darstellen. Falls eine solche Ablehnung nachweisbar wäre, in welchem Ausmaß wären dann die mißlungenen Eingriffe in die 'Lebensqualität' die Folge eines unzulänglichen Planungsinstrumentariums oder eines wesentlich fundamentaleren Versagens der 'freien Marktwirtschaft' in den gegenwärtigen Gesellschaften Westeuropas?

Notes and references

1. PRINGLE, D. (1978): Opening address to Anglo-German symposium on applied geography, Bonn, May 16, 1978
2. KENNET, W. (1976): "The futures of Europe", C.U.P., Hall, P. (1977): "Europe 2000"
3. PEET, R. (ed.) (1977): "Radical geography: alternative viewpoints on contemporary social issues", Chicago
4. HOLLAND, S. (1975): "The socialist challenge", Chicago
5. The existence of branch-plant economies and the instability in employment terms which this creates; a tendency to capital-, rather than labour-intensive activities; difficulties faced by regional planning in times of recession when the quantity of new investment is very much reduced - no more agents through which to work; economic rather than social investment.
6. BROWN, M.B. (1972): "From Labourism to Socialism: Political economy of labour in the 1970's", Nottingham
7. This does of course vary between, say, Italy and the U.K. and France and Western Germany with different levels of commitment to and involvement in public ownership and direction of large sectors of the economy.
8. ALDEN, J. & M. EDWARDS (1974): "The role of regional policy in South Wales", in: "The Valleys call", pp. 279-304
9a. BALLARD, P. & E. JONES (1975): "The Valleys call: A self examination by people of the South Wales Valleys during the Year of the Valleys, 1974"
9b. TY TORONTO (1977): "A socio-economic strategy for the Valleys of South' Wales", Aberfan

10. Unless otherwise stated the figures are taken from "A socio-economic strategy for the Valleys of South Wales", op. cit.
11. WHITELEGG, J.: "Achieving a stable industrial mix", in: "The Valleys call", op. cit. pp. 331-35
12. "A socio-economic strategy", op. cit. p. 111, para. 2.2.
13. WHYATT, A. & K. SMITH (1978): "Mondragon - wish we were there?", Undercurrents no. 28, pp. 14-16
14. Industrial Common Ownership Movement (ICOM), Woolwich/London
15. HUNTER, J. (1976): "Making of the crofting community", Edinburgh
16. Comhairle nan Eilean, 1976. Aithris na Roinne (Regional report), Department of Planning and Development
17. CARTER, I.R. (1973): "Six years on: an evaluative study of the Highlands and Islands Development Board, Aberdeen University Review XLV, pp. 55-78
18. MOORE, B. & J. RHODES (1973): "Evaluating the effects of British regional economic policy", Economic Journal 83, pp. 87-110
19. BUCHANAN, K.: "Economic growth and cultural liquidation: the case of the Celtic nations", in: "Radical geography", op. cit.
20. HECHTER, M. (1975): "Internal colonialism", London
21. HAYWARD, J.E.S. (1977): "Institutionalized inequality within an indivisible republic: Brittany and France", Journal of the Conflict Research Society VI, part I, pp. 1-15
22. PHLIPPONNEAU, M. (1967): "La Gauche et les Regions", Paris
23. HOLLAND, S. (1977): "Capital versus the regions", Basingstoke

ZUR PLANUNGSSITUATION LÄNDLICHER PROBLEMGEBIETE

mit 5 Abbildungen

GEORG KLUCZKA

Das Generalthema dieses Symposiums ist unterschiedlich interpretierbar und unter vielfältigen Aspekten zu behandeln, je nachdem aus welcher Position heraus "Planen und Lebensqualität" angesprochen werden.

Zum Begriff Lebensqualität in der Planung

Vom Standpunkt der Erkenntnistheorie ließe sich die kritische Frage vorbringen, ob der komplexe Begriff Lebensqualität nicht in jenen Bereich sprachlicher Formeln gehört, die zwar den Eindruck erwecken, Aussagen zu enthalten, aber letztendlich nicht präzisierbar und damit in der Planungspraxis nicht anwendbar sind. Im Deutschen gibt es hierfür den Begriff der Leerformel.

Man kann unter Lebensqualität jedoch auch eine aktivierende Grundforderung an die Planungsverantwortlichen verstehen, gleichsam eine Zusammenfassung dessen, was im §1 des Raumordnungsgesetzes des Bundes (1965) als Leitbild niedergelegt ist und heißt:

"Das Bundesgebiet ist in seiner allgemeinen Struktur einer Entwicklung zuzuführen, die der freien Entfaltung der Persönlichkeit in der Gemeinschaft am besten dient."

Tatsächlich war der Begriff Lebensqualität im deutschen Planervokabular noch vor 10 Jahren praktisch unbekannt, gebräuchlich dagegen seinerzeit der leichter konkretisierbare, weil ausschließlich materiell orientierte Begriff "Lebensstandard". Lebensqualität meint jedoch mehr. Das Bedeutungsspektrum dieses Begriffes beinhaltet neben materiellen auch immaterielle Faktoren der gesellschaftlichen Entwicklung und schließt neben den in der jüngsten Vergangenheit am häufigsten angesprochenen Problemen des Umweltschutzes in gleicher Weise wirtschaftliche Prosperität, Ausbau der Infrastruktur oder menschenwürdige Gestaltung der Städte und Partizipation ihrer Bürger mit ein.

Den Unterschied zwischen Lebensstandard und Lebensqualität hat H. SWOBODA treffend formuliert, indem er seiner Arbeit über "Die Qualität des Lebens" den Untertitel gab "Vom Wohlstand zum Wohlbefinden" (Stuttgart, 1973).

Bemerkenswerterweise wird von Lebensqualität überwiegend dann gesprochen, wenn es darum geht, Planungsentscheidungen mit vermeintlich negativer Auswirkung auf die Umwelt abzuwenden oder rückgängig zu machen. Dadurch wurde der Begriff Lebensqualität ungewollt in der Nähe planerischer Fehlentscheidungen angesiedelt. Die volle Ausschöpfung seiner Dimensionen und eine gezielte Umsetzung in Planungssysteme stehen bis heute aus.

Gleichwohl hat es verschiedentlich Versuche gegeben, eine Quantifizierung der Bestimmungsfaktoren von Lebensqualität vorzunehmen. Erinnert sei an die Expertise der OECD von 1973, in welcher 8 Zielbereiche mit insgesamt 24 sozialen Faktoren Berücksichtigung fanden:

— Gesundheit — Freizeitgestaltung
— Bildung — Stellung des Verbrauchers
— Arbeit — Sicherheit und Rechtsprechung
— Umwelt — gesellschaftliche Stellung

In diesem Zusammenhang steht auch die Suche nach Sozialindikatoren für das BROP (Bundesraumordnungsprogramm) von 1975, die aus einer vergleichenden Systematik abgeleitet wurden.

Mehr Lebensqualität bei zunehmender regionaler Divergenz?

Es stellt sich nun die Frage, ob die Forderung nach mehr Lebensqualität gerade im Zeichen andauernder wirtschaftlicher Stagnation realistisch ist oder präziser ausgedrückt: mehr Lebensqualität — wie auch immer substantiiert — für alle Menschen in jedem Teilraum unserer Staaten? Die Frage scheint ungehörig, geradezu provokativ, und ist doch nicht ganz unberechtigt.

Wir wissen aus der Geschichte und erleben es heute, daß es Aktiv- und Passivräume gibt; solche Gebiete, in denen sich fortschreitend Wirtschaft und Bevölkerung konzentrieren, während weite Teile des ländlichen Raumes an Substanz verlieren. Noch in der Literatur der 60er Jahre findet sich als Bezeichnung für dieses Phänomen das Begriffspaar Wohlstandsgebiete und Notstandsgebiete. In der stärker formalisierten Diskussion der Gegenwart spricht man global wie regional immer häufiger von den Zentren oder Zentralräumen und der Peripherie. Hinter einer solchen Formulierung stehen die ökonomischen Erklärungsansätze moderner Wachstumstheorien. Zentrum, d.h. überdurchschnittliche Entwicklungsmöglichkeiten, überproportionale Wirtschaftskraft, Fühlungsvorteile, qualifizierte Arbeitsplätze, Verfügbarkeit von Infrastruktur aller Art; Peripherie zu sein beinhaltet Stagnation, Marktferne, wenig differenziertes Arbeitskräftepotential, mangelnde Infrastruktur.

Das Zentrum-Peripherie-Problem ist historisch und systemunabhängig. Es wirkt sich jedoch fatalerweise unter den gegenwärtigen wirtschaftlichen Rahmenbedingungen verstärkt aus.

Wenn es eine der Hauptaufgaben der Raumordnung ist, eine Verringerung regionaler Disparitäten herbeizuführen und das Strukturgefälle zwischen wirtschaftsstarken Zentralräumen und wirtschaftsschwacher Peripherie zu reduzieren, so läßt sich heute feststellen, daß diese Aufgabe nicht etwa geringer, sondern eher größer geworden ist. Welchen Stellenwert aber hat dann angesichts der umschriebenen Situation das Thema dieses Symposiums? Ist Lebensqualität planbar und für Zentrum wie Peripherie realisierbar? Handelt es sich um einen normativen Wert oder einen variablen Relativ-Wert?

Supranationale Ansätze zum Abbau von Entwicklungsdefiziten

Was immer inhaltlich unter Lebensqualität verstanden werden möge, im Kontext mit Planung wird vor allem ihre räumliche Dimension angesprochen. Wie wir wissen, vollzieht sich räumliche Planung auf vier Ebenen: supranational — national — regional — lokal. Im Bereich internationaler Zusammenarbeit im Rahmen der EG gilt mit Errichtung des europäischen Fonds für regionale Entwicklung (1975) die Hauptaufgabe der Beseitigung extremer Strukturdefizite, wie sie z.B. im vielzitierten Mezzogiorno, im Südwesten Frankreichs oder auch in Irland und Schottland vorliegen. Hier sollen mit finanziellen Anreizen wirtschaftliche Aktivitäten initiiert werden, die ihrerseits eine allseitige Verbesserung der jeweiligen Regionalstruktur erhoffen lassen. Aber aus gesamteuropäischer Sicht — verstanden als ein großer Planungsraum — können diese Aktivitäten nur als allererster Schritt gesehen werden. Es fehlt zur Reduzierung der regionalen Ungleichgewichte weitgehend noch an gemeinsamen Zielstrategien, an vergleichenden, länderübergreifenden Strukturanalysen und an Koordination und Transparenz der laufenden Fördermaßnahmen. Bereits bei der Suche nach für den Bereich der EG vergleichbaren statistischen Daten zeigen sich fast unüberwindliche Schwierigkeiten, obwohl es ein gemeinsames Statistisches Amt der EG gibt. Vor allem aber fehlt es im Hinblick auf das Generalthema dieser Veranstaltung an gemeinsamen Überlegungen für europaweit anzustrebende Mindeststandards zur Verbesserung der Lebensqualität in den großen ländlichen Problemgebieten dieses Kontinents.

Kategorien ländlicher Problemgebiete in der Bundesrepublik Deutschland

Für den Bereich der Bundesrepublik Deutschland hat es in dieser Hinsicht bereits vielfältige Überlegungen gegeben. Sie stehen insbesondere im Zusammenhang mit den Arbeiten am erwähnten BROP, über das ich während unseres letzten Symposiums vor drei Jahren berichtet habe. Der dort ausdrücklich vertretene Ansatz, eine Verbesserung der Lebensqualität herbeizuführen, soll vorrangig und gezielt in den Problemgebieten der Bundesrepublik zum Tragen kommen.

Obwohl die großen Ballungszentren von Wirtschaft und Bevölkerung in zunehmendem Maße Verdichtungsschäden aufweisen, lagen die eigentlichen Problemgebiete der Bundesrepublick Deutschland — wie auch des übrigen Europa — seit jeher im ländlichen Raum, weil dort regional die existentielle Absicherung

der Bevölkerung unmittelbar in Frage gestellt ist. Daher wird auch in Zukunft der ländliche Raum eine besondere Aufgabe der Planer bleiben. Erste Versuche, ländliche Problemgebiete flächendeckend — soweit relevant — zu erfassen, hat es schon lange vor Verabschiedung des BROP gegeben. Insbesondere zwei Kategorien sollen hier Erwähnung finden:
— naturbenachteiligte Gebiete
— hinter der allgemeinen Entwicklung zurückgebliebene Gebiete

Als *naturbenachteiligte Gebiete,* deren Abgrenzung auf einen Beschluß des Deutschen Bundestages zurückgeht, werden seit 1961 solche land- und forstwirtschaftlich genutzten Räume bezeichnet, die folgende Merkmale aufweisen:
— geringe Bodenqualität
— extreme Klimabedingungen
— ungünstige Höhen- oder Hanglagen

Entscheidend für die Zuordnung war seinerzeit, daß die Ertragswerte unter dem allgemeinen Bundesdurchschnitt liegen. Verantwortlich für die Abgrenzung zeichnete nicht der für die Raumordnung zuständige, sondern der Bundesminister für Ernährung, Landwirtschaft und Forsten. Gefördert wurde in diesen Räu-

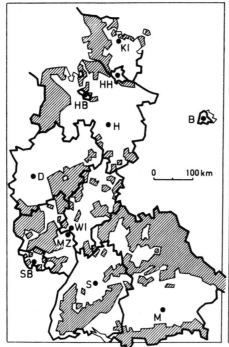

Abb. 1: Naturbenachteiligte Gebiete
Regions of deprived natural environment
Quelle: nach MALZ, F.: Taschenbuch der Umweltplanung, München 1974

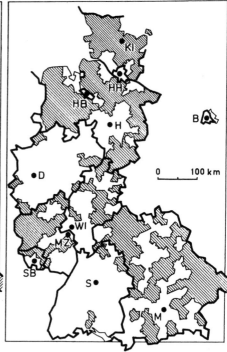

Abb. 2: Hinter der allgemeinen Entwicklung zurückgebliebene Gebiete gemäß Empfehlung der MKRO vom 16.4.1970
Backward areas

men dementsprechend mit eher punkthaften Ansätzen; vor allem waren es landwirtschaftliche Betriebe, die durch Maßnahmen der Flurbereinigung, der Aussiedlung, des Wirtschaftswegebaus und der Wasserwirtschaft subventioniert wurden.
Abb. 1 läßt sich entnehmen, daß die von der Natur benachteiligten Gebiete stärker in Süddeutschland als nördlich der Mainlinie anzutreffen sind, andererseits im nördlichsten Bundesland Schleswig-Holstein allein mehr als 50% der LN (Landwirtschaftlichen Nutzfläche) ausmachen.

Mit dem ROG (Raumordnungsgesetz des Bundes) von 1965 wurde die sogenannte Gebietskategorie der *zurückgebliebenen Gebiete* eingeführt. Sie bezeichnet jene Räume, "in denen die Lebensbedingungen in ihrer Gesamtheit im Verhältnis zum Bundesdurchschnitt wesentlich zurückgeblieben sind oder ein solches Zurückbleiben zu befürchten ist" (ROG § 2, Abs. 1, Ziff. 3). Wie für die naturbenachteiligten Gebiete ist also auch hier der Bundesdurchschnitt als Maß der Zuordnung gewählt worden.

Bereits unmittelbar nach der ersten Abgrenzung der speziell landwirtschaftsbezogenen naturbenachteiligten Gebiete hatten Mitarbeiter des Instituts für Raumordnung in Bad Godesberg Versuche zu einer umfassenderen Berücksichtigung der allgemein zurückgebliebenen Gebiete unternommen, wobei sie die Strukturmerkmale Bevölkerungsdichte, Industriebesatz, Realsteuerkraft und Bruttoinlandsprodukt zugrundelegten.

Aktueller ist eine Abgrenzung der zurückgebliebenen Gebiete durch die MKRO (Ministerkonferenz für Raumordnung), die in Erweiterung der vorgenannten Kriterien 1970 vorgelegt wurde und folgende Schwellenwerte verwendet:

— Wanderungssaldo 1961-1967: ± 0
— Bevölkerungsdichte 1968: 100 E./km^2
— Industriedichte 1968: 70 Besch./1000 E.
— Realsteuerkraft 1967: DM 118.--/E.
— Bruttoinlandsprodukt 1966: DM 6080.-- pro Kopf der Wirtschaftsbevölkerung

Das Zutreffen mindestens dreier Merkmale — gleichgültig welcher — war erforderlich, um der Kategorie der "zurückgebliebenen Gebiete" zugeordnet zu werden.

Kompliziert wurde das Verfahren dadurch, daß diese Gebietskategorie zusätzlich um solche Gebiete erweitert wurde, in denen entsprechend den Ausführungen des ROG ein Zurückbleiben zu befürchten anstand. Hierfür konnten folgende weitere Merkmale herangezogen werden:

Veränderungen 1961 - 1968
— Industriedichte: -4 Besch./1000 E.
— Bruttoinlandsprodukt: DM 1890.-- pro Kopf der Wirtschaftsbevölkerung
— Realsteuerkraft: DM 36.--/E.

Die Karte der zurückgebliebenen Gebiete (Abb. 2) zeigt die größten zusam-

ern, insgesamt also in den bis heute vorwiegend agrarisch strukturierten Räumen des Bundesgebietes. Damit ergibt sich zugleich eine starke Übereinstimmung mit den naturbenachteiligten Gebieten; und ich möchte meine Aussage wiederholen, daß aus planerischer Sicht in den ländlichen Räumen die eigentlichen Problemgebiete liegen. Beide vorgenannten Abgrenzungsverfahren können der Situation in den ländlichen Problemgebieten aber nur bedingt gerecht werden. Sie ermöglichen aufgrund der angewandten Schwellenwert-Methode keinen Vergleich einzelner Teilräume untereinander. Mit ihrem Unvermögen, die regionalen Defizite konkret aufzuzeigen, erlauben sie es auch nicht, im notwendigen Umfang gezielte Entwicklungsmaßnahmen einzuleiten.

Ein entscheidender Schritt zur koordinierten Sicht der strukturschwachen und zurückgebliebenen Gebiete und ihrer gezielten, von Bund und Ländern gemeinsam erbrachten Förderung erfolgte ab 1969 durch die Aufstellung sogenannter *"Regionaler Aktionsprogramme"* zur Verbesserung der Wirtschaftsstruktur. Sie betreffen wiederum die Gebiete, deren Wirtschaftskraft erheblich unter dem Bundesdurchschnitt liegt bzw. dahin tendiert. Seit 1971 gibt es Rahmenpläne zur Förderung der zunächst 21 Regionalen Aktionsräume. (vgl. Abb. 3). Ihr räumliches Verbreitungsmuster gleicht den beiden vorgenannten Kategorien. Die schwachstrukturierten Agrargebiete sind zugleich gewerbliche Fördergebiete. Innerhalb der Regionalen Aktionsräume können Unternehmer der Industrie Investitionszuschüsse, Darlehen, Zinsverbilligungen etc. erhalten, falls sie durch Errichtung oder Erweiterung gewerblicher Produktionsbetriebe neue Arbeitsplätze schaffen oder Rationalisierungsmaßnahmen zum Zwecke der Sicherung von Arbeitsplätzen durchführen. Gegebenenfalls können auch Arbeitsplätze im Fremdenverkehrsgewerbe, Industriegeländeerschließungen, kommunale Infrastruktur und Ausbildungseinrichtungen subventioniert werden. Das erklärte Ziel dieser möglichen Maßnahmen ist es, die räumlichen Ungleichgewichte in Deutschland abzubauen, um Chancengleichheit und Lebensqualität in allen Regionen des Bundesgebietes zu schaffen.

> Zu mehr Lebensqualität in ländlichen Problemgebieten
> mit Hilfe großräumig konzipierter Instrumente?

Damit kommen wir auf meine einleitenden Ausführungen und das BROP zurück. Lebensqualität im Sinne des BROP beinhaltet für alle Teilräume des Bundesgebietes 1. die Verfügbarkeit von Erwerbsmöglichkeiten und 2. ein ausreichendes Angebot an Infrastruktureinrichtungen, beides in zumutbarer Entfernung. Ergänzend wird eine menschenwürdige Umwelt gefordert.

Die Ungleichwertigkeit der Lebensbedingungen in den verschiedenen Teilen des Bundesgebietes wird hier erstmals durch die Anwendung eines Indikatorensystems festgestellt. Dieses erlaubt durch Konkretisierung der genannten Begriffe Erwerbsmöglichkeit (Erwerbsstruktur) und Infrastruktur die Fixierung derjenigen Regionen, in denen Defizite an Lebensqualität vorliegen.

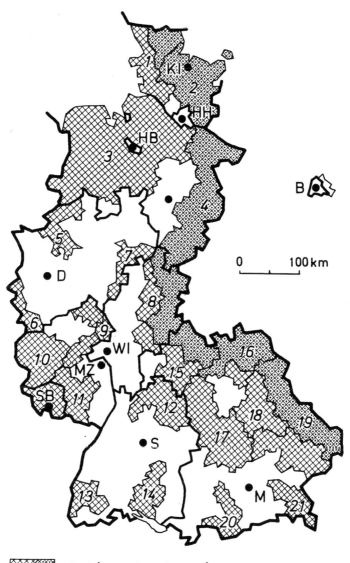

Gebiete der Gemeinschaftsaufgabe

15 Nummern der Regionalen Aktions= programme

Zonenrandgebiet

Abb. 3: Regionale Aktionsräume (Stand 1.1.1974)
Regional plans of action

Infrastrukturanalyse des BROP (1975):

 Bildungswesen   Realschüler und Gymnasiasten
             Studierende an Hochschulen
 Gesundheitswesen   Ärzte in freier Praxis
             Krankenhausbetten
 Sozialwesen   Kindergartenplätze
             Plätze in Einrichtungen der Altenhilfe
 Sport und Erholung   Turn- und Sporthallen
             Hallenbäder, Lehrschwimmbecken
 Wohnungswesen   Wohnfläche
             Wohnungen mit Bad, WC und Zentralheizung
 Verkehrswesen   überregionale Straßen
             Reisezeiten und -geschwindigkeiten im Eisenbahn-Fernverkehr
             Berufspendler mit öffentlichen Verkehrsmitteln
 Technische Ver-   öffentliche Kanalisation
 und Entsorgung   und Abwasserbeseitigung

Erwerbsstrukturanalyse des BROP (1975):

 Bruttoinlandsprodukt je Kopf der Wirtschaftsbevölkerung
 Einkommen (Lohn- und Gehaltssummen je abhängig Beschäftigten)

Abgeprüft wurden Infrastruktur- und Erwerbsstrukturindikatoren in insgesamt 38 bundesweit flächendeckenden Analyseräumen (Gebietseinheiten), die insofern eine Besonderheit und zugleich ein problemadäquates Bezugsfeld darstellen, als sie weitgehend nach dem Funktionalprinzip abgegrenzt wurden. Eine Besonderheit deshalb, weil die von mir zuvor genannten und andere planungsbezogene Raumgliederungen des Bundesgebietes nahezu ausschließlich als sogenannte homogene Räume, d.h. nach Strukturmerkmalen abgegrenzt wurden. Adäquat erscheint die Anwendung des Funktionalprinzips deshalb, weil die gewählten Indikatoren die regionalen Realisierungsmöglichkeiten der Daseinsgrundfunktionen feststellen sollen. Andererseits muß aber auf eine Schwäche in der Abgrenzung dieser BROP-Gebietseinheiten hingewiesen werden: Sie faßt innergebietlich auch konträre Zustände und Prozesse zusammen und bietet damit teilweise eine verzerrte Analyse (Nivellierungseffekt).

Im Zusammenhang mit unserer Themenstellung darf die unerläßliche Indikatoren-Diskussion vernachlässigt werden, weil wir jetzt feststellen wollen, welche Teile des Bundesgebietes sich durch besondere Mängel an Lebensqualität auszeichnen. Das BROP spricht hier vorsichtiger von "Schwerpunkträumen mit besonderen Strukturschwächen".

Bereits ein erster Blick auf Abbildung 4 läßt deutliche Übereinstimmungen mit dem vertrauten Bild der von der Natur benachteiligten und den hinter der allgemeinen Entwicklung zurückgebliebenen Gebiete erkennen. Als aktuelle ländliche Problemgebiete mit erheblichen Defiziten an Infrastruktureinrichtungen und

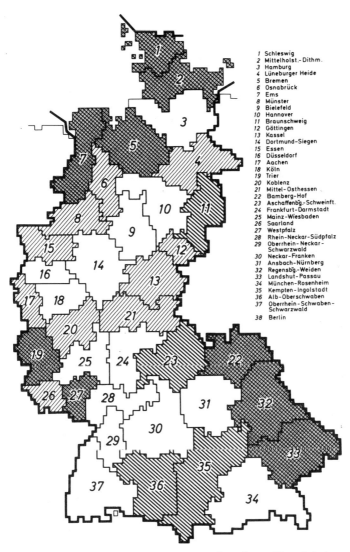

Abb. 4: Schwerpunkträume mit besonderen Strukturschwächen
Retarded areas characterized by particular structural inequities

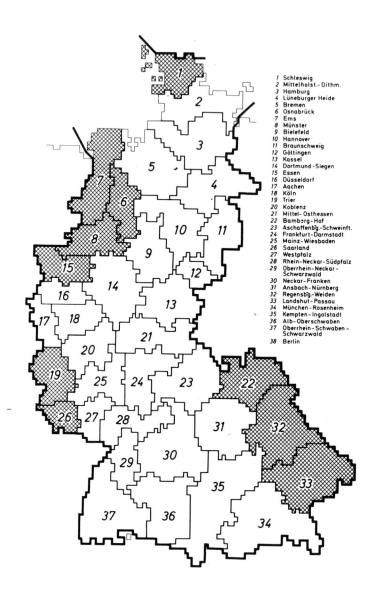

Abb. 5: Abwanderungsgefährdete Räume
Areas threatened by migration losses

Erwerbsmöglichkeiten heben sich wiederum weite Teile Norddeutschlands ab, angefangen von Schleswig-Holstein über den Unterweserraum bis ins Emsland. Ein ebenso deutliches Negativ-Bild ergeben die traditionellen Problemgebiete Nord- und Ostbayerns in gleicher Weise wie die von Eifel und Westpfalz. Es sind — wie aus der ergänzenden Abbildung 5 deutlich wird, zugleich die Problemräume flächenhafter Abwanderung. Allein in diesen extrem benachteiligten Gebieten lebten zum Zeitpunkt der letzten Volkszählung (1970) mehr als 7,5 Millionen Menschen. Wie kann ihnen seitens der Planung zu mehr Lebensqualität verholfen werden?

Das BROP gibt auf diese Frage die Antwort, daß es beabsichtigt und infolge der Erkenntnisse dieses Programms auch möglich sei, Fördermittel gezielt und schwerpunktmäßig einzusetzen. Eigens hierfür wurde das Instrumentarium der Entwicklungszentren und großräumig bedeutsamen Achsen geschaffen, das jedoch erst dann wirksam werden kann, wenn es durch die Länder ausgefüllt wird. Hierin liegt eine Crux.

Aber auch vom planungstheoretischen Ansatz und in Anbetracht der jüngsten Veränderungen der ökonomischen Rahmenbedingungen können Zweifel angebracht sein, ob die Konzeption eines großdimensionierten Planungsinstrumentariums die Probleme der strukturschwachen ländlichen Räume lösen kann.

So weist der Beirat für Raumordnung beim Bundesminister für Raumordnung, Bauwesen und Städtebau in seiner Empfehlung vom 16. Juni 1976 — also bereits ein Jahr nach Veröffentlichung des BROP — zu Recht darauf hin, daß sich die Entwicklungsaussichten vieler peripherer Gebiete deutlich verschlechtert haben, weil sich die Produktionsfaktoren der industriellen Unternehmer geändert haben.

Mit wenigen Worten zusammengefaßt heißt das: Die Standortgunst vieler Städte, die zwar in ländlichen Problemgebieten, aber immerhin an leistungsfähigen Verkehrswegen gelegen sind, hat sich im Zuge der jüngsten Konzentrationserscheinungen im sekundären, aber auch im tertiären Sektor zugunsten der großen Zentren und Zentralräume stark relativiert.

Damit wird sich das erklärte Planungsziel einer Verbesserung der Erwerbsstuktur in den ländlichen Problemgebieten auf absehbare Zeit kaum realisieren lassen. Zugleich dürfte die Abwanderungsbereitschaft und damit der Exodus qualifizierter Arbeitskräfte aus den ländlichen Problemgebieten weiter anhalten. Aber nicht nur dies: Zwei Gründe sprechen dafür, daß im Bereich der Infrastruktur eine ähnlich negative Entwicklung bereits eingeleitet ist. So haben die Zentralisationserscheinungen im Zuge der kommunalen Gebietsreform generell zu einem höheren Wege-Zeit-Kosten-Aufwand geführt, insbesondere für die Bewohner ländlicher Gebiete. Dies trifft dort in vollem Maße auf die Erreichbarkeit von Verwaltungs- und Bildungseinrichtungen zu. Des weiteren bewirken die in den strukturschwachen Gebieten rückläufigen gewerbesteuerlichen Einnahmen kommunaler Haushalte bei gleichzeitig gestiegenen Kosten einen zwangsläufigen Rückgang der Investitionen im Infrastrukturbereich, dessen Qualität damit ebenfalls nur bedingt verbessert werden kann.

Gibt es trotz aller Einschränkungen nicht vielleicht doch Wege, ein Mehr an Lebensqualität für die ländlichen Problemgebiete zu schaffen?

Die Antwort kann verhalten positiv ausfallen, wenn die künftigen Planungsaktivitäten in diesen Räumen
1. sich auf das natürliche Potential dieser Räume konzentrieren,
2. im bodenständigen Gewerbe einen Ansatz zur Verbesserung der Erwerbsstruktur sehen und
3. eine ausgewogene Re-Dezentralisierung im Bereich der Infrastruktur herbeiführen.

Summary

Regional Planning in Rural Problem Areas

This contribution deals with the framework of regional planning in rural problem areas. Based on the critical analysis of the definition of the quality of life and its application within the planning, the author poses the question, whether, in spite of growing regional disparities, the demand for an increase in the quality of life in peripheral areas can be realized.

A further train of thought has been followed with reference to the European fund for regional development. This is to aid in the reduction of retarded areas within the European Communities. It is to be noted, however, that joint European development concepts are missing. The Federal Republic of Germany already has made several proposals for the improvement of working and living conditions in rural problem areas. Decisive is the classification of these specified areas into one of the appropriate subsidized spatial categories.

Regions of natural disadvantage and retarded areas were studied with special attention being paid to their demarcation criteria and spatial distribution. Within regional activity programmes specific financial support is given to the creation of new jobs in industry in retarded areas. A final section deals with the Federal Regional Planning Programme which has the aim to improve the general working and living conditions especially in the rural problem areas. However, it is doubtful that these specifically developed planning concepts will be successful. The contribution closes with several suggestions for alternative strategies of development.

REGIONAL DISPARITIES IN WEST GERMAN AGRICULTURE

with 7 figures (one as supplement) and 2 tables

GÜNTER THIEME and HANS-DIETER LAUX

This paper is an attempt to transfer the experiences and results of two regional studies to the whole area of the Federal Republic of Germany, thereby trying to test and, possibly, generalize the results achieved. In those studies the regional differences of agrarian structures in two parts of the German "Mittelgebirge" as well as the causes of this development had been analysed (cf. THIEME 1975 and LAUX 1977).

Aims of the study

West German agriculture on the one hand can generally be characterised by low productivity and low per capita income as compared to the secondary and tertiary sectors of the economy. But on the other hand, there are striking disparities within the agricultural sector itself, which become evident by great differences of income among producers in the same area as well as by enormous regional differences in productivity, farm structure etc. Particularly the latter problem will be tackled in our analysis, which has mainly the following aims: First, a system of multidimensionally defined structural types of agriculture is to be developed. Second, it must be asked whether these structural types form a specific spatial pattern thereby allowing to divide the Federal Republic into homogeneous structural regions. Finally it is necessary to test the hypothesis that these originally static spatial types are also characterised by a different development of agrarian structures during the post-war period.

Recent development of agrarian structures in the Federal Republic of Germany

Before discussing the selection of various dimensions for our typology, it is necessary to add a few remarks on recent agricultural changes in the Federal Republic.

Proceeding from the fact that agrarian structures are essentially determined by the combination of the three most important factors of production (land, labour, and capital) farm organisation clearly demonstrates a tendency towards what may be called "minimum-cost-combination", i.e. an intention to replace scarce and expensive production factors by comparatively cheaper ones. So after an earlier period of specialisation we had a phase of mechanisation (labour being replaced by capital) in West German agriculture until the middle of the nineteen-sixties; ever since that time we have reached a phase of farm enlargement (labour being replaced by land).

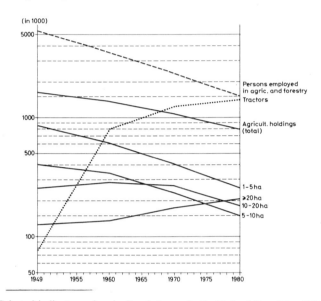

Fig. 1: Selected indicators of agricultural change in the Federal Republic of Germany

Even a brief look at figure 1 shows the enormous increase of the number of tractors (representing the production factor capital) especially during the fifties, a development which slowed down in the sixties and seventies, having come close to its saturation level. The most important changes in farm size structure, however, took place in the sixties and early seventies.

The common feature of both phases is the substitution of labour by capital respectively land so that one can say that the recent structural change is primarily characterized by the *intrasectoral* mobility of land and the *intersectoral* mobility of labour. Even the recent economic recession could only slow down, but not stop the movement of persons employed in agriculture out of the primary sector.

The process of adapting agriculture to the conditions of industrial production is basically determined by two groups of factors: on the one hand there are causes resulting from the agricultural situation itself, on the other hand there is the influence of non-agricultural development in a certain region.

Only after these considerations a problem-orientated selection of variables for the study is possible, trying to represent the following dimensions:

1. Agricultural sector
   a. physical conditions of production
   b. farm size
   c. labour supply
   d. socio-economic structure of holdings (especially the proportion of part-time farming)
   e. extent of mechanisation
   f. land-use orientation
2. Non-agricultural components
   a. degree of urbanisation/suburbanisation
   b. non-agricultural labour supply
   c. distance to urban centres

Sampling procedure and selection of data

The regional basis of our study was formed by a random sample of 3 percent of all the communities of the Federal Republic. Due to this sample size the maximum error amounts to 4 percent within the 95 percent confidence limits.

Since communities were preferred to counties it was impossible to cover the whole area of West Germany; on the other hand, communities are far more homogeneous in comparison with counties. In order to exclude the special problems of "urban" agriculture as well as horticulture, all communities with more than 20,000 inhabitants had been eliminated from the sample as well as those with a proportion of 10% or more of the cultivated land under intensive crops. Accordingly, 612 communities made up the final sample size.

In the next step of the investigation appropriate variables were selected to represent the above mentioned dimensions of agrarian and socio-economic structure. The main source of data was the vast body of official statistics from the years 1949/50, 1960/61 and 1970/72 (population, employment, and agricultural statistics). In order to eliminate the influence of the different sizes of communities, the absolute numbers were mostly converted into ratios, generally percentage rates. So for each of the 612 study units 102 variables were developed.

Regional types of agriculture (factor analysis and distance grouping)

46 of the original variables were subjected to factor analysis.[1] By means of this procedure it was to be tested whether the basic dimensions formulated above corresponded to complex factors or components, which were independent of each other.

Our factor analysis supplied eight factors which could be interpreted and accounted for 83.7% of the variability among the 46 original variables.

Instead of discussing the results of the factor analysis in detail it appears to be more appropriate to concentrate on an interpretation of factor loadings and an

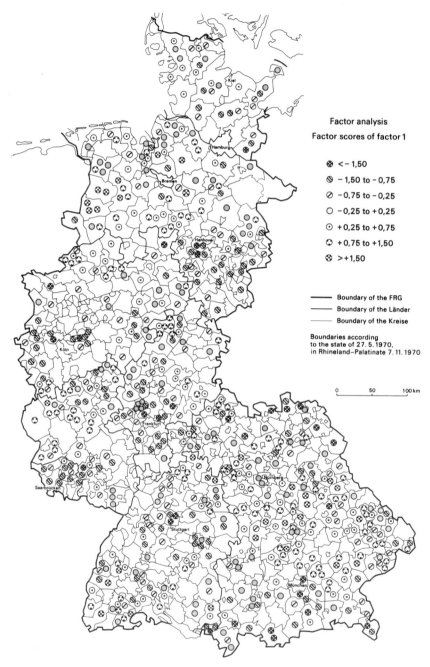

Fig. 2: Factor 1: Socio-economic structure of the communities.
Regional distribution of factor scores

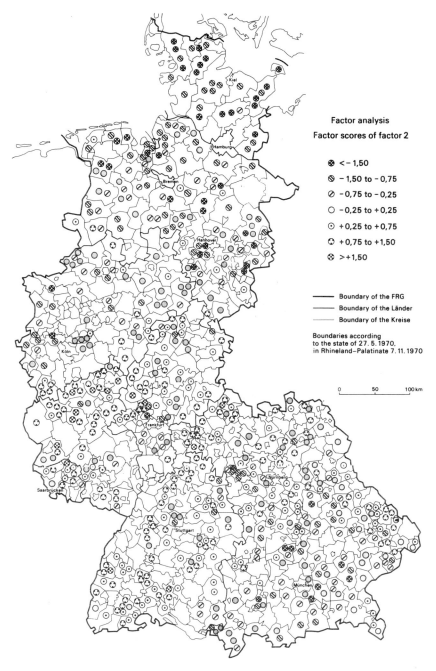

Fig. 3: Factor 2: Structure of agricultural holdings. Regional distribution of factor scores.

analysis of the regional distribution of factor scores of those four factors which were also used for the typology later on.2)

Factor 1 (figure 2) representing 25.5% of the total variance describes the socio-economic structure of the communities. In some sort of rural-urban-continuum the basically rural or even agricultural communities are characterised by high positive factor scores. Here you still have a predominance of persons employed in agriculture, employment in the secondary and tertiary sectors being lower than average; the number of persons per household is comparatively high, population density, in contrast, rather low there.

Among those areas which appear rural even today there must be mentioned western Lower Saxony, parts of the German Mittelgebirge (Eifel, mountain areas of Hesse) and vast parts of Bavaria. More or less urbanised or at least suburbanised areas are the surroundings of Hamburg, southern Lower Saxony, almost all of Northrhine-Westphalia, the Saar and the Rhine-Main-area, the central parts of Baden-Württemberg, and the Bavarian "Alpenvorland".

Factor 2 (figure 3) accounting for 22.1% of the total variance is to be interpreted as the basic dimension of the structure of agricultural holdings. It describes the contrast between communities characterised by small holdings run by part-time farmers and such areas with a great proportion of full-time farmers running holdings of at least 20 hectares in size.

The regional distribution of factor scores clearly indicates the traditional areas of undivided inheritance in northern Germany and Bavaria just as well as the old gavelkind areas in the south-west. An exception to the rule is formed by the mountainous regions of the Black Forest and the Bavarian Forest which — although traditionally areas of undivided inheritance — nowadays are characterised by comparatively small farms.

Similar to factor 2 the most significant features of factor 3 (figure 4) with 12% of the total variance are high loadings of variables from the field of farm structure. Particularly it is a high proportion of farms between 10 and 20 hectares which constitutes this factor.

Just those medium-sized farms of about 10-20 hectares today must be considered as extremely problematic, especially if run by full-time farmers. Therefore it seemed justified to define factor 3 as an agricultural problem factor.

The predominance of critical farm sizes in Bavaria and the eastern parts of Baden-Württemberg shows areas whose agrarian structures must be considerably improved, and it equally shows that there is a certain contrast between northern and southern areas of undivided inheritance with respect to their present agrarian structures.

Finally factor 6 being the last of the factors used for the following typology is to be discussed here (figure 5). It accounts for 10% of the total variance. Due to high loadings of variables representing the level of labour input per unit of land it may be interpreted as factor of labour input in agriculture.

Apart from a few regional peculiarities e.g. at the Niederrhein a look at the pattern of factor scores shows the striking contrast between north and south

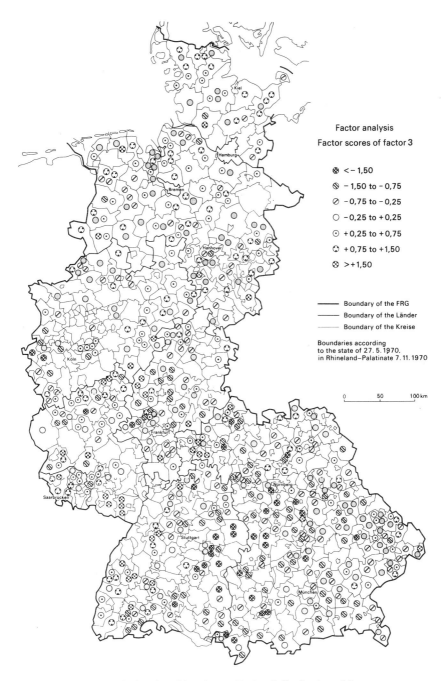

Fig. 4: Factor 3: Agricultural problem factor. Regional distribution of factor scores

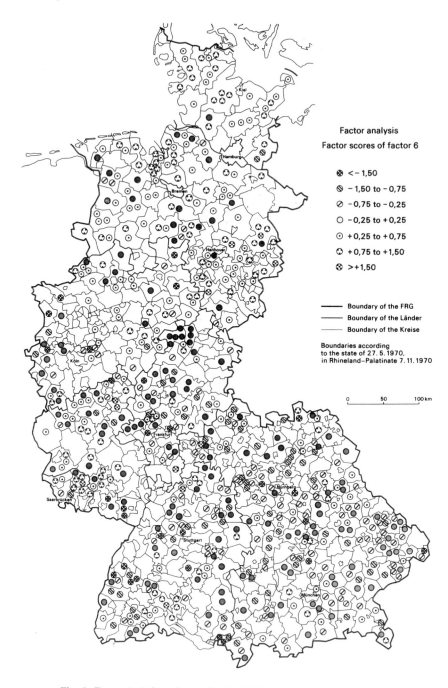

Fig. 5: Factor 6: Labour input. Regional distribution of factor scores

mentioned before. Since the relation of labour force per unit of land, the man-land ratio, is certainly a key problem of agriculture, this is another indicator of the regionally different extent of structural change to be expected.

Trying to sum up the results of factor analysis one can say that this procedure supplies a number of consistent basic dimensions of spatial structure, thereby supporting the hypothesis formulated at the beginning of this paper, and that moreover it also gives some clear evidence of the regional differentiation of agriculture in the Federal Republic of Germany.

Only by a combination of the four independent dimensions presented, however, it is possible to develop the intended typology. This task was tackled by the method of distance grouping.[3] In our case the grouping process was stopped after the 602nd grouping step, thus forming ten groups, which meant a loss of information of only 39%.

The ten groups may quite well be described through the arithmetic means of factor scores. In table 1 a very brief verbal characterisation of the different types is given, factors two and three having been summed up in one dimension. It is impossible here to give a detailed analysis of every single group: it rather seems more useful to pick out groups 1, 6 and 7 as typical examples which clearly demonstrate the differences of economic, specifically agrarian, structures.

Table 1: Distance grouping: Characterisation of the structural types

Group	Factor 1 Socio-economic structure	Factors 2/3 Farm size	Factor 6 Labour input
1	largely urban-industrial	large	very low
2	intermediate	large	low
3	urban-industrial	medium-sized to large	average
4	largely urban-industrial	small to medium-sized	rather high
5	extremely rural-agricultural	mostly large	average
6	rural-agricultural	medium-sized	high
7	largely urban-industrial	small	average
8	rural-agricultural	small to medium-sized	average
9	urban-industrial	mixed	extremely high
10	rural-agricultural	extremely small	extremely high

Group 1 is characterised by the predominance of full-time farms with more than 20 hectares and a very low input of labour. This favourable situation of agriculture is further intensified by a more or less urban and industrialised socio-economic structure of the communities.

In contrast to group 1 group 6 is marked by quite unfavourable socio-economic conditions. The high proportion of farms between 10 and 20 hectares in combination with a low proportion of part-time farms as well as the comparatively high input of agricultural labour force show that the necessary process of development has hardly started here. This group is no doubt the most problematic one with respect to both socio-economic and agrarian structures.

The situation of group 7 is completely different. The communities of this type have mostly small farms with a very high proportion of part-time farming and an average labour input. Their rather urbanised and industrial character additionally points out that employment in agriculture is only of minor significance in this group. Here as well as in group 10 with the predominance of even smaller farms the tendency towards farm abandonment with the well-known consequence of "social fallow" is particularly evident.

At first sight the spatial distribution of the single groups (figure 6, supplement) appears somewhat confusing and it seems quite difficult to distinguish clear regional patterns. We can really notice, however, some very distinct local clusters: so the north of Germany is mainly characterised by types 1, 2, 3 and 5, the south-west (Länder Hesse, Rhineland-Palatinate, and Baden-Württemberg) by groups 4, 7, 8 and 10, and Bavaria by groups 3, 5 and 6.

Considering again those structural types which have just been described in detail one can find out that group 1, which excels by favourable conditions in any respect, is strikingly concentrated in Schleswig-Holstein, Lower Saxony and the Westphalian "Börde" regions. In the whole of southern Germany, however, there are only very few representatives of this type with the exception of a certain cluster in the Palatinate and the Saar district, where recently quite impressive agricultural changes have taken place.

Group 6 also has a very distinct spatial pattern: more than 80% of all the communities of this very problematic type are to be found in Bavaria respectively the neighbouring counties of eastern Württemberg.

In contrast to this group 7 with small farms and characterised by the predominance of non-agricultural employment is concentrated — often in spatial association with group 8 — in south-west Germany and the eastern Bavarian frontier regions.

It seems justified to sum up the results of the distance grouping as follows: even if the ten different groups of communities do not form compact regions - which, due to the fact that this is a sample study, could not be expected anyway - they can - with a few exceptions and some slight reservations - be considered as regional types of agrarian structure.

Structural types and agricultural development

Now it is necessary to briefly discuss the question formulated in the beginning, i.e. whether the groups of communities defined as *structural* types are also characterised by a specific *development* of their agrarian structures. Table 2 tries to give an answer to this question. In this diagram the single groups are described by the arithmetic means of a number of selected variables. Particularly interesting in this context are the first two variables (development of the number of agricultural holdings from 1949 to 1971, and the development of the number of persons employed in agriculture from 1950 to 1970).

Being indicators of structural change in agriculture these variables had not been included in the factor analysis and therefore did not contribute to the grouping process either. All the more surprising are the eta-square values related to the two variables: these values are the result of a variance analysis[4] and for each variable show the proportion of variance "explained" by the arrangement into groups. In our case 40% respectively 36% of the total variance are explained.

The index values for the decline of the number of farms (1949 defined as 100%) vary from 81.3% (group 6) to 38.4% (group 9) and for the decline of the number of persons employed in agriculture from 54.8% (group 6) to 24.7% (group 10).

If we have a look again at those structural types chosen as examples the most striking thing is that group 6 with its very unfavourable agrarian and socio-economic *structures* is also characterised by the slowest *development* of agriculture. The insufficient mobility of land in this group can clearly be seen by the very modest progress in farm enlargement.

Groups 1 and 7, on the other hand, are among those with the most dynamic development. Differing considerably in their original farm structure, they both profit from their favourable socioeconomic situation; and the mobility of both land and labour is particularly evident by the decline of the number of holdings as well as the number of persons employed in agriculture.

In group 1 there is a strong trend towards larger farms of more than 20 hectares; medium-sized farms which, as we have heard, face the gravest structural problems are very untypical of this group, and the labour input is quite low due to the existence of non-agricultural alternatives of occupation.

A very impressive shift in farm size structure can be noticed in group 7, too, although part-time farms still dominate. It would be possible to demonstrate such characteristics of structural changes in agriculture for the other seven groups as well, but even these examples show that the *structural* types described really find their equivalents in a different *development* of their agrarian structures.

Some brief final remarks on three aspects of our regional typology should be mentioned. 1. An interesting result of our study is the fact that a number of areas formerly considered to have very favourable agrarian structures have developed into agricultural problem areas. This is true for vast parts of the southern German "Gäu"-districts as well as for some parts of the "Rheinische Schiefergebirge" (cf. LAUX 1977). Apparently, the necessary structural change has not yet taken place — one might perhaps even say because the natural conditions of production were favourable and the farm size structure originally far better than average. This stagnation can especially be noticed if non-agricultural alternatives of employment are scarce. The result is an excessive number of full-time farms of insufficient size, with almost none of them giving away substantial quantities of land, with very few of the farmers moving out of business, thereby blocking the urgently necessary process of farm enlargement.

Considering this it is evident that any kind of planning in rural areas must not be limited to the agricultural sector, the creation of non-agricultural employment being the key to an improvement of agrarian structures as well.

A second remarkable result is the effect of historical elements on the present agrarian structure in Germany. In Fig. 7 one can see the spatial distribution of customs of inheritance. The traditional division of Germany into a northern and south-eastern area of undivided inheritance separated by the south-western gavelkind area in a way has lasted until today. The areas mentioned, which also correspond to three historical variants of land tenure (Agrarverfassung), can - in

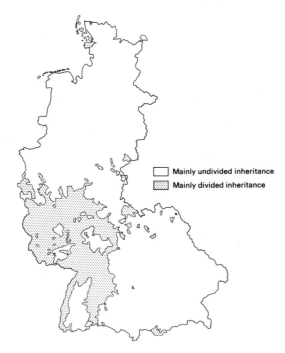

Fig. 7: Customs of inheritance in the Federal Republic of Germany 1959/60

Table 2: Selected characteristics of the structural types

Group	Developm. number of holdings 1949-1971 (1949 = 100)	Developm. number of persons empl. in agric 1950-1970 (1950 = 100)	Proportion of holdings with ... ha									Average size of holdings		Persons employed in agric. per 100 ha 1970/71	Proportion of part-time farms 1972
			1949				1971					1949	1871		
			-5	5-20	≥20	-5	5-10	10-20	≥20						
1	46,79	30,02	57,26	28,44	14,30	34,54	11,11	15,04	39,30			9,48	18,57	10,17	45,43
2	63,87	38,63	35,18	29,89	34,94	18,53	6,88	12,42	62,18			20,04	32,44	8,26	24,43
3	51,44	36,82	52,17	38,84	8,99	30,88	15,80	27,16	26,17			7,97	14,28	15,07	34,54
4	57,04	40,12	48,80	48,88	2,32	28,18	30,25	35,47	6,09			6,68	9,61	19,70	45,07
5	77,25	48,20	35,65	46,04	18,29	26,34	16,41	27,03	30,21			11,64	15,74	13,72	33,75
6	81,32	54,82	33,22	58,26	8,52	24,64	24,84	38,05	12,48			9,50	11,46	19,67	32,59
7	42,60	26,85	75,01	23,12	1,87	54,66	18,51	16,15	10,69			4,27	8,00	16,62	66,04
8	68,56	37,14	49,17	48,59	2,25	37,33	31,81	23,98	6,88			6,32	8,62	17,52	61,03
9	38,41	33,30	83,01	16,44	0,55	66,77	19,20	11,70	2,32			3,11	5,07	32,73	54,28
10	54,86	24,69	87,19	12,25	0,56	81,27	12,71	4,97	1,07			3,37	3,80	24,07	85,72
Eta-square value	0,4037	0,3634	0,5052	0,4820	0,6597	0,5690	0,4166	0,4896	0,8074			0,6116	0,7420	0,3960	0,5201

a somewhat modified form - even be detected in the results of our distance grouping. Among the 73 communities of group 1, 57 are part of the northern German area of undivided inheritance, only four of the south-eastern variant, and 12 belong to the old gavelkind area. With group 6 it is just the other way round: 63 communities of the south- eastern area of undivided inheritance are faced by 11 north German communities and 2 gavelkind communities. These examples show to what extent the persistence of historical structures has influenced German agriculture.

Finally, one last relationship might just be hinted at: our types of agrarian structure have very different shares in the spatial categories developed by the German regional planning authorities, i.e. agglomeration areas, rural areas, and rural problem areas. Here one can see again that the regions characterised by small holdings which are run by part-time farmers cause much less trouble to the planners than the areas with a high proportion of medium-sized farms: among the 76 communities of group 6 almost 60% are classified as rural problem areas, in groups 7 and 10 where the holdings are extremely small this percentage only amounts to 47% respectively 30%.

Zusammenfassung

Regionale Disparitäten in der Agrarstruktur der Bundesrepublik Deutschland

Die Agrarstruktur der Bundesrepublik Deutschland ist durch beträchtliche regionale Disparitäten gekennzeichnet. Ziel des vorliegenden Aufsatzes ist es, auf der Basis einer Stichprobe von 612 Gemeinden diese regionalen Unterschiede durch eine Typologie zu beschreiben und zu analysieren.

Ausgehend von der Hypothese, daß die Struktur der Landwirtschaft sowohl durch die inneragrarische als auch durch die gesamtwirtschaftliche Situation des jeweiligen Raumes bestimmt ist, wurden in einem ersten Schritt 46 Variable einer Faktorenanalyse unterzogen. Diese Variablen sind folgenden Bereichen zugeordnet. Agrarsektor: Betriebsgröße, landwirtschaftliche Arbeitsverfassung, sozialökonomische Betriebsstruktur, Mechanisierungsgrad, Produktionsverhältnisse; außerlandwirtschaftlicher Bereich: Urbanisierungsgrad, nichtlandwirtschaftliche Beschäftigungsmöglichkeiten und Lage zu übergeordneten Zentren.

Insgesamt wurden 8 Faktoren extrahiert, die 83,69% der Gesamtvarianz erklären. Faktor 1 ist als Faktor der sozialökonomischen Gesamtstruktur der Gemeinden zu interpretieren. Die Faktoren 2 und 3 geben jeweils verschiedene Aspekte der landwirtschaftlichen Betriebsstruktur wieder, wobei der Faktor 2 den Gegensatz von Groß- und Kleinbetrieben, Faktor 3 den Anteil mittlerer Betriebe betont. Demgegenüber wird die Arbeitsintensität in der Landwirtschaft durch Faktor 6 charakterisiert.

Mit Hilfe einer Distanzgruppierung wurde in einem weiteren Arbeitsschritt die beabsichtigte Typisierung durchgeführt. Hierbei wurden mit den Faktoren 1,

2, 3 und 6 die wichtigsten Dimensionen in die Gruppierung einbezogen. Das Resultat dieser multidimensionalen Klassifikation ist in Tabelle 1 dargestellt.

Die räumliche Verteilung der Strukturtypen (vgl. Fig. 6) läßt deutliche Unterschiede zwischen Norddeutschland (Schleswig-Holstein, Niedersachsen, Nordrhein-Westfalen), Südwestdeutschland (Hessen, Rheinland-Pfalz, Saarland, Baden-Württemberg) und Bayern erkennen. Insbesondere folgende Typen zeigen eine deutliche regionale Konzentration. Die Gruppen 1 und 2, die insgesamt eine günstige Agrarstruktur aufweisen, sind fast ausschließlich in Norddeutschland zu finden, während die Gruppe 6, sowohl durch eine problematische Agrar- wie auch eine ungünstige wirtschaftliche Gesamtstruktur ausgezeichnet, eine typische bayerische Erscheinung ist. Demgegenüber sind die kleinbäuerlichen und durch einen hohen Anteil von Nebenerwerbsbetrieben gekennzeichneten Gruppen 7 und 8 vor allem in Südwestdeutschland anzutreffen.

Bei einer Analyse der verschiedenen Strukturtypen fällt zum einen die starke Persistenzwirkung historischer Elemente der Agrarverfassung, insbesondere der Erbsitten, auf. Einige der traditionellen landwirtschaftlichen Vorzugsgebiete (vor allem die süddeutschen Gäulandschaften) zeigen allerdings deutliche Züge der Stagnation. Ein weiteres wichtiges Ergebnis ist die enge Beziehung zwischen den Strukturtypen und den Raumkategorien der Regionalplanung, hierunter vor allem den ländlichen Problemgebieten.

Notes

1. Fortran IV-program FAKAN (author: W.D. RASE, Bonn). The computing was done by means of an IBM 370/165 of the "Regionales Hochschulrechenzentrum Bonn".
2. For a detailed analysis of the factor matrix cf. LAUX, H.-D. & G. THIEME (1978), pp. 185-93
3. Program DISTZU 1 (Fortran IV), author J. BÄHR, Kiel, revised by F.-J. KEMPER, Bonn.
   The results of the distance grouping were modified by a discriminant analysis (Program MDISC, Fortran IV, SSP of IBM).
4. cf. COOLEY, W.W. & P.R. LOHNES (1971), pp. 238 sqq.

References

ANDREAE, B. (1968): "Die Minimalkostenkombination in der Landwirtschaft im Zuge der volkswirtschaftlichen Entwicklung", Ber. über Landwirtschaft 46, pp. 1-14

BARON, P. (1972): "Die Relativität des Urteils deutscher Agrarökonomen zum Betriebsgrößenoptimum und ihre Gründe", Landwirtschaft - Angewandte Wissenschaft 157

COOLEY, W.W. & P.R. LOHNES (1971): "Multivariate data analysis", New York/London/Sidney/Toronto

FOUND, W.C. (1971): "A theoretical approach to rural land use patterns", London

HERLEMANN, H.-H. & H. STAMER (1958): "Produktionsgestaltung und Betriebsgröße in der Landwirtschaft unter dem Einfluß der wirtschaftlich-technischen Entwicklung", Kieler Studien, Forschungsber. d. Inst. f. Weltwirtschaft a.d. Univ. Kiel 44

LAUX, H.-D. (1977): "Jüngere Entwicklungstypen der Agrarstruktur. Dargestellt am Beispiel des Landkreises Mayen/Eifel", Arb. z. Rhein. Landeskunde 41

LAUX, H.-D. & G. THIEME (1978): "Die Agrarstruktur der Bundesrepublik Deutschland. Ansätze zu einer regionalen Typologie", Erdkunde 32, pp. 182-98

OTREMBA, E. ed. (1962): "Atlas der Deutschen Agrarlandschaft", Wiesbaden

RÖHM, H. (1962): "Geschlossene Vererbung und Realteilung in der Bundesrepublik Deutschland", Tagungsber. u. wiss. Abhandl. d. 33. Dt. Geographentages Köln 1961

SPITZER, H. (1975): "Regionale Landwirtschaft. Die Entwicklungsaufgaben der 'Region' für Landwirtschaft und Raumordnung", Hamburg/Berlin

THIEME, G. (1975): "Regionale Unterschiede der agrarstrukturellen Entwicklung. Untersuchungen im Vorderwesterwald", Arb. z. Rhein. Landeskunde 38

PLANNING THE QUALITY OF LIFE IN RURAL COMMUNITIES

with 2 figures and 2 tables

MICHAEL PACIONE

Underlying the welfare approach to human geography, as outlined by SMITH (1974, 1977), is the question of Who gets What Where and How. In response to calls for a more relevant geography, applied geographers and planners have eagerly turned to consider the last part of this question; namely *how* to even out social inequalities and promote the individual's quality of life. However, before the quality of human life can be improved the preliminary questions of who, where and what must first be answered. This involves identifying the sections of society and the areas of greatest need. But, more fundamentally, it means identifying *what* is needed to promote life quality within these socio-spatial realms. To date much effort has gone into delimiting problem areas within countries and 'priority', 'target' and 'action' areas within cities; but far less attention has been given to the question of what constitutes a good life.

The present research set out to resolve this question with reference to an expanding commuter settlement on the edge of the Clydeside conurbation in Scotland. Within this typical metropolitan village (MASSER and STROUD 1965) two major community groups were readily differentiated along a number of social, economic and behavioural dimensions. The socio-spatial divisions of the village identified were clearly reflected in the distribution of housing class. In brief, council house tenants mainly came from the local area and had a longer association with the settlement (28 years on average) than private householders (4 years). The greater mobility of the latter group was exhibited by a disproportionately high level of car ownership (95%), the greater distances travelled to work each day, and the wider range of shopping centres frequented. In addition studies of the patterns of social interaction, and of the perceived neighbourhoods of each group served to underline the presence of two distinct communities within the settlement.

These differences in life styles between people occupying the same village space clearly pointed to the presence of some fundamental disparities in how each community perceived the village as a place to live. Individual households were therefore asked two completely unstructured questions regarding their likes

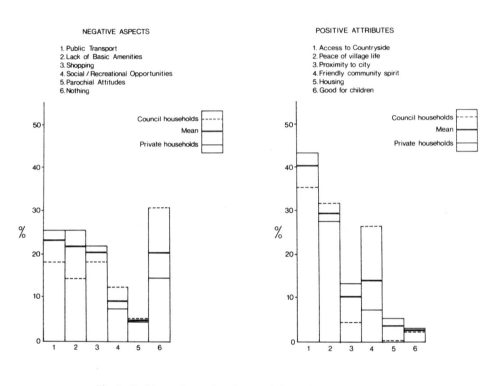

Fig. 1: Positive and negative characteristics of life in the village

and dislikes about living in the village (figure 1). The attributes most referred to by private householders centred upon the notion of 'the peace and quiet of rural country life' (71% of respondents). Proximity to the city of Glasgow, the major place of work, was mentioned by 13% of this group. The council house residents also displayed a strong preference for the village lifestyle and the rural surroundings, but significantly these were closely followed by a well defined appreciation of the friendly 'community spirit' (26%). Equally interesting from the public policy viewpoint was the fact that while 5% of private owners specifically referred to the quality of their housing as an attribute of life, not one council tenant specified this to be an attraction of life in the village. When faced with the task of listing any negative aspects of living in the village, almost one-third of the council house respondents stated that there were none, but only 15% of newcomers could find no fault. The disadvantages identified by each group closely mirrored their individual outlook and behaviour. Private householders, for example, found the lack of basic amenities such as doctors, chemists and clinics; the rural bus service; and the poor range of shops, as major irritations. Council householders also recognised these deficiencies but placed more emphasis on the absence of social and recreational opportunities. Clearly the choice of factors and the differential emphasis each community group placed on the advantages and disadvantages of life in the settlement provided an overt statement of their subjective views on what constitutes an acceptable lifestyle. This question is of course fundamental to the general concept of life quality.

Measuring the Quality of Life

Until recently most social indicators, or measures of life quality, were based upon a 'qualified observer's' judgement, seen in objective measures such as crowding indices, decibels of noise pollution, reported crimes and income levels. The limitations of such indicators have been exposed by several authors including ABRAMS (1973), and ANDREWS and WITHEY (1976) who have correctly pointed out that it is people's perceptions of their own well being or lack of well being that ultimately define the quality of their lives. Once the principle of measuring a wider range of social characteristics than are currently being observed by official bodies is accepted a decision must be made on what fundamental aspects of society should be isolated, and how these might be measured. One guideline to the first part of this question is simply that the set of indicators chosen must be broad enough to include all the most important life concerns of the population whose well being is being investigated. This has led some researchers in North America into the psychological realms of musical appreciation and the importance of love, fresh air and sunshine to perceived well being. Most geographical work, however, has tended to concentrate on more definitive concepts.

Identifying Life Concerns

MOSER (1970) has suggested that the components of a good or happy life may defy measurement but most people if asked to list the things in life which concern them would include (1) having enough to eat, (2) being healthy, (3) being housed in a congenial environment, (4) achieving work satisfaction, (5) having sufficient leisure, (6) personal security against crime. The concept of overall life quality can be regarded as the sum total of individual life concerns, although it must be remembered that the particular value or weight attached to each of the components varies from person to person and between social groups. The present study first set out to identify those concerns which were commonly held; which are relatively broad in scope; and which had some significant impact on people's sense of well being. Based on an examination of thirteen British and American studies carried out between 1965-1976, and on the preliminary investigations of life concerns described above, the investigation identified eleven major life concerns appropriate to the population under consideration. These referred to. (1) standard of living, (2) the activities of national government, (3) availability of consumer services, (4) health, (5) job satisfaction. (6) housing, (7) district,

(8) mobility, (9) amount of leisure time, (10) anticipated standard of living in the near future, and (11) anticipated local environment. The complete list of domains employed in the present study is shown in table 1. The evaluation of perceived well being presented formidable problems since feelings about one's life are clearly internal and personal. It was necessary therefore to employ a psychological scaling technique which was capable of transforming a subjective impression into an objective statistic. The measuring device adopted was the semantic

Table 1: Domains employed to measure life quality.

Variable	Domain	Operational Definition
Y	Quality of Life	Life as a whole
X_1	Standard of living	Standard of living
X_2	National government	What our national government is doing
X_3	Consumer services	The goods and services you can get in this area
X_4	Health	Own health and physical condition
X_5	Job	Job
X_6	House	House
X_7	District	This community as a place to live
X_8	Mobility	The way you can get around (to shops, work, schools, etc.)
X_9	Leisure	Amount of spare time/leisure time you have
X_{10}	Anticipated standard of living	Standard of living 5 years from now
X_{11}	Anticipated environment	Milton of Campsie as a place to live 5 years from now

differential scale, a technique which has been employed extensively in cognitive-behavioural research with good effect. Specifically each of the 124 individuals in the 12% sample population was asked to assess their position within each domain using a seven point equal interval bi-polar scale. In summary: private householders scored higher in terms of health, job satisfaction, mobility and amount of leisure time, and appeared to have a more optimistic view of their standard of living in the immediate future. The council house group scored above average in respect of the activities of the national (Labour) government and in terms of their satisfaction with the existing village community, a fact which reflects their longer association with the area. Even this latter consolation however would appear to be transitory since many of the 'established' residents saw the influx of new private housing as a serious threat to their traditional way of life.

Conceptual Models of Life Satisfaction

The assessments of the community groups provided some knowledge of the organisation and relative importance of particular life concerns. The logical extension of this was to examine the way in which individuals combined the diverse domain satisfaction scores into a general feeling of well being. The answer to this question would also indicate how well overall well being could be predicted from information on people's satisfaction with specific domains. Several structural models have been proposed to explain how individuals perform this process of amalgamation and summarisation. MCKENNELL (1971) for example hypothesised three models to explain life satisfaction. The simplest model (figure 2A) states that overall life satisfaction is a weighted sum of satisfactions with different aspects of life (domains) and that, in turn, these domain satisfactions are weighted sums of specific satisfiers and dissatisfiers. These simple principles also

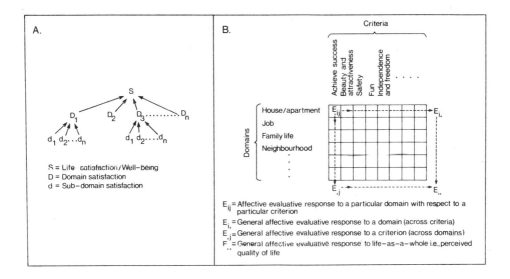

Fig. 2: Structural models of life satisfaction

underlie the model formulated by ANDREWS and WITHEY (1974), (figure 2B). Most of the conceptual models which have been suggested have some attractive features but the weight of empirical evidence at present favours the simple aggregative model described. This model suggests that somehow individuals themselves 'add up' their joys and sorrows about specific concerns to arrive at a feeling about general well being. This process appears to work in such a way that joys in one area of life may be able to compensate for sorrows in other areas; that multiple joys accumulate to raise the level of felt well being; and that multiple sorrows also accumulate to lower it. One solution to the problem of assessing the contribution of each domain to overall well being, which accords well with this conceptual structure, is the regression algorithm.

The Regression Model

In regression attention is focussed on the dependence of one variable Y on a number of other independent variables. Regression analysis thus provided a method of testing the hypothesis of which factors were associated with quality of life, and of assessing the strength of the association. The precise method adopted to test the hypothesis was a step-wise regression model. This procedure was the only one which provided an exact test for the hypothesis since in stepwise regression independent variables were ranked according to their ability to reduce the variation in the dependent variable remaining at each step. Table 2 summarises the results of the three regression analyses performed. For the population as a whole, ten domains were found to explain 38.4% of the variance. This increased to 39.2% and 50.4% for the upper and lower class sub groups respectively. These absolute figures compare favourably with the results from earlier studies. The national quality of life survey undertaken by the Social Science Research Council in 1971, for example, found that 'the best linear regression we have so far produced accounts for only 37% of the variation in reported overall life satisfaction'. In a similar study of Sunderland in 1973 the corresponding figure was 31%. In the U.S.A. CAMPBELL, CONVERSE and RODGERS (1976) employed a larger set of seventeen domain satisfaction scores to explain 54% of the variance, and suggested that this may be near the upper limit to the amount of variance that could be explained by any set of measures.

More important for the objectives of the present study however was the order in which the variables entered the regression equation. This provided greater insight into the differences between the communities in terms of the components of their global sense of well being. For both sub-groups standard of living was the most important domain underlying quality of life. This accounted for 47% of explained variance for the higher class group; and was of even greater importance for the lower class group (64%). Job satisfaction was the next most important component of life quality for both groups - accounting for 17% of explained variance for the upper class group; and 12% for council tenants. The first difference in the ordering of domains concerned those which occupied third and fourth rank. For the upper class group these places were filled by concerns with the district (16%) and amount of leisure time (7%). In contrast the lack of adequate shopping facilities in the village occupied third place (11%) for council tenants, reflecting their lower levels of personal mobility and greater dependence on local services. The prospect of the village as a place to live in the near future was of more concern to the established population (7%) than to the more recent migrants (2.5%), with some villagers specifically recording their disapproval of

Table 2: Results of the regression analyses.

	ALL HOUSEHOLDS		PRIVATE HOUSEHOLDS			COUNCIL HOUSEHOLDS		
Domain	R. Square		Domain	R. Square	Explained % Variance	Domain	R. Square	Explained % Variance
Standard of Living	0.24271		Standard of Living	0.18421	47.1	Standard of Living	0.32299	64.2
Job	0.30600		Job	0.24996	16.8	Job	0.38516	12.4
District	0.33105		District	0.31270	16.0	Consumer Services	0.43855	10.6
Leisure	0.34761		Leisure	0.34081	7.2	Anticipated Env.	0.47331	6.9
Anticipated Env.	0.35850		House	0.35935	4.7	Nat. Gov.	0.48821	3.0
House	0.37021		Anticipated Env.	0.36894	2.6	House	0.49568	1.5
Antic. St. Living	0.37607		Antic. St. Liv.	0.36655	1.9	Health	0.50001	0.9
Consumer Services	0.38030		Nat. Gov.	0.38354	1.8	Antic. St. Liv.	0.50232	0.5
Health	0.38266		Mobility	0.38951	1.5	District	0.50307	0.2
Mobility	0.38442		Consumer Services	0.39201	0.6	Mobility	0.50351	0.1
			Health	0.39240	0.1			

UPPER CLASS GROUP

$$Y = 0.29\, X_2 + 0.19\, X_6 + 0.15\, X_8 + 0.15\, X_{10} + 0.16\, X_7 + 0.63$$

LOWER CLASS GROUP

$$Y = 0.38\, X_2 + 0.19\, X_6 + 0.17\, X_4 - 0.17\, X_{12} + 0.09\, X_3 + 2.20$$

the amount of new private housebuilding. For the private householders the character of their own home was of more urgent concern than the wider village environment. This clearly indicated the 'owneroccupiers' greater commitment to their 'bricks and mortar', as well as the limited choice available within the local authority housing system. The remaining variables (domains) entered into the regression by the F value (0.01) contributed little to the overall assessments of life quality. In fact, the first five domains accounted for 92% and 97% of the explained variance for the upper and lower class sub-groups respectively. Adopting this cut-off point the final regression equations for each group took the form indicated. These well defined contrasts in attitudes towards the concept of overall well being underlined the fundamental social, spatial and behavioural differences previously identified within the settlement.

Conclusions

The concept of overall well being was found to consist of a significantly different aggregate of life concerns for the two communities identified in the village. The notion of a threshold number of five domains was able to account for a high proportion of the explained variance in both cases, but the relative importance of specific domains was singular for each group. Essentially, the predominant life concern for both groups was standard of living, followed by job satisfaction. For subsequent domains the upper class group placed most emphasis on the village as a place to live at present; in having sufficient leisure time; and on their own home. None of these domains however proved to be of any great significance for the lower class households, where greatest concerns centred on the standard of local consumer services; and the possible effects of recent changes in the village on their familiar environment in the near future.

Clearly, since different domains are important to different people and to different groups in society, serious efforts to improve the welfare of the most needy must be preceded by recognition of the practical merits of subjective investigations. Despite this the usefulness of user-attitude surveys has not yet been accepted in practice by the planning profession. It may well be true as BOLAN (1971) suggests that 'planners are not doctors, they do not deal with individuals', but the traditional practice of planning with a minimum of consultation can no longer be supported. A compromise which narrows the existing gulf between the views of the planner and those of the public is essential, and the subjective methodology described here offers an approach towards such a position. In addition, as well as being conceptually attractive, the linear additive model of overall well being may have some direct practical relevance for attempts to improve the situation of disadvantaged social groups. The compensatory principle implicit in the model suggests that, although local planning agencies may be unable in the short term to alleviate the major problems of involuntary unemployment, it might be possible for them to increase the individual's *overall* sense of well being by implementing other specific environmental improvements.

Both the planner and the public see planning as an exercise in the creation of a better environment - where they diverge is in their conception and definition of this goal. LANSING and MARANS (1969) for example found only slight correlation (r = 0.35) when they compared the evaluations of neighbourhood quality of citizens and planners in Detroit, and similar evidence has been produced in the U.K., Australia and Sweden (TAYLOR 1973; ACKING and KULLER 1973). The success of a planned environment depends on its congruence with appropriate user images and, as a step towards this, an understanding of the most important components of life quality and their relative importance would be invaluable. The lesson to be learned from perception studies, such as the one described, is that generalised absolute standards generated in isolation by professional experts may not be very useful if the ultimate aim is to improve the quality of life for recognizable social groups. To paraphrase the definition of welfare geography with which this paper began; before rushing to resolve the question of *how* to redistribute finite resources planners would be well advised to first seek information on who *wants* what where and when.

Zusammenfassung

Die Planung der Lebensqualität in ländlichen Gemeinden

Die spezifischen Forschungsziele sind: (1.) die zahlenmäßige Erfassung der unterschiedlichen sozialen Gemeinschaften innerhalb einer typischen Großstadtrandgemeinde und die Definition ihrer räumlichen Reichweiten bzw. Territorien und (2.) die Untersuchung der Lebensqualität, wie sie für eine jede Bevölkerungsgruppe besteht, sowie die Bestimmung der Bewertungen, welche eine jede Gruppe den individuellen Faktoren beimißt, die das allgemeine Wohlbefinden ausmachen. Die Studie beginnt damit, daß die Wesensmerkmale der Sozialgemeinschaften im Ort anhand sozialer und räumlicher Dimensionen menschlichen Verhaltens herausgestellt werden. Eine Untersuchung der räumlichen und zeitlichen Mobilität und die Identifizierung wahrgenommener Nachbarschaftsverhältnisse und sozialer Interaktionsmuster sind miteingeschlossen.

Zwischen den Leuten, die denselben physischen Raum bewohnen, wurden hinsichtlich ihrer Lebensstile grundlegende Unterschiede beobachtet, die eindeutig auf das Vorhandensein einiger Disparitäten bei der Wahrnehmung der Gemeinde als Lebensraum durch eine jede soziale Gruppe hinweisen. Es wurde als notwendig erachtet, die positiven und negativen Aspekte des Lebens in der Vorortsiedlung zu messen. Die erwähnten Faktoren und die unterschiedlichen Bewertungen, die jede soziale Gruppe den Vor- und Nachteilen des Lebens in der Gemeinde beimaß, ergaben klar und offenkundig eine Aussage über ihre subjektiven Ansichten dazu, was einen annehmbaren Lebensstil kennzeichnet. Diese Frage ist offensichtlich von fundamentaler Bedeutung für das allgemeine Konzept der "Lebensqualität".

Daran anschließend werden das wachsende geographische Interesse an der Lebensqualität und Gründe für eine Quantifizierung des Konzepts diskutiert, ehe die Aufmerksamkeit der Identifizierung tatsächlicher Lebensbedürfnisse zugewendet wird (d.h. der Frage: was sind die Bestandteile eines guten und glücklichen Lebens?). Diese Darstellung schließt einen knappen Überblick über frühere Versuche, diese Elemente zu isolieren, mit ein und endet mit der Herauskristallisierung von elf wesentlichen Lebensbelangen. Daraufhin werden einige Überlegungen angestellt, wie man solche zunächst nebulösen Konzepte quantifizieren könnte. Die Untersuchung wendet sich dann der Betrachtung von Modellen zur Lebenszufriedenheit zu. Es werden die bedeutenderen Modelle besprochen, die vorgelegt worden sind, um zu erklären, auf welche Art und Weise der individuelle Mensch die unterschiedlichen Zufriedenheitswerte für den ihm eigenen Lebensbereich zu einem allgemeinen Gefühl des Wohlbefindens verbindet. Die Antwort auf diese Frage zeigt klar, wie gut man die Lebensqualität insgesamt aufgrund von Kenntnissen über die Zufriedenheit mit den spezifischen Lebensbelangen oder Lebensbereichen vorhersagen kann. Im folgenden wird dann ein Strukturmodell ausgewählt und im Untersuchungsgebiet getestet; die Ergebnisse der Analysen werden vorgestellt. Abschließend werden die praktische Anwendbarkeit und die Vorzüge subjektiver Kriterien für die Sozialplanung aufgezeigt.

References

ABRAMS, M. (1973): "Subjective social indicators", Social Trends 4, 35

ACKING, C.A. & R. KULLER (1973): "Presentation and judgement of planned environments and the hypothesis of arousal", in: W. Preiser (ed.), EDRA 4, 1, pp. 72-83

ANDREWS, F.H. & S.B. WITHEY (1974): "Developing measures of perceived life quality", Soc. Indicators Res. 1, 1, pp. 1-26

ANDREWS, F.H. & S.B. WITHEY (1976): "Social indicators of well-being - American's perceptions of life quality", New York

BOLAN, R.S. (1971): "The social relations of the planner", J. Am. Inst. Plann. 33, pp. 386-96

CAMBPELL, A., P.E. CONVERSE & W.L. RODGERS (1976): "The quality of American life", Ann Arbor (Mich.)

LANSING, J.B. & R.W. MARANS (1969): "Evaluation of neighbourhood quality" AIP Journal 35, 3, pp. 195-99

MASSER, F.I. & D.C. STROUD (1965): "The metropolitan village", Tn. Plann. Rev. 36, pp. 111-24

McKENNELL, A. (1971): "Monitoring the quality of American life - commentary", unpubl. paper prepared for S.S.R.C. Survey Unit.

MOSER, C.A. (1970): "Some general development in social statistics", Social Trends 1, 10

SMITH, D.M. (1974): "Who gets what where and how: a welfare focus for human geography", Geog. 59, pp. 289-97

SMITH, D.M. (1977): "Human geography: a welfare approach", London

TAYLOR, N. (1973): "The village in the city", London

STRUKTURSCHWACHE GEBIETE AM RANDE DER REGION MÜNCHEN — DIE PROBLEMATIK VON STRUKTURVERBESSERUNGSMASSNAHMEN AM BEISPIEL DES LANDKREISES LANDSBERG/LECH

mit 4 Tabellen

Reinhard Paesler

A. Die Situation des Landkreises Landsberg/Lech in der Region München

Die Lage des Landkreises innerhalb der Region

Unter den 18 bayrischen Planungsregionen ist die Region 14 (München) mit 2,27 Mio. Einwohnern (30.9.1977) die mit Abstand größte (ca. 20% der bayerischen Bevölkerung). Es handelt sich um eine hierarchisch zentrierte Region. Um das Oberzentrum München liegen ringförmig die Mittelzentren Fürstenfeldbruck, Dachau, Freising, Moosburg, Erding, Ebersberg/Grafing, Starnberg und Landsberg, die gleichzeitig - mit Ausnahme von Moosburg - die Kreisstädte der umliegenden Landkreise sind. Der im Westen gelegene Kreis Landsberg/Lech nimmt insofern eine Sonderstellung ein, als er als einziger Kreis der Region nicht direkt an Stadt oder Landkreis München angrenzt; auch ist Landsberg die einzige Kreisstadt der Region, die keinen S-Bahn-Anschluß an die Landeshauptstadt hat. Entfernungsmäßig liegt die Stadt Landsberg wesentlich näher beim Oberzentrum Augsburg als bei München, und die regionale Zuordnung des Kreises war jahrelang umstritten. Obwohl die Stadt teilweise und der nördliche Landkreis eindeutig zu Augsburg tendieren,[1] überwog doch bei den politischen Vertretern die Zustimmung zur Eingliederung in die Region München, da man sich von der Zugehörigkeit zur Region der Metropole wirtschaftliche Vorteile versprach. Auch spielte die oberbayerische Stammeszugehörigkeit - im Gegensatz zum schwäbischen Augsburg - eine nicht zu unterschätzende Rolle.

Die raumrelevanten Bevölkerungs- und Wirtschaftsstrukturen und die Problemsituation des Landkreises

Die Region München gehört zu den wirtschaftsstärksten und, als Wanderungsziel, attraktivsten Regionen der Bundesrepublik Deutschland. Es erscheint daher zunächst unwahrscheinlich, daß hier ein "Problemlandkreis" liegen soll.

Tatsächlich gehört aber der westliche Teil des Landkreises Landsberg/Lech — einschließlich der Stadt — zum "oberbayerisch-schwäbischen Fördergebiet" der Bund-Länder-Gemeinschaftsaufgabe "Verbesserung der regionalen Wirtschaftsstruktur", und die Stadt Landsberg/Lech ist unter die Schwerpunktorte für die Schaffung neuer Arbeitsplätze mit bis zu 15% Subventionswert eingestuft.[2] Auch im Landesentwicklungsprogramm Bayern von 1976 ist der Kreis Landsberg (mit Ausnahme einiger Gemeinden am Ammersee) unter die "Gebiete, deren Struktur zur Verbesserung der Lebens- und Arbeitsbedingungen nachhaltig gestärkt werden soll", eingereiht. Es handelt sich hierbei um Gebiete, "in denen die Lebensbedingungen in ihrer Gesamtheit im Verhältnis zum Bundesdurchschnitt wesentlich zurückgeblieben sind".[3]

Abgegrenzt wurden diese Gebiete nach folgenden Kriterien, mit denen man offensichtlich versuchte, die "Lebensbedingungen in ihrer Gesamtheit" zu erfassen: Bevölkerungsdichte 1970, Wanderungssaldo 1962-1970, Löhne und Gehälter je Beschäftigten 1969, Industriebesatz (Beschäftigte in der Industrie je 1.000 Einwohner) 1970, Tertiärbesatz 1970, jeweils auf der Basis von Mittelbereichen. Für diese Kriterien wurden 5 Stufen der Abweichung vom Bundesdurchschnitt gebildet und alle Mittelbereiche, die "in mehreren Gruppen wesentlich unter dem Bundesdurchschnitt lagen", zu den Fördergebieten nach dem Landesentwicklungsprogramm gezählt.[4] Der größte Teil des Landkreises Landsberg gehört eindeutig hierzu; im Osten der Region München liegt außerdem der ähnlich strukturierte Landkreis Erding nur knapp über der Schwelle. Der Regionalbericht München von 1976 bezeichnet demzufolge die beiden Landkreise Landsberg/Lech und Erding als "fast in ihrer Gesamtheit strukturschwach",[5] u.a. anhand folgender Kriterien:
— niedriges Bruttoinlandsprodukt pro Kopf der Wirtschaftsbevölkerung,
— geringe Steuereinnahmekraft,
— niedriges Lohn- und Gehaltsniveau,
— niedriger Industriebesatz,
— hoher Anteil an Erwerbspersonen im Bereich Land- und Forstwirtschaft,
— geringer Anteil an Erwerbspersonen im produzierenden Gewerbe,
— geringe Bevölkerungsdichte.

Durch einige vergleichende Daten zur Bevölkerungs- und Wirtschaftsstruktur soll die Situation des Landkreises Landsberg/Lech näher illustriert werden (siehe Tabellen). Die Zahlen zeigen beispielhaft, daß der Landkreis tatsächlich bei den Kriterien, die allgemein zur Messung der Wirtschaftskraft und der ökonomischen Lebensverhältnisse bzw., wie es das Landesentwicklungsprogramm Bayern ausdrückt, der Qualität der Lebensbedingungen, verwendet werden, hinter dem Durchschnitt der Region und sogar Bayerns stark zurückliegt. Insbesondere ist der Landkreis weit unterdurchschnittlich industrialisiert und hat entsprechend einen noch relativ hohen Anteil landwirtschaftlicher Erwerbspersonen.

Tabellen 1 - 4:

Daten zur Bevölkerungs- und Wirtschaftsstruktur des Landkreises Landsberg a. Lech im Vergleich mit der Region München und mit Bayern

	Einwohner in Tausend				Veränderung 1950-1977	Bevölkerungsdichte 1977 (E./km^2)
	1950	1961	1970	1977		
Lkr. LL	67	64	70	76	13,4%	95
Region M	1.406	1.716	2.076	2.265	61,1%	411
Bayern	9.126	9.515	10.479	10.818	18,5%	153

	Erwerbspersonen nach Wirtschaftsbereichen in %					
	1961			1970		
	I	II	III	I	II	III
Lkr. LL	36,4	34,8	28,8	21,7	36,1	42,3
Region M	8,6	42,1	49,3	4,9	42,3	52,8
Bayern	21,4	44,1	34,5	13,2	47,2	39,6

I = Land- u. Forstwirtschaft, II = Produzierendes Gewerbe, III = Handel, Verkehr, Dienstleistungen

	Beschäftigte					
	im produz. Gewerbe			in Industriebetrieben (ab 10 Besch.) 1974		
	1961	1970	Veränderung		Besch./ Einw.	Umsatz/ Besch.i.DM
Lkr. LL	7.863	8.442	+ 7,4%	3.423	0,037	41.275
Region M	377.597	452.250	+ 19,8%	250.060	0,111	104.779
Bayern	2056.323	2264.286	+ 10,1%	1353.714	0,125	77.597

	Steuereinnahmekraft 1974 DM/Einwohner	darunter Gemeindeanteil an der Einkommensteuer
Lkr. LL	336	154
Region M	662	292

Quellen: Gemeindedaten zur Gebietsreform, Ausgabe 1978, Hg. Bayer. Stat. Landesamt, München 1978;
Regionalbericht Region München, Hg. Bayer. Staatsmin. f. Landesentwicklung u. Umweltfragen. u. Regionaler Planungsverband München, München o.J.

Die im Landkreis wohnhaften Erwerbstätigen im produzierenden Gewerbe pendeln zudem zu einem großen Teil in die Stadtregion München, zum geringeren Teil auch in die Region Augsburg; der Industriebesatz ist im Landkreis selbst besonders niedrig. Die geringe Zahl vorhandener Industriebetriebe gehört zudem überwiegend zu den weniger umsatz- und damit steuerertragstarken Branchen. Auch sind im industriellen Bereich nur geringe Wachstumstendenzen zu verzeichnen, so daß sich der Abstand zum Landes- und Regionsdurchschnitt seit 1961 weiter vergrößerte. Gleichzeitig ist auch der einheimische Dienstleistungssektor nur gering entwickelt. Die Statistik der Erwerbspersonen nach Wirtschaftsbereichen weist zwar für 1970 — nach starkem Zuwachs gegenüber 1961 — einen über dem Landesdurchschnitt liegenden Anteil von im tertiären Sektor Beschäftigten aus. Sie gehören jedoch überwiegend unteren bis mittleren Einkommensschichten an, so daß sich insgesamt ein stark unterdurchschnittliches Einkommensniveau ergibt. (Insbesondere der Anteil der Bundeswehrbeschäftigten in mehreren Standorten in und um Landsberg spielt hier eine große Rolle.) Die neuerdings in der Statistik ausgewiesene Höhe des Gemeindeanteils an der Einkommensteuer in DM pro Kopf der Wohnbevölkerung illustriert dies deutlich. Der Landkreis Landsberg überschreitet 1974 mit DM 154.- nur geringfügig die Hälfte des Regionsdurchschnitts, während selbst andere Landkreise mit "ländlichen" Teilbereichen, wie Freising oder Dachau, bei DM 181.- bzw. DM 207.- liegen.

Die Wirtschaftsstruktur hängt eng mit der Entwicklung der Einwohnerzahl und der Siedlungsstruktur zusammen. Das Gebiet des Landkreises Landsberg weist seit jeher — besonders in den südlichen Teilbereichen — eine weitmaschige dörfliche Siedlungsstruktur mit größeren siedlungsleeren Gebieten auf (Wald-, Moor-, Seeflächen). Außer der Kreisstadt Landsberg (1977 zusammen mit den sozio-ökonomisch eng verflochtenen Randgemeinden Kaufering und Penzing 28.015 Einwohner) und dem Markt Dießen am Ammersee (1977: 7.356 Einwohner) besitzt der Kreis keine größere Siedlung. Die Bevölkerungsdichte blieb bis heute relativ sehr niedrig (1977: 95 E./km^2 gegenüber 153 im bayerischen Durchschnitt), da auch in der Nachkriegszeit, abgesehen von einem Schub in der Zeit des Bundeswehraufbaus, keine wesentliche Bevölkerungszunahme zu verzeichnen war. Der Landkreis wurde auch in den letzten Jahren nur schwach in die von München bzw. Augsburg ausgehende Stadt-Rand-Wanderung einbezogen. Lediglich in den nördlichsten Landkreisgemeinden ist eine geringe Zuwanderung aus der Stadtregion Augsburg zu verzeichnen,[6] während im Osten das erst bei der Gebietsreform von 1972 in den Landkreis eingegliederte Geltendorf als Endstation einer S-Bahn-Linie nach München ein gewisses Wachstum zeigt (1970: 3.249 Einw., 1977: 3.434 Einw.).

Nach den Kriterien des bayerischen Landesentwicklungsprogramms gehört also der Landkreis zweifellos zu den Gebieten mit unzureichenden Lebens- und Arbeitsbedingungen, d.h. mit verbesserungsbedürftiger Lebensqualität. Daß man allerdings auch andere Maßstäbe anlegen kann, sollen zunächst zwei Aspekte zeigen: Für viele Münchner gehört der Landkreis Landsberg zu den "Geheimtips" unter den Naherholungsgebieten, weil er noch nicht überlaufen, dünn besiedelt und kaum industrialisiert ist, zahlreiche Naturschönheiten und große Freiflächen (Grün- und Ackerland, Wälder, Seen, Moore) enthält und eine gute interne Verkehrserschließung aufweist. Teile des Landkreises (Lechtal, Ammersee-Ufer) sind zunehmend als Standorte für Freizeitwohnsitze begehrt. Für die im Münchner Raum sehr aktiven Naturschutzvereine gelten große Flächen im Landkreis als wertvolle "ökologische Ausgleichsgebiete", Tier- und Pflanzenreservate, die es mit allen Mitteln gegen Besiedlungs- und Industrialisierungsbestrebungen, gegen Straßenbau- und andere Verkehrsprojekte und gegen übermäßige Erholungsnutzung zu verteidigen gilt. Der Landkreis wird aus dieser Richtung als noch weitgehend intakter und gesunder Lebensraum bezeichnet.

B. Maßnahmen zur Strukturverbesserung im Landkreis Landsberg/Lech

Die Ziele des Landesentwicklungsprogramms

Zu den wichtigsten Zielen des Landesentwicklungsprogramms Bayern gehört es, in allen Landesteilen "möglichst gleichwertige, gesunde Lebens- und Arbeitsbedingungen zu erhalten oder zu schaffen".[7] Wir haben gesehen, daß nach den Beurteilungskriterien der Planung der Wert von Lebens- und Arbeitsbedingungen im wesentlichen anhand der Wirtschaftsstrukturen gemessen wird. Die Entwicklungsziele für diejenigen Gebiete, die noch nicht eine mit dem übrigen Land gleichwertige Lebensqualität aufweisen, also die Gebiete, deren Struktur nach der Terminologie der Planung "zur Verbesserung der Lebens und Arbeitsbedingungen nachhaltig gestärkt werden soll", gehen allerdings darüber hinaus. Es heißt hier:

"1. Durch die Schaffung vielseitiger qualifizierter Arbeitsplätze in Wohnortnähe sollen die Beschäftigungsmöglichkeiten und die Einkommensverhältnisse der Bevölkerung verbessert werden;
2. Durch Bereitstellung familiengerechter Wohnungen, zeitgemäßer Bildungs-, Kultur-, Versorgungs- und Sozialeinrichtungen sowie eine günstige Verkehrserschließung und Verkehrsbedienung sind die Lebensbedingungen nachhaltig zu verbessern;
3. Einer Abwanderung ist entgegenzuwirken. Die Voraussetzungen einer Zuwanderung sind zu verbessern.
4. Diese Gebiete haben bei Planungen und Maßnahmen zur Stärkung des ländlichen Raums Vorrang; dabei sind der jeweilige Grad, die Art und die Ursachen der Strukturschwäche zu berücksichtigen."[8]

Über diese allgemeinen Planungsziele hinaus wird unser Beispiel-Landkreis in den "Regionalen Zielen" besonders angesprochen: Das Mittelzentrum Landsberg/Lech "ist in seinen mittelzentralen Versorgungsaufgaben ... zu stärken. Insbesondere sind anzustreben: Die Beseitigung städtebaulicher und funktionaler Mängel in der Altstadt, die Vergrößerung des industriellen Arbeitsplatzangebots."[9]

Unter den allgemeinen wie regionalen Entwicklungszielen steht die Schaffung qualifizierter Arbeitsplätze, insbesondere in der Industrie, und eine damit verbundene Verbesserung der Einkommensverhältnisse der Bevölkerung im Vordergrund; den nächsten Rang nimmt die Versorgung ein, mit Wohnungen, Sozial-, Bildungs- und Kultureinrichtungen, bis zum Verkehr. (Freizeiteinrichtungen werden überraschenderweise nicht genannt.) Vernachlässigt wird der Aspekt der Umweltqualität, obwohl es doch darum geht, "gesunde Lebens- und Arbeitsbedingungen" zu schaffen. Im allgemeinen Teil des Landesentwicklungsprogramms werden zwar unter den generellen Erfordernissen für alle Landesteile als letzter unter 6 Punkten auch "gesunde Umweltbedingungen" genannt,[10] jedoch könnte gerade für die Problemgebiete die Gefahr bestehen, daß die Ansiedlung von Industrien — evtl. von solchen, die in den Ballungsgebieten unerwünscht sind — und der Ausbau der Versorgungsinfrastruktur so sehr in den Vordergrund rücken, daß die Umweltqualität — etwa in bezug auf Luft, Wasser, Lärm, das Landschaftsbild — unvertretbar darunter leidet. Die Auswahl der Kriterien für die Abgrenzung der Fördergebiete vergrößert noch diese Gefahr, und es können Zweifel auftauchen, ob die betroffene Bevölkerung überhaupt den Wunsch hat, ihre Lebens- und Arbeitsbedingungen an den Bundesdurchschnitt angenähert zu bekommen, wenn damit zwar, um ein Beispiel zu nennen, eine größere Auswahl an örtlichen Arbeitsplätzen und eine schnellere Verkehrsanbindung an das Oberzentrum verbunden ist, andererseits aber auch der Lärmpegel im Wohnumfeld und der Grad der Trinkwasser- und Luftreinheit sich dem — schlechteren — Bundesdurchschnitt annähern.

Sozialgeographische Untersuchungen zu Fragen der Stadt- und Regionalplanung im Landkreis Landsberg

Zwei sozialgeographische Geländepraktika, die das Institut für Wirtschaftsgeographie der Universität München (Vorstand: Prof. Dr. K. Ruppert) unter Leitung des Autors in den Jahren 1976 und 1978 in der Stadt und im Landkreis Landsberg durchführte, versuchten u.a. auch, auf die obigen Fragen Antworten zu finden. Es wurde untersucht, inwieweit die Landes- und Regional-, aber auch die Stadtplanung, mit den Wünschen und Vorstellungen der Bevölkerung konform geht und inwieweit die Vorstellungen über die wünschenswerten Lebens- und Arbeitsbedingungen Unterschiede nach sozialgeographischen Gruppen aufweisen. Damit im Zusammenhang stand die Frage nach der Raumwirksamkeit kommunaler und staatlicher Strukturverbesserungsmaßnahmen. Es wurde bei dieser Untersuchung im wesentlichen mit Befragungen der Bevölkerung sowie von Meinungsführern und Vertretern der Stadt- und Gemeindeverwaltungen und der größeren Verbände und Interessengruppen gearbeitet.

Für die Stadt Landsberg kristallisierten sich u.a. folgende Ergebnisse der

Untersuchungen heraus: Die wichtigsten raumrelevanten Forderungen der Bevölkerung zur Verbesserung der individuellen Lebensqualität sind

1. Beruhigung und Luftverbesserung in der Altstadt durch Herausnahme des außerordentlich starken Durchgangsverkehrs, gleichzeitig als Maßnahme zur Hebung der Wohnqualität, die die Abwanderung an den Stadtrand verlangsamen könnte;[11]
2. Verminderung der Störungen, vor allem der Lärmbelästigungen, die durch die starke Präsenz der Bundeswehr entstehen (mehrere Kasernen, Flugplatz, Standortübungsplatz, Schießplatz im oder nahe am Stadtgebiet);
3. Verbesserung des Freizeitangebots in der Stadt (vor allem bezüglich kultureller Veranstaltungen und der Gastronomie);
4. Verbesserung der Verkehrsanbindung — vor allem im öffentlichen Personennahverkehr — an die Oberzentren München und Augsburg.

Mit der Versorgung auf der unter- und mittelzentralen Ebene ist man weitgehend zufrieden. Die aktive Unterstützung von Industrieansiedlungen wird mehrheitlich abgelehnt. Die Forderung nach weiteren qualifizierten Arbeitsplätzen im sekundären Sektor taucht überwiegend bei Vertretern der Stadtverwaltung und der Gewerkschaften auf, vor allem mit den Argumenten, man müsse die Steuereinnahmen und die Einwohnerzahl erhöhen bzw. der einheimischen Jugend nach dem Abschluß der Schulausbildung die Chance geben, am Ort einen Arbeitsplatz zu erhalten. Auspendler sollen die Möglichkeit bekommen, in eine Arbeitsstelle am Wohnort zu wechseln. Die Bevölkerung der Stadt selbst steht diesen Forderungen weitgehend indifferent gegenüber, sieht ihre Notwendigkeit vielfach nicht ein, befürchtet im Gegenteil weitere Umweltbelastungen und findet nichts wesentlich Nachteiliges dabei, daß z.B. etwa 70 - 80% aller Landsberger Abiturienten ihre berufliche Position später einmal außerhalb ihrer Heimatstadt finden werden.

Wichtig erscheint im Fall Landsberg vor allem eine starke sozialgruppenspezifische Differenzierung der Meinung über die künftige Stadtentwicklung. Landsberg wurde zu dem, was es heute ist — eine vom Militär und von staatlichen Institutionen (Strafanstalt, Kreisverwaltung, Schulen, Fachschulen) geprägte Kleinstadt mit gut ausgebildeten Versorgungsfunktionen auf der unter- und mittelzentralen Ebene — im wesentlichen durch die Gruppen der Kaufleute, Handwerker und mittleren Beamten geprägt, die den Stadtrat seit Jahrzehnten beherrschen und die in den Wiederaufbaujahren nach dem Krieg aktiv eine stärkere Industrialisierung verhinderten.[12] Vor allem die Beamten wollen auch heute noch kaum eine Veränderung dieser Situation; sie wünschen sich Landsberg als ruhige Kleinstadt in Großstadtnähe mit leistungsfähigen Versorgungseinrichtungen, aber ohne Industrie. Bei den Geschäftsleuten und Gewerbetreibenden ist in den letzten Jahren eher eine Umorientierung eingetreten; man erkennt die Chance einer Geschäftsausweitung durch Einwohnerzuwachs und Stärkung der mittelzentralen Stellung. Auch zwischen alteingesessenen Landsbergern und erst jüngst zugezogenen Einwohnern zeigen sich ähnliche Unterschiede der Auffassung über die Weiterentwicklung der Stadt. Für die relativ große Gruppe der Bundeswehrangehörigen (Berufssoldaten) sind starke Fluktuation und geringes Interesse an der Stadtentwicklungspolitik kennzeichnend.

An zwei Beispielen soll der Frage der Realisierung regionalplanerischer Ziele nachgegangen werden. Die für Landsberg geforderte "Vergrößerung des industriellen Arbeitsplatzangebots" zeigt deutlich, welche Differenzen sich zwischen den Vorstellungen der Planung über die künftige Raumentwicklung und der Bevölkerung über die gewünschte Umwelt ergeben können.

Nachdem bis in die 60er Jahre hinein teils versäumt, teils durch bestimmte Gruppen in der Stadt und durch die Raumansprüche der Bundeswehr verhindert worden war, industrielle Arbeitsplätze in Landsberg zu schaffen, bemühte sich die Stadtverwaltung in den letzten Jahren, das Versäumte nachzuholen, unterstützt durch die genannten übergeordneten Programme. Es gelang der Stadtverwaltung, ein bisher von der Bundeswehr beanspruchtes Gelände am nördlichen Stadtrand freizubekommen und als künftiges Industriegebiet voll zu erschließen. Trotz der erheblichen Vorleistungen durch die öffentliche Hand gelang es in mehreren Jahren bis heute nur, einige wenige relativ unbedeutende Betriebe mit geringer Arbeitsmarktbedeutung auf dem Areal neu anzusiedeln. Abgesehen von der allgemeinen Ungunst einer wirtschaftlichen Stagnationszeit, scheint die Industrieansiedlung gerade in derartigen Randgebieten monozentrischer Regionen schwierig zu sein. Landsberg bietet noch nicht die Fühlungs- und Verkehrsvorteile des Ballungsraums München, aber auch nicht mehr die Vorteile großstadtferner ländlicher Räume (niedriges Lohnniveau, Arbeitskräftereservoir). Lediglich Firmen, die wegen großer Flächenbeanspruchung oder gewisser Umweltrisiken keine Produktionsstätten im ansonsten bevorzugten Kern des Verdichtungsraumes errichten können, scheinen noch in Frage zu kommen.

Ein derartiger Fall trat in Landsberg ein. 1974/75 begann sich ein sehr bedeutender amerikanischer Chemiekonzern für das Landsberger Industriegebiet zu interessieren, um hier eine Produktionsstätte für Pharmazeutika zu errichten. Die Stadtverwaltung und das Bayerische Wirtschaftsministerium boten jede mögliche Hilfe, um die Niederlassung des Werkes zu ermöglichen, das eine größere Anzahl langfristig sicherer qualifizierter Arbeitsplätze aller Stufen bis zum Akademiker und eine ganz erhebliche Erhöhung der kommunalen Steuerkraft zu bringen versprach. Während des Genehmigungsverfahrens teilte sich aber die Landsberger Bevölkerung in zwei Lager, die sich wegen der Alternative bekämpften, eine möglicherweise umweltbedrohende Produktionsstätte zu errichten — was vom Werk und von Gutachtern energisch bestritten wurde —, die aber mit Sicherheit wirtschaftliche Vorteile und neue Arbeitsplätze bringt, oder auf jedes Risiko zu verzichten und dafür wirtschaftliche und stadtentwicklungspolitische Stagnation in Kauf zu nehmen. Die vor allem von der erwähnten Gruppe der Beamten geführte Bürgerinitiative gegen das Pharmawerk, die mit der Gefahr von Luft-und Trinkwasserverschmutzung argumentierte, erhielt Hilfe von der angrenzenden Gemeinde Kaufering und besonders von der Stadt Augsburg, die 30 km lechabwärts liegt und eine Bedrohung ihrer Trinkwasservorräte bei übermäßiger Belastung dieses Vorfluters befürchtete. Die Verwaltung der Stadt dagegen sah die einmalige Chance eines wirtschaftlichen Aufschwungs für Landsberg und betonte, die Stadt als Fördergebiet könne die Arbeitsplätze nicht ausschlagen, ohne sich völlig unglaubwürdig zu machen. Die Frage löste sich schließlich von selbst, da die Firma nach längerer Verzögerung durch Einsprüche, Auflagen und Gerichtsverfahren das Interesse verlor und ihre Planungen aufgab.

Als zweites Beispiel sei die Erfüllung der "mittelzentralen Versorgungsaufgaben" angesprochen, deren Verbesserung ebenfalls regionalplanerisches Ziel ist. Landsberg gehört zu den historischen Städten, deren zentralörtliche Bedeutung durch die sozio-ökonomischen Umschichtungen des 19. und 20. Jahrhunderts, insbesondere durch die Verlagerung der Verkehrsströme im Eisenbahnzeitalter, rapide abnahm. Die Stadt, die einmal "oberzentrale" Funktionen erfüllt hatte, war schließlich in den 60er Jahren, vom Angebot und von der Reichweite her gesehen, nur noch als schwaches Mittelzentrum anzusprechen. Nicht nur die Bewohner der Randgebiete des Landkreises, sondern selbst die der Stadt und ihrer Nachbargemeinden suchten zunehmend die Oberzentren München und Augsburg auch zur Deckung zentralörtlicher Bedürfnisse der mittleren Stufe auf, da Landsbergs Angebot unzureichend war.[13]

Inzwischen wurde durch Eigeninitiative des Landsberger Handels und gezielte Maßnahmen der Stadtverwaltung (Verbesserung der Infrastruktur für Handel und Dienstleistungsbetriebe, Werbemaßnahmen, Schaffung eines ausreichenden Parkplatzangebots usw.) das mittelzentrale Angebot nach Breite und Tiefe und die Benutzungsmöglichkeiten für die potentiellen Kunden so stark verbessert, daß der Einzugsbereich stabilisiert, zum Teil sogar wieder ausgebaut werden konnte. Insbesondere im Bereich privater Dienstleistungen (z.B. medizinische Versorgung) ist Landsberg heute wieder ein voll entwickeltes und in Anspruch genommenes Mittelzentrum. Die auf weitere Stärkung dieser Funktion gerichtete Planung steht offenbar in Übereinstimmung mit den Wünschen der Stadt- und Umlandbevölkerung, die nicht auf die Oberzentren fixiert ist, sondern sich, bei Vorliegen eines entsprechenden Angebots und guter Erreichbarkeit, "zurückgewinnen" läßt. Weitere planerische Anstrengungen in dieser Richtung — z.B. Verbesserung der Erreichbarkeit in zeitlicher Hinsicht — dürften erfolgreich sein.

C. Sozialgeographie und Planung der Umweltqualität

Für die Sozialgeographie, die sich in starkem Maße bemüht, praxisorientierte Forschung zu betreiben,[14] ergeben sich aus den vorstehenden Erörterungen und Beispielen einige Erkenntnisse, die stärker als bisher in die Raumplanung einbezogen werden sollten.

Die Planung ging bisher davon aus, daß über die Notwendigkeit der Wirtschaftsförderung in sog. strukturschwachen Gebieten und über die Art der Förderung mit Hilfe von Infrastrukturausbau und Schaffung neuer Arbeitsplätze, vor allem in der Industrie, allgemeine Übereinstimmung herrscht. Diese Annahme ist offensichtlich revisionsbedürftig. Es gibt größere Bevölkerungsgruppen — die sich durch sozialgeographische Forschungsmethoden abgrenzen lassen —, die von ihrer Wohngemeinde eine hohe Versorgungsqualität und gesunde Umweltbedingungen erwarten, weniger dagegen Bevölkerungs- und Wirtschaftswachstum oder vielfältiges Arbeitsplatzangebot. Daß z.B. die Güte der Versorgung auch von der Bevölkerungszahl, der Wirtschafts- und Steuerkraft der Gemeinde abhängt, wird häufig ignoriert. Im Fall eines Widerstreits zwischen verschiedenen Landschaftsnutzungen werden die Umwelt-, die Wohn- oder die Freizeitqualität der Kulturlandschaft gegenüber ökonomisch orientierten Nutzungen vorgezogen, wenn diese die genannten Qualitäten zu beeinträchtigen drohen, auch wenn dies auf Kosten stärkerer wirtschaftlicher Entwicklung der Wohngemeinde geht. Die weniger geographische als moralische Frage, inwieweit eine solche Haltung unter Umständen auch auf Kosten von arbeitslosen oder wirtschaftlich schlechter gestellten Mitbürgern geht, soll hier nicht weiter erörtert werden; aber für die Planung ist es wichtig, zu berücksichtigen, daß die staatliche und kommunale Wirtschafts- und Strukturförderungspolitik — Landsberg steht hier nur stellvertretend für viele andere Beispiele — zunehmend von Teilen der Bevölkerung behindert wird. Die Planung müßte in Zukunft stärker als bisher die unterschiedlichen Interessenlagen der verschiedenen Bevölkerungsgruppen gegeneinander abwägen und in ihre Überlegungen einbeziehen, anstatt pauschal Fördergebiete aufgrund rein ökonomischer Kriterien und mit Hilfe von Bundes- oder Landesdurchschnittswerten festzulegen. Entscheidend ist, daß aus einer "Planung für einen Raum" stärker eine "Planung für die Menschen in einem Raum" wird, d.h. die Verbesserung der Lebensbedingungen, die die Planung anstrebt, muß weniger raum- als einwohnerbezogen gesehen werden. Auf diese Weise dürfte sich auch am ehesten der weitverbreitete Argwohn gegen das "Verplantwerden" — man denke z.B. auch an in Einzelfällen allzu schematisch durchgeführte Gebietsreform — abbauen lassen.

Summary

Retarded Areas at the Periphery of the Munich Region. Problems of Structural Improvement Measures: the Example of the Landkreis Landsberg/Lech.

This paper deals with the questions that arise out of the situation that a structurally weak area exists within a region that is economically healthy, with a sound income structure and a monocentric orientation towards one agglomeration centre. The example of this situation dealt with here is the "Landkreis" Landsberg/Lech in the west of the Bavarian planning region 14 (München), between the dominant central places of München and Augsburg. The Bavarian regional planning programme classifies this "Landkreis" among those areas with an insufficient quality of life, due to the fact that population density, job availability ratio, and economic capacity with a particularly small amount of industry, are well below average. Therefore, specifically in the "Kreisstadt" Landsberg, policies of structural advancement are being carried out with the aim of creating new qualified jobs within the secondary and tertiary sectors of the economy.

The difficulties of putting these aims into practice in the agrarian peripheral area of a monocentric region will come under closer scrutiny. Through the illustration of two cases an attempt will be made to show what goal-conflicts may arise in reality, when in theory one tries to attain, within the framework of a regional planning programme, equality of living and working conditions in all areas of a region. In the case of Landsberg/Lech it was a citizens' interest group for environmental protection that brought about the cancellation of the establishment of a pharmaceutical plant. The building of this plant would have brought about an increase in the number of qualified jobs and an increase in tax income for the area but it would also have increased the risk of environmental damage. A further aim of regional planning that was carried out to help support the position of Landsberg as a second order centre has been registered as quite successful, due to the fact that city administration, citizens and private services worked hand in hand.

Social geography therefore draws the consequence that planning must consider more strongly the differing ideas of the affected population, with regards to their living and working sphere, according to social groupings. It is especially in the rural circumference of metropolitan agglomerations, that under certain circumstances, environmental quality may take priority over the goal of reaching the federal average of economic standard.

Anmerkungen und Literaturhinweise

1. RUPPERT, K. u.a. (1969): "Planungsregionen Bayerns — Gliederungsvorschlag", Teil 1, München
2. Akad. f. Raumforschg. u. Landesplanung (1969 ff.): "Daten zur Raumplanung", Teil II D, Hannover
3. Bayerische Staatsregierung (1976): "Landesentwicklungsprogramm Bayern (LEP)", Teil A II. 4.1 bzw. Begründung zu A II. 4.1
4. LEP, Begründung zu Teil A II. 4.1
5. Bayerisches Staatsministerium f. Landesentwicklung u. Umweltfragen u. Regionaler Planungsverband München, (o.J.): "Regionalbericht Region München", München S. 55
6. SCHAFFER, F. u.a. (1975): "Randwanderung im Raum Augsburg", Beitr. z. Statistik u. Stadtforschung, Augsburg, Nr. 2, S. 24 ff.
7. LEP, Teil A II. 1.1
8. LEP, Teil A II. 4.2.1 - 4.2.4
9. LEP, Teil C, Region 14, I. 4.2.7
10. LEP, Teil A II. 1.2
11. POSCHWATTA, W. (1977): "Wohnen in der Innenstadt", Augsb. Sozialgeogr. Hefte 1, insbes. S. 123 ff.
12. PAESLER, R. (1970): "Der zentrale Ort Landsberg am Lech", Mitt. d. Geogr. Ges. in München 55, S. 114 ff.
13. PAESLER, R.: "Der zentrale Ort Landsberg am Lech", a.a.O., S. 105 - 22
14. MAIER, J., R. PAESLER, K. RUPPERT, F. SCHAFFER (1977): "Sozialgeographie", Braunschweig, S. 157

THE TEXTILE REGIONS OF WESTERN EUROPE AS PROBLEM REGIONS

with 3 figures and 4 tables

M. Trevor Wild

This paper focuses attention on the textile manufacturing regions of Western Europe as a specific, yet widely represented, type of problem region. Though there is an abundance of interesting and informative local studies, it is at first sight rather surprising that a topic so obvious as this, has attracted little attention from both academic geographers and persons concerned with the broader issues of regional development. Perhaps the explanation for this lies in our present approaches to the recognition and understanding of industrial problem regions. Within the context of Western Europe, comparative interest in these is often of a very general nature, with regions being considered only in terms of their overall characteristics; i.e., economic structures, economic dynamism, central place systems and rather more tentatively, economic and social 'health'. Rather too commonly the special characteristics of particular branches of industrial activity have been ignored or left undetachable from general situations. Important exceptions to this criticism can be found in studies in the regionalisation of coal mining, and to a lesser extent, iron and steel production. Here, interest has been justifiably attached to their high geographical concentration, their importance as basic industrial resources, their tendency in the past to dominate regional employment structures, and, in the case of coal mining, the drastic reductions in the labour force. There is a case, however, for adding textile regions to this list, bearing in mind that information on this industry is rather less forthcoming, and its labour force has a very high female component.

The strongest argument for upgrading our interest in textile regions is afforded by the figures in table 1. These show for the period 1954 - 74, a net loss of 929,000 textile jobs in the United Kingdom, France, and West Germany, a figure not much less than the 996,000 decline in coal mining employment. Indeed, since 1966 the absolute fall in textile employment in these three countries has been the more severe, with 502,000 jobs being lost compared with 436,000 in coal mining. Furthermore, if one also includes commonly associated industries such as clothing and textile engineering, the situation is little short of catastro-

Table 1: Employment in textiles, clothing and coal mining: United Kingdom, West Germany and France, 1954 - 74

(in 000s)

	1954	1956	1958	1960	1962	1964	1966	1968	1970	1972	1974
Textiles	2288	2240	2149	2076	1978	1971	1861	1685	1656	1466	1359
Clothing	1463	1422	1427	1323	1355	1350	1327	1229	1212	1166	1039
Coal Mining	1620	1594	1603	1504	1378	1325	1060	898	790	692	624

Source: National Statistical Yearbooks.

phic, with well over a million workplaces being withdrawn since 1964. It has been argued that this was cushioned by the more dispersed character of the textile industry. It is dangerous, however, to take this too far and to ignore the basic facts of distribution. Over Western Europe, textile manufacturing is admittedly fairly widespread, but it is also true that there are some major regional concentrations. The most extreme examples are in the United Kingdom, where around three quarters of the country's total textile production and employment is to be found in West Yorkshire and Lancashire. Of the three countries, West Germany has the most diffuse distribution, though heavy concentrations are represented in the Wuppertal and Mönchengladbach districts, North Westphalia, Swabia, South Wurttemberg and Upper Franconia.

The characteristics of textile regions

Because of the antiquity and geographical continuity of textile working areas, much of their distinctive character has developed from historic traditions. This is particularly noticeable when one considers their surviving distribution over Western Europe (figure 1). The first point to be established is that they have each undergone a similar sequence of formative growth, though this of course has varied considerably in historical timing, scale, and geographical expression. The earliest stage goes back to the Middle Ages, when the combination of market attraction, defensive needs and occupational interest, brought about an initial concentration of craft industries into many important towns and cities. This was then followed by a general 'urban exodus' of textile working, a distributional trend which is certainly recognisable in England from the late fourteenth century onwards. The stimulus for this movement came from the expansion of the industry and its growing occupational demands. In the woollen industry, the shift from urban to rural environments and particularly upland valleys, was further encouraged by the increasing use of water power in the fulling process. The seats of textile working during this long period of pre-technical industrialisation, were almost invariably areas of fairly pronounced environmental difficulty, but paradoxically also, where earlier settlement processes had produced a high densi-

Fig. 1: Textile regions of Western Europe

ty of rural population. Though some lowland districts, such as parts of Flanders, northeastern France and North Westphalia, were represented, the most common environments were those of the upland fringes, notably the Pennines flanks, the foothills of the Alps, and the West European 'Middle Hills'.

The third and final growth stage is better known, involving the spatial responses to the transition from cottage to factory and the use of water, steam, and later electricity power. It can be noted, however, that the industrial revolution did not produce any really new textile region, though some of the most poorly situated of the established areas were forced into an early decline (e.g. the English Cotswolds and East Anglia). Geographical continuity, in its broadest sense, owed much to the strength and tradition of pre-technical industrialisation, and particularly the development of native skills and basic organisational systems. In most cases the most striking geographical changes took place on a highly localised scale, emphasising the new communications axes, but leaving intervening tracts of countryside largely untouched. The classic illustration of the spatial response to each of the three stages is in East Lancashire, where Manchester, the original urban focus, lies on the periphery of a textile belt whose broad regional outlines were created during the period circa 1500 - 1800, but whose general human landscape and culture owes the most to the nineteenth century. The settlement structure of this and most other textile regions, therefore, shows a clearly differentiated pattern of (i) historic organisational centre on the edge of the manufacturing region, (ii) a 'rash' of small villages and hamlets created during the initial agrarian occupance and the period of pre-technical industrialisation, (iii) the concentrated development and urbanisation of the industrial revolution, representing the present manufacturing core.

The nineteenth and early twentieth centuries of course embraced the decades of fastest growth in the textile industry and its associated employment generation, population increase and urbanisation. With this in mind it is important to note, how much the first of the series of death blows to the industry in the 1920s truncated formative development, leaving most textile areas in a 'fossilised' state. This produced a residual situation in which obvious environmental and structural problems were aggravated by severe employment contraction, declining population, and the ageing of such artifacts of fixed investment as housing, industrial premises, communications, and service institutions. Each of these problems are typical of what are often described as 'outworn industrial areas'. In textile country, however, they are normally more strongly represented for two basic reasons; first, the acceleration in industrial growth, population increase and building had come rather earlier than in most other major manufacturing regions, so that by the twentieth century the 'ageing' trend was much more advanced. Secondly, the location of most textile areas aggravated difficulties. To appreciate this, one has to turn once again to the facts of historical development, for it is these which explain the common allegiance to the upland parts of Western Europe. Such environments contain an obvious element of physical remoteness, often inhibiting communications and general access. This situation, however, has been accentuated by further geographical coincidence, namely the configuration of Western Europe's nation states, and the tendency for most textile regions to occupy peripheral positions. This is most clearly exemplified in France, where the Nord, Vosges. Lvonnais and Pvrenees areas are each situated in the remoter corners of the country . In West Germany, the associationship can be seen in North Westphalia, the Aachen district, Upper Franconia, Swabia, and the southern Black Forest. In England, the concentration of textile working in Yorkshire and the North West and, apart from the Nottingham-Leicester-Derby area, its virtual exclusion from the Midlands and South has contributed much to regional disparities.

Since the inter-war years, the decline of textile capacity and employment in Western Europe has been unrelenting, apart from a short-lived recovery in the late 1940s and early 1950s. The reasons for this, contraction of export markets, penetration of home markets by foreign competitors, low investment, and general pessimism of future prospects, have been well publicised. The most adverse trends are to be found in the United Kingdom, where the number of workers, after reaching a peak of around 1,300,000 in the late 1920s, fell to 750,000 by 1946. After recovering to just over the million mark in 1950, the downwards movement was resumed once again; 840,000 textile workers were recorded in 1964, and 513,000 in 1976 (table 2). Furthermore, this trend does not allow for the increase

Table 2: United Kingdom, employment in textiles and clothing, 1930 - 76

(in 000s)

	1930	1936	1940	1946	1950	1956	1960	1964	1970	1976
Textiles	1317	1266	1183	750	1013	1002	906	840	731	513
Clothing	n.a.	694	699	500	701	716	609	582	508	381

Source: Central Statistical Office, Annual Abstracts.

in short-time working, which by the 1970s amounts to between a fifth and a quarter of the total number of jobs. Opinions on the future of the industry, expressed both in the past and during the recent debates on the M.F.A. (Multi-Fibre Arrangement) and European Commission proposals on further import controls, range from the common economists' view that textiles represent an outdated and inefficient activity unsuitable for advanced economies, to the sentimental view, that they represent a highly valued trade which given the right conditions can contribute substantially to the national wealth. In support of the latter, some points can be made regarding the situation of the British textile trade. Here, textile products in 1977 contributed 5.3% to national exports. Imports, however, cancelled this out by nearly two times, so that the resultant loss to our overall balance of trade was higher than in any other branch of manufacturing industry.

It is clear, therefore, that the single overriding problem of textile regions — the calamitous losses in full-time employment — can only be resolved by government intervention designed to ensure at least a stable future. With international market forces still dominating over regional sentiment, this is as unlikely today as it was in previous decades. Even those problems of textile areas which plausibly could be solved at the regional level, have received only intermittent attention. In the United Kingdom, Development Area status was not conferred on any predominantly textile area until the early 1960s (Central Lancashire, Weaving Belt). It was a whole decade later before the rest of the Lancashire textile belt and the neighbouring region of West Yorkshire was able to qualify for this type of assistance, and one feels that this was granted not so much because of the demise of their staple industry but more through their location in 'provincial' Britain. Complaints such as these are by no means unique to these two areas, for neglect was to be found in several other West European textile regions.

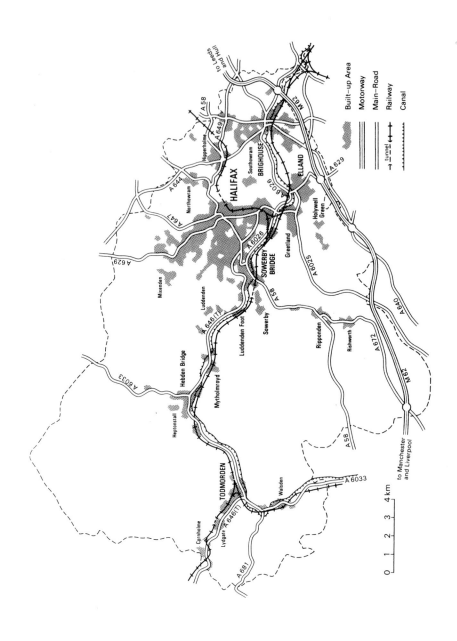

Fig. 2: Halifax and Calder Valley
from: Yorkshire and Humberside Economic Planning Council and Board, "Halifax and Calder Valley", H.M.S.O., 1968

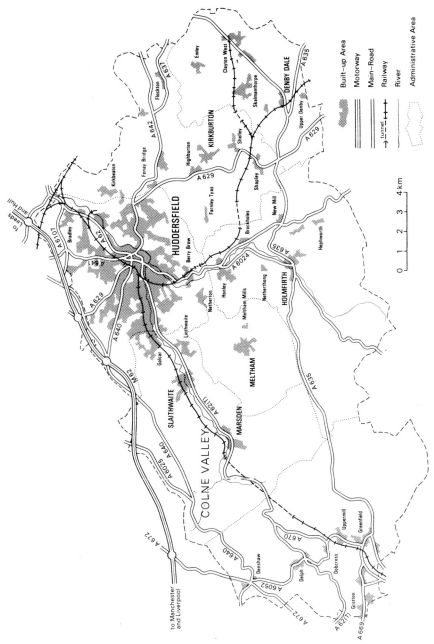

Fig. 3: Huddersfield and Colne Valley
from: Yorkshire and Humberside Economic Planning Council and Board,
"Huddersfield and Colne Valley", H.M.S.O., 1968

The example of the Halifax-Huddersfield Area of West Yorkshire

The various difficulties affecting major textile regions can be illustrated more clearly by looking in closer detail at a particularly severely afflicted area — the Halifax and Huddersfield districts of West Yorkshire. Paradoxically, this heartland of the British woollen and worsted trade represents one of the few textile areas to attract special planning reports. These, the Yorkshire and Humberside Economic Planning Council and Board's *'Halifax and Calder Valley Study'* (1968) and *'Huddersfield and Colne Valley Study'* (1969) highlighted the following main problems encountered in the two areas in the late 1960s:

I *Employment structure and trends:* - high leaning towards declining industries.
II *Low job security:* - high mortality of industrial firms and incidence of short-time working.
III *Low incomes:* - mainly reflecting low wages of the textile industry.
IV *Population decline:* - high level of out-migration, especially amongst school leavers: low birth-rate due to demographic ageing.
V *Settlement and central place structure:* - diffuse distribution of towns and villages: isolation from major regional centres (Manchester, Leeds).
VI *Services:* - inadequate and outdated infrastructure, reflecting central place pattern and low investment.
VII *Communications:* - difficult topography and antiquity of established system.
VIII *Local government structure:* 15 Local Authorities.
IX *Housing:* - residue of nineteenth and early twentieth century growth.
X *Climatic and topographic conditions:* - upland environment.

Measurements of the strength of some these problems are given in table 3, where special note can be taken of (I) the 14.4% decline in population from 1931-1966, (II) the heavily imbalanced employment structure with textile still occupying 30% of the active population and tertiary activities comparing very unfavourably with the national average, (III) the adverse employment trends, showing losses in textiles and other manufacturing industries outweighing gains in tertiary activities, (IV) the high proportions of unfit, poorly valued, and aged housing.

Despite its methodological imperfections, the Assessment Scores in table 4 provide a general evaluation of the area's most prominent economic, social and environmental features. As one would expect, the questions of employment structure, earnings, job security, quality of industrial buildings, and housing each appear in poor light. Some other features, however, such as the quantity of industrial buildings, community life, educational services, and countryside and recreation, came out well enough to be regarded as regional advantages, and in one way and another these have done much towards assisting the restructuring process.

Table 3: Halifax and Huddersfield Districts; Statistics from 1968/69 studies

A. LOCAL GOVERNMENT STRUCTURE

County Boroughs:	2 (Halifax, Huddersfield)
Municipal Boroughs:	2 (Brighouse, Todmorden)
Urban Districts:	10 (Colne Valley, Denby Dale, Elland, Hebden Royd, Holmfirth, Kirkburton, Meltham, Ripponden, Saddleworth, Sowerby Bridge)
Rural Districts:	1 (Hepton)

B. POPULATIONS

1901	459,500
1911	455,600
1921	436,800
1931	430,000
1951	406,840
1961	376,000
1966	369,950

C. AGE-SEX STRUCTURE 1966 (MALES AND FEMALES)

	Halifax-Huddersfield Districts	England and Wales
0-14 years	21.8%	23.2%
15-39 years	30.9%	32.6%
40-59 years	29.9%	28.9%
Over 60 years	17.4%	15.3%
% females	52.4%	51.6%

D. SOCIO-ECONOMIC GROUPS, ACTIVE MALES 1966

	Halifax-Huddersfield Districts	England and Wales
Managerial and Professional	13.7%	15.3%
Non-manual workers	14.1%	18.2%
Skilled manual workers	44.4%	39.5%
Unskilled manual workers	27.5%	24.9%
Others	0.3%	2.1%

E. EMPLOYMENT STRUCTURE 1966, AND % CHANGES 1959-66

	Employment structure as % of total employment, 1966		% changes, 1959-66	
	Halifax-Huddersfield District	Great Britain	Halifax-Huddersfield District	Great Britain
Primary activities	2	4	-18	-33
Textiles	30	3	-11	-11
Clothing	4	2	-3	+6
Other manufacturing industries	31	33		
Tertiary activities	33	58	+11	+12

F. HOUSING

Unfit dwellings, 1965, as % of existing stock:
    Halifax District: 17.4%
    England and Wales: 5.5%

Rateable values of dwellings:

	Below £30	Above £30
Halifax District, 1967	56.6%	43.4%
Huddersfield District, 1968	47.7%	52.3%
England and Wales, 1968	15.4%	84.6%

Age of housing, 1967, Huddersfield district:

	Pre 1914	1914-45	1945-67
Holmfirth U.D.	65.9%	13.9%	20.2%
Saddleworth U.D.	65.7%	18.5%	15.8%
Meltham U.D.	63.6%	6.0%	30.4%
Huddersfield C.B.	49.5%	28.2%	22.3%
Kirkburton U.D.	47.1%	33.4%	29.5%
Colne Valley U.D.	45.4%	36.8%	17.8%
Denby Dale U.D.	24.6%	47.9%	27.5%

Sources for tables 3 and 4: Yorkshire and Humberside Economic Planning Council and Board, 'Halifax and Calder Valley', and 'Huddersfield and Colne Valley', Department of Economic Affairs, H.M.S.O., London, 1968 and 1969.

Table 4: Assessment scores 1967

Range: 0 (Very poor) to 8 (Very good)

This is a modification of the original system employed in the two studies, allowing the amalgamation of results for both districts.

	Housing	0
	Employment structure	2
	Earnings	2
	Job stability & prospects	2
	Quality of industrial buildings	2
	Dereliction	3
	Public utilities	4
	Health services	4
	Education facilities	5
	Quantity of industrial buildings	6
	Community life	6
	Countryside & recreation	6

Some comments on the restructuring process in the Halifax-Huddersfield area

From the economic point of view this has had a long but undistinguished history. New industries, some indirectly associated with the textile trade and others, such as chemicals, food and drink, metal working, and light engineering (excluding textile engineering), were certainly making some ground in this area as early as the inter-war period. During the 1950s, the pace of development quickened a little with several new firms capitalising on the inheritance of cheap labour and availability of old but solidly built industrial premises. These were particularly useful assets, which as later experience was to show, were unfortunately never utilised to the full advantage. In the main the vacated textile mills and their labour were taken up by small, poorly financed and vulnerable firms, employing less than a hundred workers and seeing little significant expansion. There were happily a few notable exceptions, such as Mackintosh-Rowntrees at Halifax, Brooks Motors at Huddersfield, David Brown at Meltham, and I.C.I. (Dyestuffs Division) at Bradley Mills. The expansion of tertiary activities, particularly during the late 1950s and 1960s, has done more towards stabilising employment trends. However, partly reflecting the Central Place structure of the area, these have been predominantly of the lower ordered type, with Local Authority employment in labouring and clerical work figuring the most strongly. This has meant that there is a general paucity of the more lucrative tertiary occupations, particularly in professional and major office services.

Though doing much towards arresting the pace of economic decline, the infusion of new industries and the growth of tertiary activities in the area, has done little to alter basic social patterns. Changes here have come from another direction, namely through the discernible trend from an overwhelmingly industrial to a dormitory function. Activating this movement, which one should stress is only really at its beginnings, have been a number of recent developments, amongst which importance can be attached to, (I) the opening of the M62 motorway from Liverpool to Hull, whose route passes west to east across the area; (II) further advances in personal mobility; (III) the nation-wide inflation of house prices which has not reflected itself very much in the costs of the older property so characteristic of this area; (IV) the amalgamation of the 15 Local Authorities to form the new Metropolitan Districts of Calderdale (centred on Halifax) and Kirklees (centred on Huddersfield); (V) the inclusion of these two districts within the new framework of Assisted Areas; (VII) changes in residential and environmental preferences, so that given the cheap costs of the more traditional types of housing, the dramatic local landscapes, and the now easier access to Manchester and Leeds, there is a growing attraction to predominantly middle class incomers; (VII) the extension of improvement grant systems for the modernisation of old residential property.

Not surprisingly, therefore, since the late 1960s, the rate of population decline in this area has been sharply checked, though there is still a modest net outflow of people.[1] This has not been matched by any slowing down in employment decline, which over the last three years has, in fact, accelerated. Obviously, since the publication of the two studies, social changes have been quickly outpacing economic design. There are obvious manifestations of this to be seen in the local landscape where the neo-georgianisation and sandblasting of humble weavers' cottages and even millworkers' terraces are widespread. Other historical incongruities confirm the trend, for example, Morris dancing in Heptonstall, skiing in Todmorden, yachting in Saddleworth, and several other forms of imported behaviour. The mechanics of the local housing market, working in associationship with the developments just described, was recently illuminated by the journalist ROBERT WATERHOUSE. Writing in a March issue of the Guardian, and referring to what he had just observed in Hebden Bridge, he commented,

"Very few of the Hebden Bridge top-and-bottom houses[2] now sell at more than £5,000 ... Because of this amazing cheapness, and because of the abundance of empty property, the town has now a flourishing community of young outsiders, many of them squatters, who have brought their long hair and health foods into a stronghold of Yorkshire conservatism (where many things indeed are worth conserving). Mutual tolerance is under great strain, a strain not aided by the smart young professionals who have snapped up picturesque Heptonstall just over the hill"

The example of the Halifax and Huddersfield districts serves to illustrate four fundamental points which are undoubtedly commonly represented in most textile regions; they run in more or less chronological order, and it is indeed tempting to suggest a form of cyclic change.

1. the strength and wide range of inherited problems —
2. the slow, unregulated pace and character of economic reconstruction —
3. due to the years of decay and neglect, the ironic emergence of certain valuable local assets —
4. the uncontrolled exploitation of these assets, and the creation of a new series of problems.

Zusammenfassung

Die Textilindustriereviere Westeuropas als Problemregionen

Diese Studie ist gedacht als eine Aufforderung zur allgemeinen Diskussion der Frage nach der "Lebensqualität" in den alteingesessenen Industriegebieten. Die Aufmerksamkeit wird auf die Textilindustriereviere Westeuropas und die mit ihnen verbundenen geographischen Charakteristika und sozio-ökonomischen Probleme gelenkt. Ferner wird Kritik an der gleichgültigen Behandlung solcher Gebiete durch die Regierung und auch an ihrer erstaunlicherweise geringen Beachtung durch die akademische Welt geübt. Die Notwendigkeit, sich mit ihrer "Lebensqualität" zu beschäftigen, zeigt sich klar am Beispiel des Halifax-Huddersfield Distrikts in West Yorkshire, heute einem unserer größten und problematischsten Textilindustriereviere. Hier lassen sich insgesamt zehn Problempunkte aufzählen, aber trotzdem gibt es auch einige positive Dinge — Gemeinschaftsgeist in der Bevölkerung, Naherholung, Bildungseinrichtungen und billige, allerdings verbesserungsbedürftige Wohnmöglichkeiten —, die dem unmittelbaren Eindruck vom schlechten örtlichen Wohnungsstandard widersprechen. Weiterhin am Beispiel von Halifax-Huddersfield wird dem Umstrukturierungsprozeß in den Gebieten der Textilindustrie Aufmerksamkeit geschenkt: erst im Hinblick auf den Zuzug neuer Industrien und das Wachstum auf dem teritären Sektor; dann aber, am Schluß dieser Arbeit, im Sinne der gegenwärtig wachsenden Spannung zwischen der allgemein unter Druck geratenen ortsansässigen Bewohnerschaft und den neuen Zuwanderern. Gerade die letztere Gruppe zeichnet sich nämlich durch ihre unterschiedlichen Lebensstile und durch ihre andersartige Beziehung zu diesem Raum, der immer noch eine überwiegend vom 19. Jahrhundert geprägte Industrielandschaft bleibt, aus.

Notes

1. Between 1951-1961, the population fell by 7.7%, exactly seven times the rate for the decade 1966-1976.
2. The old style of workers' cottages in this area were characterised by a lower house of two floors facing down the valley slope, and under the same roof, an upper house facing backwards into the hillside.

References

BRISCOE, L. (1971): "The textile and clothing industries of the United Kingdom", Manchester

Central Statistical Office (various years): "Annual Abstract of Statistics", H.M.S.O., London

H.M.S.O.: "Annual statement of the overseas trade of the United Kingdom 1977", London

Institut National de la Statistique et des Études Économiques (various years): "Annuaire Statistique de la France", Paris

National Economic Development Office (1969): "The strategic future of the wool textile industry", H.M.S.O., London

P.E.P. (1934): "Report on the British cotton industry", London

Statistical Office of the European Communities (various years): "Eurostat: National Accounts", Luxembourg

Statistical Office of the European Communities (various years): "Eurostat: Quarterly Bulletin of Industrial Production", Luxembourg

Statistisches Bundesamt (various years): "Statistisches Jahrbuch für die Bundesrepublik Deutschland", Stuttgart & Mainz

Yorkshire and Humberside Economic Planning Council and Board (1968): "Halifax and Calder Valley: an area study", H.M.S.O., London

Yorkshire and Humberside Economic Planning Council and Board (1969): "Huddersfield and Colne Valley: an area study", H.M.S.O., London

WILD, M.T. (1972): "The Yorkshire wool textile industry", in J.G. JENKINS (1972): "The wool textile industry in Great Britain", London

WILD, M.T. & G. SHAW (1975): "Population distribution and retail provision: the case of the Halifax-Calder Valley area of West Yorkshire during the second half of the nineteenth century", Journal of Historical Geography 1, 2, pp. 193-210

PUTTING BACK THE LAND —
THE ADAPTATION OF ENVIRONMENT AND SETTLEMENT IN FIFE, SCOTLAND, TO THE CLOSURE OF COAL MINING.

with 6 figures, 2 fotos and 5 tables

ANDRES H. DAWSON

Place as an Academic and a Practical Problem

In its beginning and at its end Geography is about places. Systematic studies, aiming to establish regularities, trends and models, are merely a superstructure of knowledge raised on what happens to a limited range of phenomena in a restricted number of particular places; and, when they have all been completed, the task of building up their findings into coherent wholes remains. One traditional product of that endeavour in Geography has been the recognition on the earth's surface of what have been considered to be different places. As J.H. PATERSON has said

> "The regional geographer is essentially a gatherer of Other Men's Flowers, It is not, usually, the transmission of new facts that justifies his authorship, so much as the rearrangement into more significant patterns of facts which are already known."

However, in the absence of any knowledge of an allembracing system of existence and behaviour, the recognition of places — "the rearrangement into more significant patterns" — must involve a leap of judgement, and the places which are recognised must be individual synthese — the property, as in any other work of art, of their composer. But, if the places which are discovered and set forth find acceptance in, and bring order to, the hitherto jumbled perceptions of the earth's surface in the minds of others, such synthese may not be totally arbitrary.

Nor need they be mere academic doodlings. Great efforts have been made by Man troughout the world and in many ages to alter the nature of the place in his control and the syntheses of them which are common in the minds of others, of which successive redesigning of landscape gardens in post-Renaissance Europe and the shrill advertisements of the package holiday firms are but some of the more extreme examples. Nowhere has both the need to do this been felt more

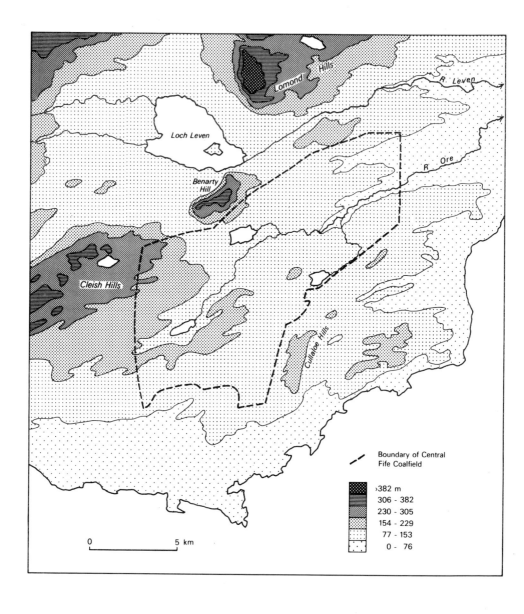

Fig. 1: Central Fife Coalfield, physical

strongly nor the effort employed to achieve a change been greater than in the case of the coalfields of Britain (BARR, J., Civic Trust, Ministry of Housing and Local Government, Oxenham), and, in particular, that in central Fife (figure 1). By the 1960's that area was a mess. A century of large-scale coal mining had created a place which was repulsive. Writing of the Lochgelly District of County[1] in the *Third Statistical Account* of Fife in 1952 ALEXANDER SMITH felt obliged to say

> "Unlike so much of the remainder of the county, this is a drab countryside for the most part, and very soon it was to be made worse by the inevitable and unsightly evidence of colliery workings."

Moreover, mining, which employed more than fourteen thousand of the population of seventy thousand in the late 1950's, was declining rapidly. New jobs were required, but the local authority (Fife County Council) believed that industrialists and entrepreneurs would not come to a place of dereliction and ugliness, and GOULD and WHITE confirmed this view when they showed that, in the opinion of the South of England in 1967 — one of the chief sources from which new industries might be attracted — central Fife was amongst the least attractive places in the United Kingdom. A new place had to be created and advertised.

The Character of Central Fife

What was the nature and scale of the job? The central part of the Fife coalfield, covering 120 km² between Dunfermline in the southwest and the New Town of Glenrothes in the northeast, occupies a depression between a broken line of hills to the north and a less pronounced line to the southeast. The difference in altitude between the floor of the depression and the crests of the hills is not great, being about two hundred metres in the north and seventy in the southeast, but the slopes to those crests are sufficient to give the impression, both on entering the area and from within it, that, save at its eastern end, it is enclosed.[2]

Before coal mining was anything more than the small surface scratchings which had gone on since medieval times the landscape of the area was bland and drab. More than a century of agricultural improvement had filled it with large, rectangular fields, copses, shelter belts and tidy, stone farmsteads, set amongst trees (*New Statistical Account*). More than four fifths of the area had been 'improved' by 1854, including the bed of one of the larger lochs, which had been drained; rough grazings occupied the small areas of rocky, steeper slopes which divide the depression into three broad, shallow valleys, and some of these valley lands where drainage was still difficult; and woods were largely on the higher margins of the area, thus emphasizing them and adding to the area's sense of gentle enclosure and identity (table 1 and figure 3). In brief, it was but one example of a scene and type of place which is still widespread in the east of Scotland more than a hundred years later - that of a lowland Howe or Strath.

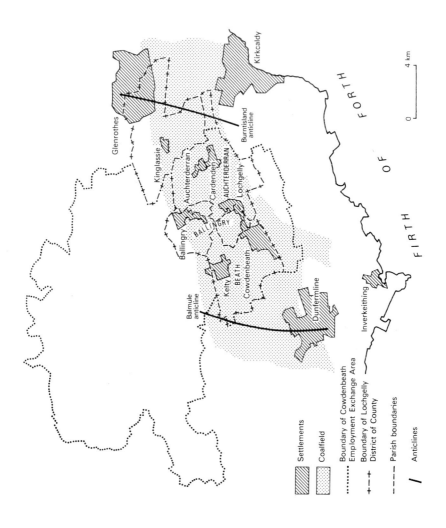

Fig. 2: Central Fife Coalfield, boundaries and settlements

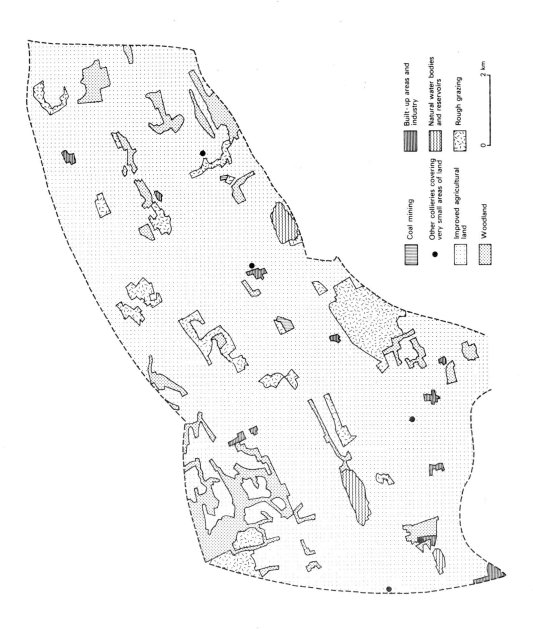

Fig. 3: Central Fife Coalfield, 1854 land use
Source: Ordnance Survey 1 : 10, 560 (1854)

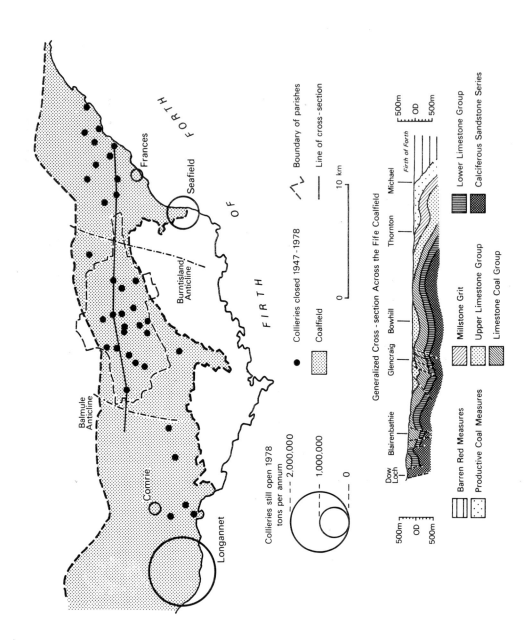

Fig. 4: The Fife Coalfield
Information supplied by the National Coal Board

Deep shaft-mines changed all this. The population of the three parishes of Auchterderran, Ballingy and Beath, which cover fifty-five percent of the area, grew at a rapid and accelerating rate from the middle of last century until the outbreak of the First World War (table 2 and figure 4). Hamlets grew into sprawling rows of miners' cottages, pits and tips. Each coal company built its own settlement replete with all these elements, so that the country lane of 1854 from Dunfermline to Ballingry became an almost unbroken line of houses, collieries and railway installations, eighteen kilometres in length; and large, but separate, pit villages developed at Auchterderran, Cardenden, Kelty and Kinglassie. Meanwhile, the land between the settlements began to sink, so that in 1923 Loch Ore reappeared, but as a stagnant, smelly, dirty pool (WHITTINGTON, 1966).

In 1957 there were eighteen collieries at work, raising about four million tons each year. By 1967 all were closed (figure 4). Declining demand for coal, the sinking of new pits of greater size, efficiency and easier geological conditions,

Table 1: Central Fife Coalfield - Land Use (Percentages of the area)

	1854	1978
Improved land, farmsteads and shelter belts	84	61
Rough grazing	6	2
Woodland	7	10
Natural water bodies	1	1
Built-up	1	10
Mining	—	9
Public open space	—	4
Derelict	—	2

Sources - Ordnance Survey 1:10,560 (1854) and personal fieldwork.

Table 2: Auchterderran, Ballingry and Beath Parishes, Fife - Population

Year	Population	Year	Population
1841	3,322	1911	51,112
1851	5,130	1921	54,349
1861	6,583	1931	48,541
1871	8,533	—	—
1881	10,839	1951	54,073
1891	16,758	1961	50,418
1901	28,694	1971	43,319

Source - Registrar General for Scotland, Census of Scotland 1971, Fife, Table 5, Edinburgh.

Fig. 5: Central Fife Coalfield, major areas of land made derelict by mining
Source: Second Land Utilisation Survey (1964); Ordnance Survey 1:10,560 (1966); and Scottish Development Department, Classification, Analysis and Monitoring of Derelict Land — Fife County, Edinburgh (1974)

underground flooding and the working out of seams were the causes of this sudden change (MCNEIL 1973). Eight percent of the central Fife coalfield lay derelict, and, as the population began to move away, the towns and villages began to decay. Although the area covered by landscape elements of mining origin was less than a quarter of the whole, thirty-seven parcels of land larger than two hectares lay derelict, of which five exceeded fifty hectares and the largest covered four hundred, with the effect that everywhere there loomed in view the black and smoking tips of colliery spoil and silent pithead winding gear (figure 5).

The New Place

At least two types of place might have been created from this mess. The pyramidal tips might have been left, and the opportunity taken to clear away the dirty, broken details of the landscape — the miners' rows, colliery sheds and fences — around them, and to redesign the settlement and routeways on a larger, more 'free-flowing' scale. Such a scale would have been commensurate with the existing, vertical forms, which might, by such a design, have been emphasized, and which, in turn, echoed the dominant features of the natural topography — the twin volcanic plugs of the Lomond Hills. Such a conception might have created a greater sense of spaciousness, mobility and modernity in the landscape, which might have been attractive to industrialists from elsewhere, and, in an era in which the spread of placelessness is increasingly feared (RELPH, 1976), preserved in one area the boldest and most distictive elements of a landscape type — the late nineteenth-century and early twentieth-century coalfield — which everywhere is being swept away. Only the winding tower of the Mary Colliery was allowed to survive — a piece of outdoor sculpture — to remind the viewer of what the place had briefly been.

But, if the idea was ever considered in the early 1960's, it was rejected. Some of the bings held deepseated fires which it was necessary to expose and quench; some of the spoil was required to fill the marshy depressions which had developed through subsidence; it was suggested that the people who stayed behind in central Fife when the mines closed wished to be rid of reminders of its recent history; and, much of the land under the tips could be put back to agriculture. Above all, however, was the belief that new jobs would not come to a place which bore the marks of a coalfield. Nobody objected to the cleaning up, and a second type of place prevailed.

This was a throwback to the nineteenth century. More than half the land treated in the major reclamation schemes carried out by the local authority was returned to agriculture (table 3 and figure 6). Land which had been covered by spoil heaps and marsh was regraded into gentle slopes and sown to grass, thus restoring the wide vistas down to Loch Ore and to the surrounding hills which had existed in the early nineteenth century, so that, except for the intrusion of the

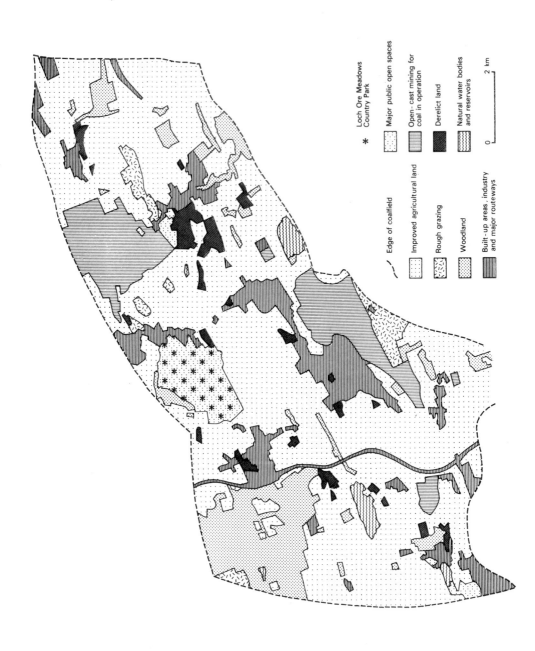

Fig. 6: Central Fife Coalfield, 1978 land use

Table 3: Major land reclamation schemes in Central Fife Coalfield 1963 - 1978, carried out or planned by Fife County Council or Fife Regional Council

NAME	AREA (HA.)	QUANTITY REGRADED ('000m³)	COST (£000)	DATE	FROM: DERE-LICT	FROM: POOR PASTURE (Hectares)	FROM: POOR WOOD-LAND	TO: AGRI-CULTURE	TO: WOOD LAND (Hectares)	TO: OTHER USES
Hill of Beath No. 1	9	23	7.5	1963	9	—	—	9	—	—
Hill of Beath No. 2	40	192	37	1964	26	14	—	21	15	4
Jenny Gray Colliery	15	230	39	1964/5	15	—	—	15	—	—
Lochore Meadows - Phase										
1 Nellie Colliery	73	192	80	1967/8	40	17	9	50	12	11
2 Glencraig Colliery	83	1,533	190	1969/70	61	21	—	82	—	1
3 Mary Colliery	233	650	104	1971/3	87	63	—	—	—	233
4 Aitken Colliery	171	1,000	210	1973/4	106	—	—	129	16	26
5 Lumphinnans No. XI Colliery	39	900	194	1974/5	32	—	1	37	2	—
6 Lindsey Colliery	40	565	250	1975/6	35	—	—	40	—	—
Newton Colliery	6	61	14	1973	4	2	—	6	—	—
Dundonald Colliery	35	371	130	1976/7	23	—	—	34	—	—
Lumphinnans No. 1 Colliery	26	60	110	1978	26	—	—	24	2	—
Minto Colliery	—	—	—	1979	—	—	—	—	—	—
Wee Mary Colliery	—	—	—	—	—	—	—	—	—	—
Kinglassie Colliery	—	—	—	1978/9	—	—	—	—	—	—

Source - Fife Regional Council, Glenrothes.

towns, the substitution of post and wire fences for the pre-existing hedges and walls, and some new blocks of woodland — as yet still saplings — the land has been put back.

Within the coalfield settlements a different, though no less intensive, form of landscape alteration was pursued. The last of the miners' rows, with their harsh, rectangular uniformity and unsurfaced roads, have been replaced by local authority housing at lower density, giving space for gardens. Moreover, short stretches of the margins of the main roads from the south have been subject to detailed examination and improvement in which individual buildings, hoardings and even walls have been demolished, repainted or otherwise given a facelift, and small plots of land within and around the settlements have been tidied or planted with tress (MCNEIL 1973).

Meanwhile, promotional activities were pursued by the local authority with a view to attracting industry. Literature was produced which made mention of the new Loch Ore Meadows County Park and the recreational facilities it offered within a few kilometres of industrial estates (figure 6). External recognition was sought for the extent of the change of landscape which had occurred and the new standards of facilities which had been achieved from the Countryside Commission for Scotland. In all, about £3,000,000 (at 1978 prices) has been spent by the authority on reclamation, renovation and promotional activities (much of which has been made available by central government).

An Evaluation

How successful has it been? The question requires to be answered on several grounds. Although some miners travel daily to the few collieries which remain open in the east and west of Fife (figure 4)[3], and although many other miners left the area, some accepting transfers to coalfields in England (MCNEIL 1973), the area is still bedevilled by a very high level of male unemployment — a level which has remained consistently above those of all other Employment Exchange Areas[1] in Fife since the closure of the mines (table 4). This has been caused in part by the redundancies in mining, in part by the lack of mining jobs for boys on leaving school, and, in consequence of the loss of both population and income, a decline in the number of jobs in the tertiary sector of the central coalfield. In these circumstances it is not surprising that the population of the two largest settlements (Cowdenbeath and Lochgelly) sank substantially between 1951 and 1971 (table 5).

New Industries have been attracted. Indeed, during the periods of relative buoyancy in the Brithish economy in the late 1950's and early 1960's Fife attracted far more of the immigrant firms to Scotland than either its area or its population might have warranted (WELCH 1970)[4]. Between 1958 and 1971 115 new industrial establishments appeared in that part of Fife lying south and west of the river Leven (figure 1). Fifty-five of these were in Glenrothes, were, unlike in the central coalfield, Special Development Area inducements were on offer[5] (of which the availability of advance factories has been shown to have been of particular importance in attracting firms (MCNEIL 1974)), twenty-four were in the Inverkeithing area, but only twelve, none of which employed more than five hundred in 1967, were in the area of the central Fife coalfield (MCNEIL 1973 and 1974). Since that date the major sources of new jobs have been on the coast of

Table 4: Unemployment (mid-year)

Year	Coalminers in Fife	Coalminers in Cowdenbeath E.E.A.	Year	Coalminers in Fife	Coalminers in Cowdenbeath E.E.A.
1959	173	70	1969	716	178
1960	245	106	1970	762	177
1961	1798	76	1971	731	181
1962	530	115	1972	569	130
1963	631	322	1973	634	200
1964	578	339	1974	523	204
1965	320	174	1975	415	145
1966	328	193	1976	483	178
1967	481	273	1977	460	179
1968	1,000	245			

Employment Exange area	1977 (January) total	%	men	%	1978 (January) total	%	men	%
Cowdenbeath	1,745	21.0	1,190	23.7	2,022	23.1	1,409	26.9
Inverkeithing	214	5.1	130	5.0	247	5.8	150	6.0
Dunfermline	2,171	6.4	1,273	5.5	2,328	6.8	1,315	5.9
Burntisland	192	7.9	127	7.2	280	10.2	183	9.0
Kirkcaldy	1,966	6.6	1,234	7.1	1,968	6.6	1,281	7.4
Glenrothes	1,578	9.1	919	9.2	1,641	8.2	907	8.5
Leven	1,592	12.9	1,042	14.3	1,893	14.8	1,365	18.0
Fife	10,464	8.0	6,569	8.3	11,541	8.8	7,372	9.3
Scotland	183,418	8.4			203,629	9.2		
U.K.	1,390,218	6.0			1,484,687	6.4		

Source - Manpower Services Commission, Edinburgh.

Table 5: Cowdenbeath and Lochgelly Burghs 1951 - 71

Population	1951	1971	Change 1951 - 71 absolute Change	Change caused by Migration
Cowdenbeath	13,153	10,464	-20%	-3,260
Lochgelly	193	155	-20%	—
Fife	5,563	5,025	-10%	—

No. of service establishments

Cowdenbeath	300	254	-15%	—
Lochgelly	193	155	-20%	—
Fife	5,563	5,025	-10%	—

Rateable value of service establishments

Cowdenbeath	£ 14,200	£ 101,000	x 7.1	—
Lochgelly	£ 7,900	£ 42,500	x 5.4	—
Fife	£ 274,000	£ 2,227,000	x 8.1	—

Sources - Registrar General for Scotland, Census of Scotland 1971, Fife. Table 4, Edinburgh and Fife County Council, Valuation Rolls for 1951/2 and 1971/2, Cupar (1951 and 1971).

Fife, associated with the North Sea Oil industry, and only one proposal has been submitted for a large new industrial development in the central coalfield — for a petrochemical plant south of Cowdenbeath which would employ 350 people — apart from the opencast mining operations which have continued since 1961. Moreover, many of the new jobs in the coalfield have been for women, and those for men have been but a small proportion of the total which was lost through the closure of the pits.

Similarly, farming will regain only a modest part of that which it has lost since 1854; and much of the land which has been restored, though better drained in some cases now than in last century, is only covered by a skim of seventy-five millimetres of topsoil, which will restrict its use to grazing for many years to come. Only in areas at present undergoing opencast mining, which were in agricultural use immediately prior to the opencast operations, will a full soil profile be restored when mining is complete. In all other cases the cost of reclamation, at six to twenty times the value of the land for agriculture, will never be recouped. No private individual or business could have taken on the task of restoration, save with a philanthropic end in view, and thus, on all these grounds, it would seem that the policy of 'putting back the land' has not been a complete success.

Why has the outcome been disappointing? Perhaps it is too soon to judge for, although most of the dereliction in the area has been removed and all the major sites will have been cleared by 1980, it is unlikely that the image of the area in people's minds will change as fast. The Loch Ore Meadows — the largest single coalfield reclamation scheme in Britain — have attracted awards, and the local authority's chief planning officer, Mr. MAURICE TAYLOR — whose idea it was — and the driver of the bulldozer which moved the burning bings have been decorated, but almost all the publicity which central Fife has received has emphasized the size of the task of putting back the land, while the local authority itself has made great play of the contrast between 'before' and 'after' scenes within the area. In consequence the public outwith Fife has been reminded constantly that, whatever the area might be in the process of becoming, it has been and, to some extent, remains a coalfield. The coalfield image has not yet been exorcised.

Such reminders of its past may not be helpful for, even in the periods of greatest economic growth, Fife must compete for industry with almost all of Scotland, Wales and much of England, which all can offer similar financial inducements. In these circumstances it is unlikely that coalfield towns, no matter how they have been tidied up, will be obviously more attractive to entrepreneurs, their skilled workers who may be transfered from existing factories, and to wives and families than New Towns, rural shires and pleasant market towns, all lacking both the history of mining and the stigma of labour militancy which was attached to central Fife (SMITH 1952). In fact, there has been very little economic growth to spread across the needy parts of Britain during the 1970's, and even less industrial investment.

Furthermore, it was only in 1978 that the Loch Ore Meadows Country Park, with its rural, open-air character, yachting, fishing and picnicking facilities, was finally recognised as such and designated by the Countryside Commission, thus marking its restoration to an agreed, acceptable level of amenity and public utility[6]; and the full effect of this achievement on the public's image of the area cannot have occurred yet. Nor have the by-products of the opencast mining appeared yet. When the sites south of Cowdenbeath and Lochgelly have been fully worked not only will the derelict area of the Dora and Foulford collieries have been cleared away, but the foundation of the East Fife Regional Road, linking the M 90- motorway to Kirkcaldy and Glenrothes, will have been laid, as will that of an eighteen-hole golf course. And yet, despite the incomplete nature of the work, the population of the area seemed already to have reached a stable, if a lower, level by the middle 1970's (Fife Regional Council 1977), and speculative building of houses for sale, which may indicate a broadening of the social character of the settlements, was proceeding[7].

Foto 1: The Central Fife Coalfield before ...

Foto 2: ... and after "putting back the land".

Central Fife and the Quality of Life

However, before the reclamation has finished, a challenge has appeared to it. Because no private person or body would accept responsibility for cleaning up what private industry had begun, the local authority felt obliged to tackle it, and, in return, it has retained the ownership of almost all the land it has improved. The land has been rescued, but technology and the economy move on. Much coal was left at shallow depths in central Fife when mining was more primitive or facing harsher market terms, but now new opencast techniques can extract coal which previously would have been unprofitable. Some of this lies under reclaimed land, including the Loch Ore Meadows Park, and the National Coal Board Opencast Executive has sought permission recently to explore the possibilities for new mining in this area (Scotsman 1976). What should the authorities do? What price should the people of Fife demand for any new disruption and scarring, even if it were only to be for the usual four-year period required by opencast mining in Fife, of the new place which they have created so recently, or is the land, by virtue of the fact that it has been rescued by the public through their elected bodies, sacrosanct to the uses to which it is now put?

In other words, in what does the quality of life reside - the appearance of the place in which we live, its recreational facilities, its social composition or the opportunities of employment which it offers, or wealth from the exploitation of its natural resources, or in something else? What places have a higher quality of life, and what do not? For those industrialists who did not come to central Fife, and for those people who lived in this place but who left it, the quality of life would seem to be superior elsewhere; for those industrialists who did come, it would seem that in their view their lives would be improved by lower costs for, and better chances to expand, their businesses (MCNEIL 1974); and, for those who lived in this place and stayed, though in many cases unemployed, the opportunities of movement seem to have weighed more lightly than the costs and losses to them of leaving it.

The conclusion must be that the quality of life, like beauty, lies in the eye of the beholder rather than in what is to be seen; and that therefore geographers may find it necessary to turn away from the 'totting-up' approach to its measurement which has been adopted by DREWNOWSKI and SCOTT, LEWIS, KNOX and others, and look instead at what the people do. Is it too simple to suggest that people only see two types of place — those which would offer them, in their belief, a higher quality of life, and those which would not — and then only one of these types at any time; and is it too simple to suggest that, in the case of central Fife, people's choices, as revealed by their movements over time, have shown that this place has offered both a better and a poorer life within the last hundred years, that perhaps in the late 1970's it may be emerging from a period in which its quality of life has been too low, and that any new mining should only be permitted if it can be shown that it would not jeopardise the area's improving image? And, if such a test by migration should prove to be more widely applicable as a measure of the quality of life in any place, does it not mean that, as with people, so with places it is true to say that the poor are always with us?

Zusammenfassung

Die Restauration einer Landschaft — Die Wandlung von Siedlungsraum und Umwelt in Fife nach der Schließung der Kohlengruben

Geographie handelt von Orten. Systematische Studien in der Geographie geben Material an die Hand, aus dem unter Umständen ein zusammenhängendes Ganzes geformt werden kann, und gewöhnlich ist ein Resultat solcher Synthesen die Erkenntnis über verschiedene Orte. Jedoch sind Geographen nicht die einzigen, die sich mit dem Begriff des Ortes auseinandersetzen. Große Anstrengungen sind in der Landschaftsgestaltung unternommen worden, um Orte einem Schönheitsideal anzupassen oder um die Leute zu überreden, daß für sie bestimmte Orte attraktiv oder der Aufmerksamkeit würdig seien. Nirgendwo anders hat man die Notwendigkeit, dies zu tun, stärker wahrgenommen als im Fall der britischen Kohlenreviere, und besonders in jenem von Zentral-Fife. Zwischen 1957 und 1967 wurden in einem Gebiet von 120 km² die Bergbaubetriebe stillgelegt, wobei 14.000 Beschäftigte aus ihren Arbeitsstellen entlassen wurden. Neue Arbeitsplätze wurden gebraucht, um die 70.000 Einwohner zu versorgen, aber die Kommunalbehörden glaubten, daß Industrieunternehmen nicht an einen Ort ziehen würden, der für seine durch die Industrie selbst verursachte Verwahrlosung und Häßlichkeit bekannt war. Ein neuer Ort mußte geschaffen und öffentlich angepriesen werden.

In dieser Studie werden die alternativen Landschaftstypen, die man hätte schaffen können, beschrieben und der bis 1978 erzielte Fortschritt bei der Rekultivierung der früheren Agrarlandschaft dargelegt. Es wird das Scheitern der Bemühungen aufgezeichnet, den Niedergang der Bergbaustädte zu verhindern und ein Andauern der hohen Arbeitslosenraten in der Region zu unterbinden. Ferner werden die Schwierigkeiten aufgezeigt, mit denen die Kommunalbehörden bei ihrem Versuch konfrontiert waren, neue Industrie anzuziehen, sowie die Herausforderung in Gestalt eines neuerlichen Genehmigungsantrags für den Kohleabbau in den bereits rekultivierten Gebieten vermerkt.

Es wird die Schlußfolgerung gezogen, daß die "Lebensqualität" von Räumen in einigen Fällen am Bevölkerungsverhalten gemessen werden könnte und daß Wanderungen den Umstand widerspiegeln könnten, daß man einige Orte entsprechend der wahrgenommenen Lebensqualität höher als die anderen einschätzt. Unter Zuhilfenahme dieses Kriteriums wird gezeigt, daß Zentral-Fife während der vergangenen einhundert Jahre zuerst bessere und dann, in der jüngsten Vergangenheit, schlechtere Lebensbedingungen bot. Ausgehend von diesem Beispiel wird die Vermutung geäußert, daß es scheinbar wie mit dem Menschen so auch mit den Orten ist: die Armen sind stets mit und um uns.

Notes

1. The boundaries of the central section of the Fife coalfield do not coincide with those of the areal units which are used for administrative purposes in the area and for which various types of statistics are available (figure 2). However, the central Fife coalfield, for which the Burntisland and Balmule anticlines have been taken as the eastern and western boundaries, may be represented by
   (a) the parishes of Auchterderran, Ballingry and Beath, which lie almost entirely within the central coalfield, occupying fifty-five percent of its area, and containing very few inhabitants in their non-coalfield parts (see also figure 4);
   (b) the Lochgelly District of Country, which also includes the parish of Kinglassie; and,
   (c) the Cowdenbeath Employment Exchange Area (E.E.A.) which, although it includes the whole of the former County of Kinross, the parish of Auchtertool and part of the parish of Dunfermline, much of which are not on the coalfield, had a population of about 52,000 in 1971 of which 45,000 lived within the central part of the Fife coalfield.
2. The central Fife depression is bounded by intrusive and resistant igneous rocks of Permo-Carboniferous age forming the bounding hills to the north and southeast. It was excavated probably as a result of differential erosion of the less resistant carboniferous sedimentaries underlying it during Tertiary times by marine, sub-aerial and fluvial processes. The depression and the slopes of the hills, though not their summits, are covered by boulder clay. The river Ore and the Lochty Burn occupy broad, shallow valleys which are of pre-glacial origin.
3. The distances from Cowdenbeath to the Longannet group of collieries in the west of Fife and to Seafield Colliery are twenty and fifteen kilometres respectively.
4. Between 1945 and 1968, 362 firms from outwith Scotland established industrial plants in Scotland which survived until at least the latter year. Of these, 42 were in Fife. Those established between 1960 and 1968 contributed 231 and 38 to these totals respectively (WELCH).
5. Financial and other assistance to industry in central Fife has been available since the passing of the Local Employment Act of 1960. Grants of up to forty percent were available for investment and up to thirtyfive percent for buildings to firms in the area together with rax relief on investment and assistance with movement into the area from more prosperous areas. A Regional Employment Premium has also been payable since 1967 to firms in Development Areas, but since that date central Fife has been obliged to compete with the Special Development Areas in which further financial assistance has been available.

6. Country Parks are defined by the Countryside (Scotland) Act 1967 as a "park or pleasure ground in the countryside, which, by reason of its position in relation to major concentrations of population affords convenient opportunities to the public for enjoyment of the countryside or open air recreation".

7. In 1974 the housing stock of Cowdenbeath and Lochgelly was composed as follows:

	Local Authority, S.S.H.A. and National Coal Board	Owner-occupied
Cowdenbeath	86%	13%
Lochgelly	87%	10%
Scotland	54% *	33%
U.K.	29% *	52%

(Central Statistical Office and Fife County Council 1974)
* National Coal Board houses excluded

References

BARR, J. (1970): "Derelict Britain", London

Central Statistical Office (1975): "Social Trends" 6, p. 155, London

Civic Trust (1967): "Derelect land", London

DREWNOWSKI, J. & W. SCOTT (1968): "The level of living index", Ekistics 25, pp. 266-75

Fife County Council (1959): "Retrospect", Cupar

Fife County Council (1974): "Valuation roll for the year 1974-75", Cupar

Fife Regional Council (1977): "Population estimates 1976", Glenrothes

GOULD, P. & R. WHITE (1974): "Mental maps", pp. 69-74, London

KNOX, P.L. (1975): "Social well-being: a spatial perspective", Oxford

LEWIS, G.M. (1968): "Levels of living in the north-eastern United States about 1960: a new approach to regional geography", Transactions I.B.G. 45, pp. 11-37

MCNEIL, J. (1973): "The Fife coal industry 1947-1967", S.G.M. 89, pp. 81-94 and pp. 163-79

MCNEIL, J. (1974): "Factors in industrial location: the Fife case 1958-71", S.G.M. 90, pp. 185-97

Ministry of Housing and Local Government (1963): "New life for dead lands", London

New statistical account (1845), vol. IX, Fife-Kinross, pp. 168-9 and 177, Edinburgh

OXENHAM, J.R. (1966): "Reclaiming derelict land", London

PATERSON, J.H. (1960): "North America", author's note, Oxford

RELPH, E. (1976): "Place and placelessness", London

Scotsman (31st March 1976), Edinburgh

SMITH, A. (1952): "Third statistical account of Scotland - Fife", pp. 419-20, Edinburgh

WELCH, R.V. (1970): "Immigrant manufacturing industry established in Scotland between 1954 and 1968: some structural and locational characteristics", S.G.M. 86, pp. 134-48

WHITTINGTON, G. (1966): "Land utilisation in Fife at the close of the eighteenth century", S.G.M. 82, pp. 184-93

OXENHAM, J.R. (1966): "Reclaiming derelict land", London

PATERSON, J.H. (1960): "North America", author's note, Oxford

RELPH, E. (1976): "Place and placelessness", London

Scotsman (31st March 1976), Edinburgh

SMITH, A. (1952): "Third statistical account of Scotland - Fife", pp. 419-20, Edinburgh

WELCH, R.V. (1970): "Immigrant manufacturing industry established in Scotland between 1954 and 1968: some structural and locational characteristics", S.G.M. 86, pp. 134-48

WHITTINGTON, G. (1966): "Land utilisation in Fife at the close of the eighteenth century", S.G.M. 82, pp. 184-93

BRO UND BLAENAU IN INDUSTRIAL SOUTH WALES: RECONCILING THE IRRECONCILEABLE?

with 2 figures and 1 tables

Philip N. Jones

Introduction

The South Wales Coalfield has been identified as a sub-region where the 'Quality of Life', as measured by various objective social indicators, is retarded.[1] The most fundamental cause is the poor access to jobs, which severely constrains income levels. Nevertheless many discontinuities appear between identified needs and the actions of various public policies which suggest that existing solutions are both partial and inadequate. The paper examines the general background to spatial contrasts in quality of life in industrial South Wales, and exemplifies these with reference to the Upper Afan Valley. The latter has been the location of a Home Office-sponsored Community Development Project (CDP), and, stemming from the writer's Doctoral research into the morphogenesis of colliery settlement in the South Wales coalfield,[2] the impact on the landscape of catastrophic colliery closures, rapid population decline, and subsequent environmental improvement schemes can be evaluated over a fifteen-year period.

The Spatial Dimensions of Social and Economic Disparities in South Wales

Regional development problems can only be analysed in terms of the totality of physical forms, social and economic structures, and historical evolution. Industrial South Wales, a major regional entity of closely similar areal dimensions to the Siedlungsverband Ruhrkohlenbezirk in West Germany, personifies the existence of sharp spatial inequalities, and is a region in which reversals of economic fortune have been rapid. In its most elemental form the Region, with a 1971 population of 1.8 million, comprises two contrasting sub-regions — the Coalfield and the Coastal Lowlands; historically these corresponded to the Blaenau, a bleak gritstone upland plateau dissected by steep-sided valleys, and very sparsely settled, and the Bro, a rich lowland of good farming, agrarian villages and small

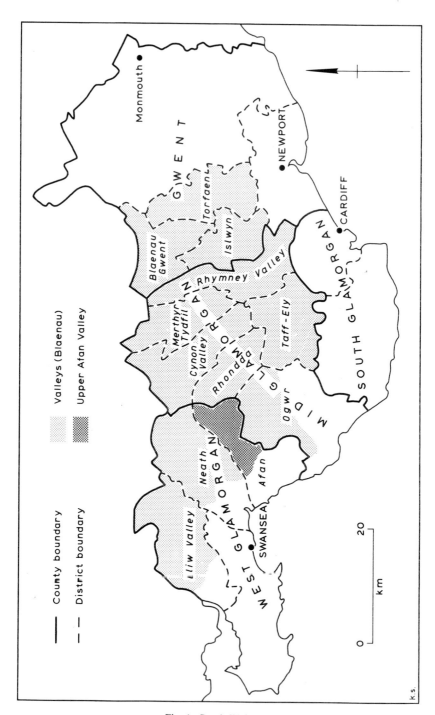

Fig. 1: South Wales

market towns. The nineteenth century industrialization brought the iron industry and coalmining to the Blaenau, accompanied by extremely rapid population growth. With no equivalent of a "Hellweg" urban system to guide it, settlement was largely amorphous, functionally disordered, and indifferently planned. The inter-war economic depression initiated a process of contraction in the iron and coal industries, which with temporary interruptions, has severely eroded the economic base. We are now approaching the end of a cycle of economic development that has in some parts taken barely 100 years from initiation to peak to extinction. The Bro, modestly stimulated by the growth of exporting ports in the nineteenth century, has assumed the key role in the present century, and particularly since 1945. In a period when development prospects and the quality of life, existing and potential, are increasingly bound-up with the urban hierarchy and the physical land resources for factory construction, this favours the accumulation of investment in the expanding cities and towns of the Coastal Lowlands at the expense of the declining, difficult environment of the coalfield.

This albeit brief sketch of the cycle of economic development[3] forms the scenario in which government policy has operated in the phase of active regional development policy since 1945. Although there is no formal Regional Plan, Government policy has vacillated between its implied commitment to prevent the continued decline of 'the Valleys', and encouraging the inexorable economic pressures which attract industrialists and other investments to the Coastal Lowlands. As elsewhere in Western Europe the 'coal crisis' triggered a rapid contraction of the coalmining industry after 1957, which is illustrated by employment statistics for coalmining in the South Wales coalfield:

Year	Employment
1957	102,000
1960	80,000
1965	65,000
1970	43,000
1976	30,000

In 1967 the Welsh Office, in its only definitive document on regional planning issues in Wales, felt obliged to state: "For both economic and social reasons the Government reject any policy which would assume the disintegration of the substantial valley communities".[4] Yet, despite these ostensibly firm words, the decline in population and economic activity has continued. The Central and Eastern Valleys, with a population of 680,000 in 1951, had fallen to 652,000 in 1966, and 632,000 in 1972, although this trend masks substantial internal contrasts, as ALDEN has shown.[5] Indeed the severity of the decline has been such that Professor HAROLD CARTER (Aberystwyth) was prompted to write of the Valleys as being in "a state of incipient disintegration" in 1975.[6]

This state of affairs stems both from fundamental structural weaknesses within the coalfield, and from the inadequacies of governmental policies. As an example of the former case, HUMPHRYS has drawn attention to the rationalization trends in the services and administration sector, progressively favouring the Coastal Lowlands with their cohesive urban system: employment in services actually declined by some 7,000 between 1965-1970.[7] Infrastructural investments in motorways, ports, and other major facilities, has concentrated in the Coastal Lowlands (M4 especially). Major industrial estates and other industrial facilities designed to attract industry to Industrial South Wales as a whole have been concentrated in the interface zone between coalfield and Coastal Lowlands, as part of the 'Valley Mouth' strategy. Bridgend, Llantrissant, Treforest, Cwmbran are examples of what the TY TORONTO study has termed the 'Marginal Shift' component of government policy.[8] Whilst industrial estates have been built in the Coalfield, industrialists, especially major ones, have shown a preference for the big sites and better communications of the 'Valley Mouth' sites — the most recent is Ford Motor Co. Ltd., which has selected Bridgend. Without positively admitting as such, the general strategy has been that of the 'Growth-point', and a basic assumption of policy has been to provide industrial jobs at Valley Mouth estates within commuting distance of the Coalfield communities. On the other hand, the corresponding programme of advance factory construction and industrial estates within the coalfield has been progressively weakened by the erosion in the amount of differential financial assistance available vis à vis the Coastal Lowlands.[9]

The Valleys of the Coalfield are therefore doubly-disadvantaged by the concentration of job-losses and their less favourable position to attract new employment. A physico-economic hierarchy exists within the Region from Valley — Valley Mouth — Coastal Plain, a sequence that is bound together by patterns of spatial interaction which merely add confirmation to the gradients of inequalities which exist. Yet, ultimately, even more than just observed inequalities are at stake. As HERBERT[10] has reminded us, much more is involved than indices of population decline, levels of facilities and so on; we are witnesses to the impending destruction of traditional, place-oriented communities which are the epitome of the uniquely Welsh industrial culture, and that the expanding communities of the Coastal Lowlands share all the apparent characteristics of similar societies elsewhere in Britain, lacking any real distinctiveness. In a sub-region as large as the South Wales Coalfield, this picture can only be a generalisation, and one of the major contributions which the geographer can make is to investigate the critical interactions between scale and geographical specialization, since these lead to very considerable differences in innate development potential and measurable performance. The valley chosen to illustrate the problems at 'close quarters' must therefore be seen in this light.

The Upper Afan Valley: The Emergence of the problem

The Upper Afan Valley highlights in an acute way both the spatial inequalities introduced by differential economic trends in Industrial South Wales, and the effects of selective trends in public investments which have consistently fa-

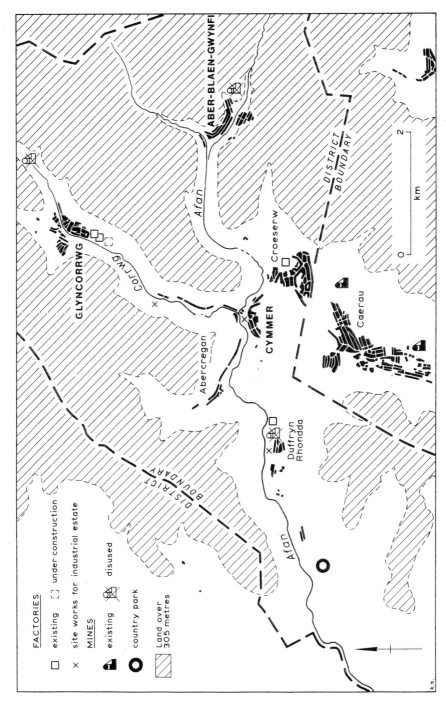

Fig. 2: The Upper Afan Valley

voured the Coastal Lowlands — in this case the major industrial town of Port Talbot. Although affected by the inter-war depression, the Valley in 1945 had basically survived with its economic pattern unscathed — an almost total dependence on coalmining. This continued until a catastrophic sequence of colliery closures affected all three mines in the Valley between November 1966 and May 1970. The total number of local jobs declined from 2,978 in 1961 to 745 in 1971, reflecting these closures and the paucity of other employment.[11] Although most eligible coalminers were offered alternative jobs in collieries in other valleys, the decline in resident miners was equally sharp — from 1,720 in 1961 to 534 in 1971, a pattern of drift out of the industry consequent upon closure which closely parallels similar situations in South Wales, such as the Dulais Valley.[12] Effectively the raison d'être of the Upper Afan Valley communities had disappeared in four years and the population declined accordingly:

census 1961	9,368
census 1971	8,647
estimate 1974	8,240

The severity of the decline in basic employment was however accentuated by the specific context: the Upper Afan Valley, like so many valleys, was not entirely typical, and two sets of factors stand out. Firstly, the settlement pattern is very fragmented and functionally weak, due to a combination of extremely severe relief, the chronological development of coalmining, and spatial relationships with older industrial communities.[13] As such it is characterized also by physical remoteness and remains one of the least-developed valleys in the Coalfield. There was therefore no adequate functional base upon which tertiary employment could develop, and the sparse introduction of manufacturing industry has been fraught with difficulties.[14] Secondly, the Upper Afan Valley (coincident with the former Glyncorrwg UDC), suffered from a planning policy of neglect for some twenty vital years 1945-65, before the onset of colliery closures. The Valley was dismissed by the old Glamorgan County Development Plan as an area of coalmining, and "It is intended that an expansion of Cymmer shall be the main centre for the Afan Valley and that, except for the completion of already approved housing schemes, in general no new building shall take place elsewhere in Glyncorrwg Urban District" (Glamorgan CC Development Plan, Area No. 1, Written Statement, 1952). As a corollary to this negative attitude the Plan favoured wellmeaning but retrospectively ill-advised programmes of clearance of older housing, followed by rehousing at the central settlement of Cymmer, and this made severe inroads into the physical environment and community structure of smaller, isolated settlements such as Abercregan. The sum total has been the development of concentrated social deprivation in the Upper Afan Valley, ironically juxtaposed and now administratively joined to the richest industrial town in Industrial South Wales, Port Talbot. Yet the interaction between valley and coast has been more difficult than might be anticipated, since long, awkward journeys of

10-15 miles face those fortunate enough to obtain employment in the major industrial concentrations of Port Talbot, Bridgend, Kenfig and Neath.

Indicators of Social Malaise

These have been intensively researched by the Upper Afan Valley CDP, who stress that the existence of this social deprivation does not only affect the immediate quality of life of the population, but vitally weakens any hopes of correcting the situation since it lowers the ability of the population to compete in the crucial market for jobs.[15] Among the most important characteristics identified by the CDP were:

1. High unemployment (about 11%) and low household incomes: an estimated one-third of all households are dependent on Social Security for a major part or the totality of their income.
2. Outmigration affecting predominantly the younger economically active population.
3. Poor accessibility to jobs in time and cost, the latter becoming particularly significant in a population with low household incomes. 70% of economically active residents worked outside the Area by 1971 (cf. only 30% in 1961), yet car ownership levels (at 1/3 of all households) lag seriously behind national average. Public bus transport is inadequate and (despite a rate subsidy) is costly for work journeys. It also seriously diminishes the internal mobility of residents in relation to other facilities. Some employers (e.g. NCB, BP Chemicals) arrange free bus transport, but this is not common. Rail passenger transport disappeared with the colliery closures in the 1960s.
4. Poor educational facilities and achievement levels e.g. sixth form and further educational facilities are centralized at Port Talbot.
5. Inferior shopping and entertainment facilities. No settlement ranked higher than 'Settlement with complete neighbourhood Services' in a classification developed by the writer on a coalfield-wide basis. This is perhaps understandable in view of the fragmentary settlement pattern, which effectively results in 3 major settlements and a number of smaller ones:

	Population (1974)
Cymmer-Croeserw	3,361
Glyncorrwg	1,576
Abergwynfi and Blaengwgnfi	2,023
Abercregan	362
Duffryn Rhondda	403
Heol-y-Glyn	262
Craig	192
Cynonville	143

Source: Upper Afan CDP Final Report, 1977

The functional poverty can be illustrated further by a facilities count of Glyncorrwg 1978 — 1 public house, 2 social clubs, 2 food stores, 1 hardware store, 1 sub-Post Office cum general store, 1 confectionery and tobacco, 1 hairdressers (ladies). A measure of the decline is that in 1963 the same settlement also possessed a large Cooperative Society "emporium", a part-time Bank branch, and 4 public houses.[16] A similar situation is found in other settlements — higher order shopping and recreational facilities must be sought outside the area — in Port Talbot, Neath or Maesteg.

Towards a Solution

Solutions to seemingly intractable spatial inequalities must realistically be examined in terms of the changing relationships between functional organization and geographical scale, and different levels of public policy. All interact upon one another, although there appears to be a reluctance to recognize the full implications of this interaction. Two critical scales are the local and the regional.

The Local Scale: the Draft Upper Afan Valley District Plan

The commitment of West Glamorgan County and Afan Borough District Council seems firm: "the communities have a viable future and... every effort should be made to assist their adjustment to the events of recent years", and: "... the District Plan has been directed towards the achievement of stability, and, in particular, the halting of the current trend of population out-migration".[17]

It is impossible to give a complete summary of policy proposals covering all aspects, but in relation to our major theme the following are of major importance:

1. Although it is considered impracticable to provide jobs within the Valley for all, or even a majority, of the working population, nevertheless a vigorous programme of industrial site preparation has been proposed, and is being currently implemented with financial assistance from the Welsh Development Agency (WDA). These all involve reclaiming old colliery sites, tips and other derelict land, as at Duffryn Rhondda, Avon Colliery, Cymmer, and Glyncorrwg; at the latter an Advance Factory is nearing completion. It is expected that most people will still be dependent on finding work outside the Valley, especially at Port Talbot, and this should be related to (4) below.
2. The Plan categorically reverses the former clearance policy of the old authority, favouring rehabilitation and in situ reconstruction where clearance is unavoidable. Abercregan earmarked for new housing. Moreover land is to be allocated for private house building. GIAs are proposed in the 3 major centres (none have been declared), but in the meantime improvement of older properties under existing Housing Act legislation will continue.

3. Work on improving the general quality of the environment will continue, especially continuing the excellent work already achieved in the Afan Argoed Country Park (in conjunction with the Forestry Commission), which also houses the Welsh Miners Museum, a purely local initiative.
4. On the transport situation the Plan is more pessimistic, in the light of a constant financial squeeze exerted by Central Government. It proposes to continue the existing level of financial subsidies to transport operators, but sees little scope for any positive improvements, and indeed envisages little more than a holding operation to prevent further deterioration. This clearly has serious implications in an economically marginal community.

The Regional Scale

The District Plan is realistic in its assessment, at least, pointing out that it does not control industrialists' powers of decision making, cannot offer extra financial aid to industry, and cannot legislate for the ups and downs of manufacturers' fortunes. The differential financial assistance in favour of SDAs has been whittled away to almost vanishing point, whilst the extension of Development Area status to South Glamorgan has effectively eliminated spatial discrimination. Moreover the increasing concern with the 'Inner City' has introduced yet another competitor for scarce government resources and limited amounts of mobile manufacturing employment. It should also be borne in mind that geographical scale effects must be considered within the Valleys.[18] What level of job diversification can reasonably be expected within a community of 8,200 total population? This implies that for reasons of job accessibility (in terms of quality and choice) a considerable degree of commuting must be anticipated, and planned for, regardless of hoped-for successes in the attraction of manufacturing firms to valley sites. The TY TORONTO study suggests that searching investigations must be made into new ways of subsidizing transport costs to widen choice. The Upper Afan CDP devoted much time and money in demonstrating the effectiveness of direct subsidies for work journeys, but was unable to gain wider acceptance of this principle in West Glamorgan. Yet until a satisfactory way is found of removing the cost burden of the 'friction of distance' from Valley communities, their populations will be effectively discriminated against, with results that no official bodies ostensibly desire! It is also arguable that even within the restraints of a 'mixed economy' more direct and positive action in 'hard-core' problem areas to support marginal manufacturing industry can be justified, such as reserving or guaranteeing government orders — after all, the precedence of shipbuilding and aircraft ordering practices is well-established.[19] Positive discrimination in other spheres, such as the Rate Support Grant, should also be increased, but here precise identification of the areas to be assisted becomes an important problem in itself.[20]

Conclusion

Studies conducted in the declining coalfield or Valleys communities of Industrial South Wales emphasise their stable and cohesive social characteristics, despite the severity of economic and population decline. The major issue by far in their 'quality of life' is the relatively limited access which they have to sufficient jobs, both in quantity and quality, although the neglect of positive measures in the post-war years must also carry much of the blame. Without more radical measures to overcome their disadvantages and increase their competitiveness in the labour market other actions will inevitably appear 'cosmetic' in character. Experience to date suggests that neither sufficient resources, nor co-ordination of policies exists to overcome these problems.

Zusammenfassung

Bro und Blaenau im industriellen Süden von Wales: Vereinbarung des Unvereinbaren?

Akute räumliche Disparitäten bezüglich der sozialen und wirtschaftlichen Verhältnisse herrschen in den Industriegebieten von Südwales zwischen dem Kohlenrevier-Plateau (oder 'Blaenau') und den küstennahen und randlichen Tiefländern (oder 'Bro'). Im Zeitraum seit 1945 hat die Bro die Schlüsselrolle für das regionale Wachstum und den Wohlstand eingenommen, bedingt durch ein Zusammentreffen ihres für eine Expansion der Industrie und der Infrastruktur günstig verfügbaren Flächenpotentials mit dem Vorhandensein großer und gut integrierter Stadtzentren, die als Wachstumspole für ein zusammenhängendes Dienstleistungsangebot fungieren. Die Blaenau hingegen ist zweifach benachteiligt, einmal dadurch, daß sie über eine amorphe und funktionsschwache Siedlungsstruktur verfügt, und zum anderen dadurch, daß sie eine schwere Rezession in ihrem Hauptindustriezweig, der Kohlegewinnung, erlebt.

Die Regierung hat, in der Hauptsache durch ihre regionalen Industrieförderungsmaßnahmen, das miserable wirtschaftliche Schicksal der Blaenau zu wenden versucht. Trotz einer scheinbaren Bekräftigung des Interesses an der Erhaltung der großen Kohlenreviergemeinden hat jedoch die Masse der durch die Regierung finanzierten Industrieexpansionen außerhalb des eigentlichen Kohlenreviers in randlichen Grenzorten stattgefunden, wo sie nur den Trend anderer öffentlicher und privater Investitionen verstärkt. Als eine Folge davon sind lange und kostspielige Pendelwege aus den Kohlenreviergemeinden zu den Arbeitsstätten allgemein üblich geworden. Darüberhinaus sind die finanziellen Anreize, deren sich gewisse Teilgebiete des Kohlenreviers erfreuen, während der siebziger Jahre zunehmend abgeschwächt worden.

Die gegenwärtige Situation ist daher nicht vielversprechend für die Gemeinden der Blaenau, die nichtsdestoweniger klassische Beispiele einer authentischen walisischen Industriekultur bleiben und deren Verfall bedauerlich wäre. Der ihnen drohende Niedergang durch die gleichzeitige Auswirkung der wirtschaftlichen Vernachlässigung und der unzureichenden raumordnungspolitischen Korrekturmaßnahmen wird mit Bezug auf das obere Afantal (Upper Afan Valley), das einen wirtschaftlichen und sozialen Verfall von ganz außergewöhnlichem Ausmaß erlitten hat, herausgestellt. Ehemals blühende städtische Bergbaugemeinden sind in Gefahr, zu wahrhaftigen 'Geisterstädten' abzusinken, da die Bevölkerung konstant abwandert. Wegen ihrer Abgeschiedenheit und wegen ihrer geringen Einwohnerzahl hat es sich als schwierig erwiesen, neue Industrien anzuziehen, die genügend Arbeitsplätze schaffen könnten. Mit Entschiedenheit bemüht sich zur Zeit der 'District Council' um eine Verbesserung der Wohnverhältnisse und der Umwelt allgemein; aber wird dies ausreichen, um eine grundlegende Kehrtwendung im Niedergang des Tales zu bewirken? Angesichts des teuren, unattraktiven und schlechter werdenden Angebots öffentlicher Verkehrsmittel, die in nur sehr geringem Grad Zugang zu den Arbeitsplätzen und öffentlichen Einrichtungen der Küstenstädte und dortigen Industrien gewähren, erscheint Pessimismus angebracht.

Notes and references

1. Uwist CPD Research Team (1976): "A descriptive study of the special development areas in South Wales", Working Paper 14
2. JONES, P.N. (1965): "Some aspects of the population and settlement geography of the South Wales coalfield 1850 - 1926", unpubl. Ph. D. thesis, University of Birmingham
3. for fuller accounts see: MANNERS, G. ed. (1964): "South Wales in the sixties", HUMPHRYS, G. (1972): "Industrial Britain: South Wales"
4. Welsh Office (1967): "Wales: The way ahead", H.M.S.O. London
5. ALDEN, J. (1977): "Economic problems facing urban areas in South Wales", Regional Studies II, pp. 285-96
6. CARTER, H. (1975): "The crisis of the Valleys and its challenge", in: BALLARD, P. & E. JONES eds.: "The Valleys call", Ferndale, Mid-Glamorgan
7. HUMPHRYS, G. (1972), op. cit.: An indication of the functional poverty of the Valley is provided by the shopping study carried out by the former Glamorgan County Council in the mid-1960s, in which only 4 out of 35 major service centres were current or former coalmining centres.

8. TY TORONTO (1977): "A socio-economic strategy for the Valleys of South Wales", Aberfan
9. ibid.: Further development areas have also been declared in other parts of Britain, imposing still further demands on resources, and further competition for scarce industry.
10. HERBERT, D.T. (1972): "Population mobility and social change in South Wales", Town Planning Review 43, pp. 327 - 42
11. West Glamourgan County Council and Afan Borough Council (1977): "Upper Afan Valley Draft District Plan"
12. SEWELL, J. (1975): "Colliery closures and social change: a study of a South Wales mining valley"
13. JONES, P.N. (1969): "Colliery settlement in the South Wales Coalfield 1850-1926", University of Hull Occ. Papers in Geography 14, examines the morphology and processes of colliery settlements in selected areas of the Coalfield, including the Upper Afan Valley.
14. There are (1978) four small factories operating in the Upper Afan Valley, all employing under 100. One factory opened and closed within a three-year period, a typical experience of branch plants in development areas.
15. See particularly PENN, R. and J. ALDEN (1977): Upper Afan CDP Final Report to Sponsors which summarizes the work of the CDP, its aims, achievement, problems etc. This report also contains a comprehensive bibliography of the Project's voluminous publications.
16. Data derived from personal fieldwork surveys undertaken in 1963, 1968, 1978 in the settlements of the Upper Afan Valley and elsewhere.
17. "Upper Afan Valley Draft District Plan", op. cit. on which these remarks are based.
18. A very difficult and contentious problem which was perhaps not given sufficient evalution in the TY TORONTO "Socioeconomic strategy...." op. cit.
19. This remark is prompted by the fact that the major new factory in the area, a book-binding firm, was forced to contract its labour force from 350 to 50 between 1970 and 1972. Could not the Government have redirected some binding work in view of its ever-expanding output of official reports etc? A full assessment of this factory set-back, and its impact on the community, is found in: Uwist CPD Research Team (1975): "Impact study of a plant redundancy in a depressed area on workers and community", Working Paper 13
20. PENN, R. & J. ALDEN op. cit.

INDUSTRY VERSUS ENVIRONMENT IN THE METROPOLITAN FRINGE

ANDREW BLOWERS

Themes

The relationship between environmental protection and economic growth is often portrayed in terms of conflict. For example, a recent review of the problems of the countryside concluded, 'The problem is, then, one of conflicts: between urban and rural; between socio-economic development and the needs of landscape and amenity; between costs and benefits (whether real or perceived)'.[1] Seen in this light the task of planning is to reconcile these competing interests by establishing priorities and weighing short term pressures against long term interests. The spatial solution of this conflict has usually been to restrain development in areas where environmental needs are paramount and to concentrate growth at specific locations. This approach has underpinned both regional and local planning strategies. An alternative view is that economic and environmental aims are complementary. The economic basis of rural life has endured a long term decline and is exacerbated at times of economic recession. The decline in employment, the loss of services and public transport and the increasing social imbalance of rural population can be attributed, in part at least, to restrictive planning policies. The maintenance of an attractive environment may depend on a more positive conception of planning which attempts to intervene to arrest the decline of some rural areas.

These two views represent different ideologies of planning. The idea of planning as fundamentally concerned with environmental values emphasises the control of development and is suited to conditions of economic and population growth. The other approach is permissive and stresses the entrepreneurial role of planning that is necessary at a time when resources are more limited and the economy is stagnant. These contrasting ideologies are, to an extent, reflected in different planning styles. On the one hand there is the comprehensive, long term approach which represents the future in spatial and environmental terms relying on measures of planning control to direct pressure towards growth points. Alternatively, there is the more indicative approach which focuses on economic processes and stresses uncertainty and the need for continuous monitoring and review so that planning policies can respond to changing circumstances. These ideologies and styles of planning are not mutually exclusive and may be present within individual plans. But examination of plans poses the question whether planning is responding sufficiently to the problems facing the economy. In particular are planners still relying heavily on the negative aspects of control at a time when positive measures are required to stimulate economic revival?

South East England provides a suitable context in which to explore the interaction of styles of planning which attempt to respond to environmental and economic aims. Superficially the protection of the environment and the promotion of economic development may appear complementary in the context of a metropolitan region. If the decline of the metropolis is to be checked then restraint elsewhere in the region could contribute to this aim. But, if restraint proves successful without concomitant growth in the metropolis, there could be a gradual erosion of the economic vitality of the region as a whole. It is not a simple issue of earmarking areas for development and areas for restraint as was the practice in earlier plans but of applying sensitive judgements at the local level which do not prejudice economic needs or long term environmental considerations.

Although some plans do not appear to have responded to the changing economic circumstances this is less significant than at first appears. There is a considerable difference between the rhetoric of planning and its reality. Many policies are open to interpretation and, when tested, may prove flexible. Much future development may be committed by past decisions or outstanding planning permissions. The power to implement plans does not lie with those who formulate them, rather with many agencies, public and private. 'Power also resides, within much wider limits than are sometimes recognised, with a variety of private developers, large and small, who can be effectively restrained from developing, expanding or investing in certain areas but cannot be positively directed to carry out any operations unless they so wish'.[2] Although plans may be equivocal, subject to interpretation and lacking the power to ensure implementation, it would be unwise to underestimate the influence of planning both on the form and quality of the environment and upon economic performance and social well-being. What is needed is an analysis both of planning policy and its implementation in order to evaluate its potential influence on economic development and environmental conservation.

South East England — The changing circumstances

The demographic and economic changes in South East England are, to some extent, similar to those experienced in other metropolitan regions. The decline of London's population has been continuous though it has accelerated in recent years.[3] Until recently this decline has been more than compensated for by growth in the region as a whole. It is currently anticipated that the fall in the birthrate together with net outward migration will result in a static population of 17M. with London's share continuing to decline possibly below 6M. by 1990.

Although the South East has consistently performed better than other parts of Britain, a recent assessment placed it only 17th of 49 regions in the EEC.[4] In common with the rest of the UK it has suffered high inflation, unemployment and cuts in public expenditure. There have been long term structural changes reflected in the decline of manufacturing employment and the growth of the service sector. The scale of manufacturing decline in London has given rise to concern and to the thesis that it results from specific processes described as the 'London Factor'.[5] Between 1961 and 1974 employment in London fell by 34% (489,000 employees) as against a national fall of 5%. Half the decline was accounted for by the closure of firms, about a quarter by the shedding of manpower and the remainder by the transfer of jobs from London (16% to the new and expanding towns). Although the decline of London's population was more than keeping pace with its loss of jobs,[6] parts of London were exhibiting the combination of unemployment and lack of skilled workers that has become common in many areas.

Elsewhere in the South East population and, though with a slight time lag, employment have continued to rise. A small part of this growth has been accommodated in London's new and expanding towns designed to relieve congestion in London by a process of planned dispersal to self contained and socially balanced communities. The bulk of the out-migration has been voluntary, a 'ripple' effect spreading further from the metropolis into towns and villages beyond the Metropolitan Green Belt. This growth aroused apprehensions about the effect on the environment and agriculture and by the 1970s there was a perceptible hardening of public attitudes in favour of the conservation and protection of the countryside.

The two fears, one concerned about London's decline, the other with the effect of growth on the countryside surrounding the capital, represented a powerful combination in favour of a reappraisal of planning policy. Combined with fundamental changes in national economic and political circumstances the pressure for a new direction may seem overwhelming. The local authorities in the region expressed the situation as follows, 'It is our view that planning in the South East has reached a watershed. The situation facing the region differs in critical respects from that within which planning has operated since the war. Many long standing assumptions, objectives and policies concerning the relationships of London to the rest of the region and of the region to the rest of the country are no longer appropriate. A change of direction is necessary, involving new objectives and policies'.[7]

The Changing Policies

a) Industry

Since the war planning policy has been based on a national effort to redistribute industry in favour of the Assisted Areas[8] where the problems of unemployment, lower incomes and the physical symptoms of decline are most in evidence. The South East with its problems of congestion was an obvious source of industry for the regions. Within the South East some internal redistribution of population and industry was to be encouraged through planned dispersal, providing the opportunity for urban renewal in the form of redevelopment in London. Thus the Abercrombie plans for London and the region[9] were predicated on declining densities in London, the 'cordon sanitaire' of green belt and dispersal to new and expanding towns. By the 1960s it was apparent that population growth had been much greater than expected resulting in much unplanned dispersal. Regional policies while contributing to the development of infrastructure and economic activity of the regions had not been able fully to compensate for the structural decline of industry or staunch the dynamic growth of the South East. As a result regional policies were strengthened and the Assisted Areas enlarged to include more than half the country.

By the 1970s a series of processes were identified which suggested a shift in planning policy. Most fundamental was the recognition that the economy as a whole was performing badly and more specifically that the industrial basis of the nation was being undermined. The causes were seen as a combination of low investment, shortage of appropriate skills, declining profitability and government policy. At national level this led to the government's 'Industrial Strategy'[10] which aimed to reassert the salience of manufacturing and to encourage a high growth, high wage economy. The strategy did not amount to a national plan (an attempt at this in the 1960s had proved abortive but rather attempted to create a social reform depends'. In terms of spatial policies this suggested a shift from negative planning controls designed to restrict industrial activity towards a more industrial base on which the Government's whole programme of economic and social reform depends'. In terms of spatial policies this suggested a shift from negative planning controls designed to restrict industrial activity towards a more permissive and flexible attitude by planning authorities. 'It will be clear to authorities that too rigid an adherence to old style development plans could impede the life of an area and damage industrial firms'.[11]

b) The inner city

At about the same time the whole strategy of post war urban dispersal and renewal policy was being challenged at national and regional level. Various statements on housing policy urged the virtues of rehabilitation rather than comprehensive redevelopment.[12] In the South East the Greater London Council began to question some of the fundamental assumptions of policy. Although only about 10% of the gross emigration from London was to the planned new and expanding towns the GLC argued that these towns had attracted the most skilled sources. This might have been justifiable while population and public expenditure were still rising but this was no longer the case. The GLC proposed that the sources. This might have been justifiable while population and public expenditure were still rising but this was no longer the case. The GLC proposed that the new towns programme should be stabilised, that the new towns should look elsewhere than to London for their industry, and that resources should be redirected towards London to tackle the economic and social problems of the inner city, notably of the Docklands in East London.

This clarion call was echoed by a government statement on new towns which argued, 'But to allow the new towns to beggar the cities they serve by taking only the relatively fortunate members of society and leaving the least fortunate behind would be likely to increase rather than diminish the social problems of these cities'.[14] New towns should become more concerned with absorbing disadvantaged groups and accommodating second generation families and retired people. This was the prelude to a reappraisal of government thinking. In a seminal statement in Manchester in 1976, the Secretary of State for the Environment outlined the consequences of the dispersal policies for the inner city areas and suggested that 'powerful, countervailing action' was needed. He commented on the various programmes intended to overcome inner city problems, 'Crucial though all these programmes have been, they have to some extent dealt with the symptoms and not the causes of the decline of the inner cities'.[15] The causes were revealed in a series of inner city studies. The symptoms — unemployment, housing stress, dereliction, poverty, immigration — varied in degree, the causes were economic and social. 'The poverty stems from the persistence of divisions of status and income in society at large'.[16] The problems would have to be tackled on a national scale through employment, welfare and income policies. At the local level the studies urged a 'total approach' which would attempt to integrate programmes, would achieve positive discrimination and lay greater emphasis on small scale community planning rather than on highly bureaucratised, remote and impersonal strategic planning. 'There needs to be a new and more sensitive style of working geared to the management of, small-scale urban change'.[17] Failure to tackle the problems of the inner city quickly and effectively 'could lead to a situation when conditions would become too difficult and costly for us to retrieve'.[18]

A major example of an area suffering the composite problems of the inner city is London's Docklands where massive structural change in the economy has been brought about by the rundown of the docks resulting in a decline of dock workers from 26,000 to 9,500 since 1967.[19] Docklands is a series of isolated riverside communities with a combined population of about 56,000. The *Strategic Plan for the Docklands* has set itself the objective, 'to use the opportunity provided by large areas of London's Dockland becoming available, to redress the housing, social, environmental/economic and communications deficiencies of the Docklands area ... and thereby, to provide the freedom for similar improvement throughout East and Inner London'.[20] To achieve this, industry must be attracted and the vast areas of disused and derelict land cleared and developed. This will require massive investment in infrastructure including major road schemes, a possible crossing of the Thames and an extension of the underground system. Altogether the investment required is estimated to be of the order of £2,000M. more than half of it from the public sector.

Changing attitudes to traditional planning policies culminated in a series of policy pronouncements. The economic crisis had forced the government to halt the growth in public expenditure in 1976 and to take a close look at its priorities. Local authorities were advised to restrict their expenditure. To ensure compliance the government established guidelines, set cash limits and reduced its proportion of financial support thus forcing the authorities to depend somewhat more on the resources they could raise locally through rates.[21] At the same time the government's Rate Support Grant was redistributed in favour of the metropolitan areas, notably London. The effects of such a redistribution should not be exaggerated since in relation to the existing expenditure it is likely to have a marginal impact. London already absorbs a disproportinate share of public sector spending on such items as housing and transportation.[22]

A policy for the inner cities was announced in 1977 which would increase the expenditure on urban programmes from £30M. to £125M. by 1979/80. The policy stresses the need for programmes to be 'given an inner area dimension and priority in order to assist the regeneration of these areas'.[23] Perhaps the most striking innovation is the concept of partnerships between the government and certain selected inner city areas where a combination of loans, grants and other measures will aim to attract industry and achieve environmental improvements.[24] There is also the concession that location of industry policy should have an inner city as well as a regional dimension. In future the partnership areas of inner London and inner Birmingham will, after the assisted areas, take precedence for the attraction of mobile industry. At the same time efforts will be made to promote office development in these inner city areas. This marks a further retreat from established policies which attempted to control industrial development through the issue of industrial development certificates, (idc's) and offices through office development permits (odp's). In practice few idc's were refused. Although industrial mobility has been low and the controls have been applied flexibly, the official commitment to a new strategy is a radical departure from previous planning nostrums.

c) The rural areas

Reciprocal changes in policy have shifted the emphasis in the region surrounding London. Lower population forecasts and the concern for the plight of the inner city encouraged a review of the new towns programme and in 1977 the government announced that although the momentum of the new towns would be sustained in the short term, the latest new towns would have lower population targets and would be expected to contribute more to the relief of inner city stress.[25] Other policies reacted to the problems of population pressure on the predominantly rural areas surrounding London. In 1975 a White Paper, *Food from our own Resources*, underlined the significance of agriculture at a time of rising world demand for food and higher prices and set a target of an annual increase in productivity for agriculture of 2½%. Although some loss of land to other uses was inevitable the White Paper urged that 'wherever possible, agricultural land of a higher quality is not taken where land of lower quality is available'.[26] Outside London 13% of the land is urbanised and 69% is devoted to agriculture. The region has a higher proportion of its land in the highest grades than the average for England and Wales.[27] Apart from the need to protect agricultural land there are other physical constraints on development. Large areas of the region are designated as areas of landscape value, or as green belt and parts of the coastline and nature reserves are also protected against development. It is estimated that only about 40% of the land in the South East outside London is not subject to one or more of these various physical constraints.

d) Policy conflicts

By the mid 1970s there were clearly established attitudes and policies which favoured the revitalisation of the metropolis and especially the inner city and which sought to restrain and restrict growth in the surrounding region. Given the complexity of the situation in detail, the level of existing commitments and the limitation imposed by the shortage of resources no simple strategy was likely to emerge which could reconcile all the land use conflicts in the region. The change in the direction of policy was itself a matter of debate. There were those who argued that the established policies of dispersal still offered the best scope to improve conditions within London and to offer better opportunities to those who wished or could be persuaded to move. It would be a 'cardinal mistake', they argued, to treat the problems of the inner city in isolation. 'Both the people and the businesses who remain in the inner city area ... are increasingly those falling by the wayside in our society. We must beware of compounding their plight by attempting to restore the urban pattern of the past, for this could only be done by subjecting the poor to still greater pressures upon their living space'.[28] However, the policy of attempting to restore the economy of the inner city and to protect the metropolitan fringe from the pressures of growth appeared to respond to changing circumstances and to strike a popular political chord. Whether it could be achieved would depend, in part, on how broad initiatives were interpreted by planning policies at the local level.

The changing planning process

Planning methods have shifted from a predominant concern with a fixed future pattern of land use to be secured by the application of development control towards a more indicative style characterised by flexibility and continuous review. There are several reasons for this changing emphasis. One is the problem of providing adequate and accurate forecasts. Another is the recognition that the powers to implement plans are weak and that there are difficulties inherent in co-ordinating the various activities necessary to achieve the objectives of a plan. At a more ideological level the early plans were based on assumptions about social processes which incorporated a naive environmental determinism which has been shown to be misguided. At best this belief in the ability of plans to enhance the quality of life enabled planners to assert the values of self containment and social balance in the new towns, the environmental importance of green belts and the preservation of good landscapes and historical towns and villages. At worst slavish adherence to simplistic and little understood concepts of social planning was partly responsible for the problems of high rise development, social segregation and loss of community. Evidence of plans failing to achieve the solutions they professed left planners vulnerable to blame for problems which are inherent in society. The problems with which planning has to deal are exceedingly complex and do not conform to the notion of a long term strategic blueprint. During the 1960s the traditional land use development plan was abandoned in favour of a more indicative approach which takes into account social and economic processes, the availability of resources and which is subject to monitoring and review. Strategic plans — called structure plans — consist of a series of assumptions and forecasts about the future and indicate the broad spatial structures and environment that may result if the predictions are fulfilled. Monitoring is intended to ensure the adjustment of policies as conditions alter.

These structure plans are produced by each county planning authority and form the basis for more detailed local plans. They are expected to 'interpret national and regional policies'. A major problem here is that the lower tier of local authorities, the district councils, are responsible for local plans. Considerable energy is absorbed in disputes between the two tiers. There is no regional level of government and consequently regional strategies drawn up by regional bodies[29] are advisory and have to depend on the local planning authorities for their implementation. In the South East region, which covers a third of the country's population, there are thirteen county planning authorities including the Greater London Council. By 1978 all but one of these had produced structure plans, at least in draft form though only three plans (one of them covering part of a county) had been approved by the Minister for the Environment.[30] The prevailing climate during their preparation was one of uncertainty in conditions of economic restraint and this was reflected in the plans which exemplified the new style of planning. While the Structure Plans were being prepared it was decided to review the

Strategic Plan for the South East which had been approved in 1971. A major issue was how far all these plans would reflect the new national political attitudes to industry, the environment and the inner city. More specifically, would they be capable of providing a framework which both enabled industrial revival to take place and which did not jeopardise the regeneration of the inner city or the preservation of agricultural land and the rural environment?

The Strategic Plan for the South East

The *Strategic Plan for the South East* (SPSE) was an early example of the new approach to planning. It offered a framework for structure plans, a recognition of the uncertainties with which it was dealing and a consciousness of its inherent weakness as a decision making document, 'decision-making in a free society can only be influenced and not determined by Government and local authorities who, however, create the context for decision-making by controls of various kinds, grants and allocations of resources to public investment'.[31] Thus it set objectives which could be met in broad terms in the period after 1981 when the strategy would begin to bite. Among these objectives were, to maximise existing resources, to combine flexibility with the need for a reasonably robust plan, to match population and employment growth and to promote more or less self-contained city regions within the South East, to protect the countryside and agriculture and to provide wide opportunities in employment, housing and mobility. Since population was expected to continue growing there was no attempt to suppress the dispersal from London, rather an attempt to ensure that it was steered towards defined growth areas. Five major growth areas were designated — South Hampshire based on Southampton and Portsmouth; Milton Keynes, the latest and largest of the new towns, together with Northampton being expanded as a new town just beyond the boundaries of the region; the Reading/Wokingham/Aldershot/Basingstoke cluster of towns west of London in a rapidly developing area soon to become known as 'Area 8' after its zonal classification in the strategy; the Crawley area centred around the new town and Gatwick, the major airport between London and the south coast; and south Essex, an area where employment and better infrastructure were needed especially if the then proposed airport at Maplin was built. In addition medium growth areas were designated at a number of places with potential for growth which did not conflict with other planning objectives, at Ashford, Maidstone/Medway, Eastbourne/Hastings, Aylesbury and Chelmsford. By concentrating growth, the rest of the region could be subject to sufficient restraint to ensure the preservation of landscape and agriculture. The problems of London had not yet forced themselves on the planners' attention and the subject was treated summarily with continued redevelopment and rehabilitation expected to yield better living conditions for the residents of the capital. The strategy was, in effect, a synthesis of post war planning policy adapted to the trends in growth that were identified in the region.

Although the plan shaped attitudes towards growth and restraint in the region it was quickly overtaken by events which altered the premises on which it had been constructed. Apart from the downturn in economic and population forecasts, two major projects, the airport at Maplin and the Channel tunnel were abandoned. By 1974 it was recognised that a major rethink was necessary and a Review of the Strategic Plan was published two years later. The Review claimed, however, that a completely new strategy was not necessary and that 'the basic framework of SPSE remains sound but ... the time was ripe for updating and developing it in view of the far-reaching implications of the changes which had occurred'.[32] Some critics were more sceptical arguing that an advisory regional plan could not hope to be implemented by the structure planning authorities. 'What is needed is a fully operational regional planning team, working on a continuous basis, reporting to a regional authority with executive power over regional finance, transportation and planning'.[33]

The Review was heavily guarded about the prospects of achieving objectives. 'Phasing and programming of plans can be related to available resources to produce a flexible system capable of meeting uncertain situations by aiming to achieve objectives in increments or stages which are themselves largely self-contained: though incremental development must be seen as part of a planned whole and not merely as ad hoc or piecemeal development'.[34] Throughout, the Review insists on continuous monitoring, the avoidance of options that cannot be changed and the value of 'flexibility'. As a result the Review virtually abandons the concept of a strategy altogether and opts for what it describes as a 'contingent' approach, 'that is to say, choices which need not be exercised immediately or in the short term are so far as possible deferred for resolution later, when the effects or recommendations made in the short term can be more clearly assessed'.[35] The idea is to 'take an attitude' about the immediate future and, in the fashion of Micawber, to see 'how the situation evolves'. The Review is 'neutral and cautious' and we might be forgiven for assuming that its fear of committing itself amounts to an understandable fear of being proved wrong by events. But such a craven approach hardly provides guidance for the structure plans, still less does it adopt the kind of positive stance that might facilitate industrial revival.

A strategy that attempts to balance the needs of the economy and environment faces a number of difficulties. The very substantial unimplemented planning permissions[36] and the tendency for authorities to release land in response to demand often at the cheapest locations make it difficult, if not impossible, to relate development to specific growth areas. Conversely, if housing and employment are restricted in areas of restraint this can lead to inflated house prices or lack of employment opportunity which will affect the least mobile and less well off. If firms are discouraged from expanding locally they may become less efficient or go out of business altogether. Not surprisingly the Review is tentative, aware of the problems less certain of the solutions.

There are some specific proposals in the Review. For instance, it urges the relaxation of industrial and office controls in London. These controls have not been removed altogether and, outside the partnership areas, London remains one of the low priority areas. Although there appears to be a flexible attitude in the granting of permission to firms wishing to remain in London, and for those firms which can demonstrate that they cannot locate in an assisted area, it appears that speculative developments will be limited in most parts of London.[37] In general the Review of the Strategic Plan reaffirms existing policy with certain changes in emphasis. It suggests that restraint should be strengthened to protect agriculture and amenity. It recognises that the growth areas will have lower population than in the original strategy and fulfil different functions.[38] They are conceived less as counter magnets to the metropolis and more as subregional centres to relieve surrounding areas of restraint. There is greater flexibility than in the original strategy in the recognition that, apart from areas of growth and restraint, there are areas which can accommodate housing and employment to meet local needs. There remain inherent conflicts between growth and restraint, of economic development and environmental conservation at the local level which must be reconciled in the structure plans for the various parts of the region.

The emerging pattern

Although the structure plans offer a wide variety of interpretations of the Strategic Plan, each claims to conform to its general principles. Some adopt a contingent strategy, some provide a long range view, and all stress the importance of monitoring and review. Each plan has been subject to extensive consultation and public participation and has been endorsed by the elected representatives of its local authority. They are political documents reflecting general public attitudes as well as the values of the local population. There is a pervasive attitude of restraint and low growth. All the plans recognise the problem of applying restraint while attempting to meet the need and demand for local employment and housing through the existing planning commitments. There is a difference of emphasis between those plans most concerned to preserve the environment and those which stress the importance of the local economy.

The difference in emphasis stems partly from the geographical circumstances of the areas covered by each plan. It is possible to identify three different approaches to the key relationship between environment and economy. First, there are those plans covering areas which do not contain either growth areas or areas of restraint where the satisfaction of local needs is the dominant theme. Then there are those plans covering areas of growth and restraint where complementary policies are combined. Finally, there are plans for areas of restraint where the protection of the environment is seen as the paramount aim.

1. Local needs strategies

Two structure plans covering Oxfordshire and Bedfordshire on the northern edge of the region fall within this group. Both counties have experienced rapid population growth in the past, both have a balance between jobs and resident workers and both have a high dependence on a small range of activities, notably vehicle manufacturing. The economic aims of both plans are similar, 'to maintain the viability and effectiveness of existing industry and commerce in the county' (Bedfordshire);[39] the provision of conditions conducive to industrial and commercial prosperity' (Oxfordshire).[40] They also underline the need to achieve restraint by concentration of future development. Oxfordshire's spatial strategy is based on the growth of some of its country towns in order to spread economic activity while preserving the environment around Oxford and over much of the rural area. Bedfordshire has opted for concentrating future development around the major towns of Luton and Bedford, again to relieve pressure on the countryside. Although both could be said to conform to the regional strategy, they contain controversial elements. For instance, Bedfordshire's insistence on the potential for growth at Luton aroused opposition from neighbouring Hertfordshire which claimed such a policy could stimulate a 'growth spiral' which would prejudice Hertfordshire's attempts to restrain development. Conversely, Bedfordshire claimed that Hertfordshire's restrictive attitude could transfer pressures for housing development northwards into Bedfordshire. Such border skirmishes indicate the problems of reconciling neighbouring plans when they are motivated by different attitudes.

2. Combined strategies

This is the largest group and contains the major and medium growth areas and each proposes to use these growth points to concentrate future development beyond existing commitments. But each varies in the degree of restraint it seeks to apply, some recognising a need to allow some economic and housing development in their rural areas, others advocating a much tougher line.

Buckinghamshire proposes a sharp distinction between Milton Keynes, a major growth centre which should accommodate three quarters of the future growth, and the rest of the county where severe restraint will be applied. 'Its philosophy is to pursue those successful regional growth schemes which are well under way but otherwise to concentrate on resolving local problems where possible in conjunction with solutions to regional problems'.[41] Aylesbury, one of the medium growth areas, will concentrate on local needs, and future housing and employment pressures in the green belt in the south of the county will be diverted further north. Although this could be disruptive to industry and those in housing need the plan claims that 'the disadvantages can be minimised and are outweighed by the advantages of preserving the green belt'.[42] The South East Economic Planning Council countered this by urging Buckinghamshire to consider 'whether the economic loss to the county was effectively compensated by any subsequent environmental gain'.[43]

A similar 'blanket' approach was presented by Hampshire, a county containing two major growth areas. Although the principle of major growth was accepted in the earlier plan for the Southampton and Portsmouth area by the time plans for mid and north east Hampshire were drawn up attitudes had hardened in favour of restraint. Mid Hampshire is predominantly rural an area of restraint though policies for employment are reasonably permissive supporting the needs of local industry. The plan for North East Hampshire covering part of growth area 8 was stridently anti growth. 'North East Hampshire should no longer be considered as a "growth area" '. Consequently the policies echo this restrictive attitude — 'To limit employment growth in North East Hampshire', 'To restrict totally all development in the countryside'.[44] This approach is justified on the grounds that commitments are sufficient to enable a contingent approach to be adopted up to 1986. The presence of a major growth area in the south of the county, and the pressure of public opinion to resist growth in the buoyant area 8 explains an attitude which appears to contradict the regional strategy.

Berkshire also covers a substantial part of area 8 and also has a tripartite plan. East Berkshire is an area of restraint having grown rapidly in the past owing to its location near the prosperous part of London. The plan for this area called for 'modified limited growth' which would 'provide a strategic framework within which the local economy can be maintained, while restricting further employment growth in accordance with the area's regional role as a restraint area'.[45] It is not altogether clear how a policy of severe restriction on employment growth can be accommodated in a plan which emphasised flexibility. The central Berkshire plan covering the growth area is intended to complement that for the east of the county but adopts a cautious approach leaving options open to be decided later. Like Hampshire it regards the term 'growth area' no longer appropriate and settles for 'limited growth' though the level of existing commitments (possibly 30,000 jobs) is considerable. Despite contrasts in presentation and analysis the plans for Hampshire and Berkshire seem little different in practice for both are cautious about growth beyond commitments and prefer the contingent approach which allows trends to develop before embarking on a specific course.

West Sussex contains the major growth area of Crawley based on Gatwick airport which is likely to grow rapidly as a result of the government's airports strategy.[46] This plan also makes the customary rejection of the concept of a major growth area but accepts that Crawley should concentrate on local rather than regional pressures as suggested in the Review of the Strategic Plan for the South East. West Sussex adopts a very short time horizon (3 or 4 years) up to its first review during which no further land will be released. Future growth in jobs will need to be related to the local work force and it is argued that the labour shortage can be exaggerated since 'West Sussex firms are used to making a little labour go a long way'.47) Although it recognises that some development will occur around Gatwick it seems that the physical restraints applied in the area may inhibit its economic potential. Over most of the county the plan proposes restrictive policies to ensure the protection of the environment and agriculture.

The East Sussex and Kent structure plans are more permissive in tone. The future economy of East Sussex is described in the following terms, 'Future growth of economic activity in the County will lie largely in the expansion of professional firms and services, higher education, agriculture and forestry, tourism and conferences, and the provision of facilities for retired people'.48) Employment will be related to housing and efforts will be made to encourage activity in the less buoyant parts of the county, notably around Hastings, one of the medium growth areas. Although restraint will be exercised over much of the county including Brighton where there already exist considerable employment commitments, there is a recognition that some employment should be provided in the rural areas. The problem in East Sussex is seen as one of redistribution necessary to achieve a better balance between different parts of the county.

This theme of imbalance underlies the structure plan for Kent. The combined strategy here is to achieve conservation over much of rural Kent and to concentrate growth both in areas with potential (the medium growth areas of Maidstone and Ashford) and in the economically weaker but populous areas of Thames-side, the Medway towns and Thanet. In such a large county conservation and growth are seen as compatible rather than conflicting aims. The economic aims of the plan are expressed more vigorously than in any other structure plan for the region, 'The principal theme of the strategy, therefore, is the encouragement of growth of economic activity and employment in the county'.49) The approach is summarised as follows, 'a principal focus of the Structure Plan should be to seek gradual increase in the growth of economic activity in the County, through policy objectives of encouraging the realisation of the apparent employment potentials and improving prospects in areas where economic activity levels in the workforce are low, taking into account environmental considerations. This would reflect the national economic situation, would be in the interests of those parts of Kent which do not share in the high levels of prosperity found elsewhere in the South East, and would be a suitable response to current and likely future population growth pressures where employment increases have lagged behind'.

The group of counties which have adopted mixed strategies recognise, in common with the first group, that some development will be necessary to meet local needs. The structure plans of the third group express profoundly different philosophies.

3. Strategies of severe restraint

Two counties, Surrey and Hertfordshire, have adopted aggressively restrictive policies. Apart from their location in the green belt on London's borders they have other features in common — rapid population growth in recent decades, strong and diversified economies, and (especially in Surrey) an environment which has attracted commuters who work in London.[50] Hertfordshire has been one of the main reception areas for London overspill and contains four of the original eight London new towns. Past growth, current pressures and the environmental and political features of the two counties account for their parsimonious attitudes towards future growth.

Hertfordshire's public participation resulted in a strategy which favoured 'lower physical and economic growth than in the past coupled with action to consolidate and improve the existing physical and social structure'.[51] Its rather enigmatic theme of 'consolidation with security' is inspired by fear of the 'growth spiral' which is defined as 'the continuous and repetitive demand for the use of land and other resources for homes and jobs which, if fulfilled, can create any further consequential demands and so on. This spiral creates a continuing situation of unfulfilled demand for either housing or jobs, together with deficiencies in roads and other services, and leads to the progressive erosion of the environment'.[52] To counteract the pressures from its buoyant economy, Hertfordshire proposes to ban new office development and research activities and will encourage the relocation of firms outside the county. The coup de grâce of the plan is to extend the green belt to cover the whole county outside the areas already committed for urban development. A major criticism of the plan was that 'while priority should continue to be given to growth areas, the current economic situation made it impracticable to try to restrict growth, as strictly as the County appeared to intend to do, in one of the few areas of current industrial vitality'.[53]

Surrey's population growth reached its peak in the 1950s., its employment growth in the 1960s., and the 'ripple' effect from London has now passed beyond its borders. During the period 1951-71 population and jobs increased by a third and housing by half as the level of commuting rose. The whole county will be covered by a policy of restraint and designated green belt. Employment growth will be limited largely to commitments, firms from outside the county will be resisted though some provision will be made for local needs. 'The overall intention of the Employment Policies is to exercise strict restraint on the increase in the number of jobs, so that regional policies are upheld and the Green Belt preserved by attempting to keep demand for labour to a minimum and thereby not contributing to increasing pressure for housing. At the same time the policies are designed to meet certain essential local needs of Surrey's residents and of particular types of firms and establishments and, where possible, overcome identified problems'.[54] No provision is made for those parts of major growth areas 8 and

Crawley which lie inside the county in a plan heavily orientated to environmental protection. The defence of the plan lay in the complementarity of its role as a restraint area to London's need for revival. 'What we have proposed, therefore, is a careful policy framework to embrace green belt restraint, the need to acknowledge some economic growth, the intention to arrest the deterioration in the conditions of those sectors of the population against whom restraint policies would, unduly discriminate, and the need to allow some growth of local firms'.[55]

Conclusions

At the regional level there would appear to be compatibility between a strategy for developing London's economic base and attempts to confine growth in the rest of the region. The use of planning controls to relieve pressure and divert it elsewhere has been a traditional part of regional planning policy. The apparent success of that strategy aroused London's fears of decline though the causes of decline are complex. The direction of policy has now begun to alter, employment growth in parts of London is to be encouraged, the new towns programme is being reduced and the authorities around London are adopting policies of restraint in which economic development is limited mainly to local needs.

The planning authorities are still relying heavily on controls as the means of achieving their policies. While it may be argued that controls are the only effective weapons they possess it is questionable whether such an approach is any longer relevant to the economic circumstances of the late 1970s. The government's industrial strategy, if it is to succeed, will depend on a permissive and positive approach by planning authorities. It may be that restrictive attitudes, while justifiable in environmental terms, could stifle activity in the only places where it is likely to develop (such as Hertfordshire and Surrey for example). The crucial issue confronting the planning authorities is how to achieve a balance between the needs of the region and the less prosperous parts of the country, between London and the rest of the South East, and between short term economic needs and long term environmental conservation.

There is certainly a potential conflict between national economic strategy and local planning policies in the South East region but it would be premature to reach any firm conclusions on the outcome. The review of the regional strategy has not been endorsed by government and most of the structure plans have yet to be approved. Although attitudes and policies may have changed markedly in the past few years they are still in a stage of transition.

This transitional phase is marked in most plans by the contingent approach adopted in many of the plans. Options should not be foreclosed, rather time should elapse to see what economic and demographic trends are emerging before fundamental changes are made. The long term master plan approach has been abandoned in favour of continuous monitoring and review. Policies tend not to be precise but are hedged around by considerable ambiguity leaving scope for varying interpretations. The inherent continuity of past policies with their legacy of planning commitments limits the short run choices available and indicates a gradual rather than sudden shift in direction.

The outcome of planning strategies hinges on the experience of implementation. If a more positive role for planning is envisaged then planning authorities will require more control than they currently possess and more than is, perhaps, politically feasible. Planning in the UK has always been divorced from investment and hence co-ordination of the various agencies, public and private, responsible for implementation has been weak. It is weakest at the regional level where there is only a tenuous relationship between the various public authorities responsible for housing, transportation, education, health and so on. The regional strategy is purely advisory, though ministers would be expected to stand by it in cases of conflict with structure plans. At the local level implementation is substantially in the hands of the second tier authorities which hold responsibility for housing and local plans. Influence over the private sector is weak, planning authorities may encourage development but cannot guarantee it. It is too early to judge whether the Community Land Act which places the control of development land in the hands of local authorities will alter the relative influence of the private sector on planning outcomes. Up to now the implementation of plans has become out of step with forecasts and large unimplemented permissions preempt future decisions. Implementation responds to local political and economic circumstances, and is essentially a short term incremental process.

The ebb and flow of planning policies in the South East and the problems of implementation suggest that a long term co-ordinated approach is impossible. The planning authorities lack either the willingness or the capacity to adopt a positive rather than a responsive role. The rhetoric as well as the reality of planning policy can be important in moulding attitudes. Although in reality the policies of the current crop of structure plans can be eroded or evaded, their rhetoric can act as a powerful psychological deterrent to industrial activity in the region. If the attitude of low growth and conservation becomes pervasive then it can become self fulfilling.

During the 1970s there has been a major shift in the economic and demographic parameters on which planning forecasts and policies are based. It is quite conceivable that within a few years there could be equally fundamental changes. Consequently the planning authorities will attempt to maintain their basic strategies while increasing the flexibility of plans to provide a greater sensitivity to future changes. But there must be a limit to the changes that current strategies can accommodate. Any marked changes in economic prospects, in energy costs, or in social values will have to find expression in planning policies. At a more obvious level major planning decisions will disrupt regional and local calculations. The likelihood of major airport development at Gatwick and Stansted already threatens to stretch the credibility of the Strategic Plan. At the local level it is likely that structure plans will play a significant but not a decisive role in the relationship between economic and environmental values.

Zusammenfassung

Das Verhältnis von Industrie und Umwelt im Großstadtrandbereich

Zur Verfolgung von Umweltschutzinteressen sind regulierende Eingriffe und Kontrollmaßnahmen in der Landesentwicklung angewendet worden, aber solche Raumordnungspolitik kann im Widerspruch zu der Notwendigkeit stehen, das Wirtschaftswachstum zu fördern. Bei der jetzigen Wirtschaftsstagnation und Bevölkerungsstabilität hat man gesehen, daß Umwelt- und Wirtschaftsinteressen sich gegenseitig ergänzen und voneinander abhängig sind. Die räumliche Konzentrierung der Wirtschaftsentwicklung macht es möglich, andernorts Schutzmaßnahmen zu ergreifen. Aber eine Raumordnungspolitik, die einerseits Wachstum, andererseits Entwicklungsbeschränkungen herbeiführt, ist hinsichtlich ihrer Verwirklichung abhängig von vielen verschiedenen Planungsträgern und Behörden, und deshalb können sich unter Umständen die Ergebnisse nicht mit den ursprünglichen Zielen eines solchen Planungskonzeptes messen. In dieser Arbeit werden die sich ändernden politischen Einstellungen zur Wirtschaft und zur Umwelt behandelt und die raumplanerischen Probleme bei der Durchführung entsprechender Maßnahmen im Südostteil Englands untersucht.

Der Südosten beherbergt ein Drittel der Landesbevölkerung und ist die wohlhabendste Region, obwohl er unter den insgesamt 49 "Regionen" der Europäischen Gemeinschaft nur an 17. Stelle rangiert. Innerhalb dieses Gebietes ist eine Abnahme der Bevölkerung und der Beschäftigtenzahl in London eingetreten (34% der Arbeitsplätze gingen zwischen 1961 - 1974 verloren), während es in der Umgebung der Metropole zu einem Wachstum in diesen Bereichen gekommen ist. Diese Ab- und Zunahme hat zu einem Überdenken der Planungsmaßnahmen geführt. Aus Furcht vor einem Rückgang der Industrie — und dies besonders in den größeren Städten — hat man die Strategie der Bevölkerungsumverteilung und Industrieumsiedlung aus dem Zentrum an die Peripherie in Frage gestellt. Vorrang ist nun einer Wiederbelebung des produzierenden Gewerbes in der Innenstadt gegeben worden, was durch eine Verringerung der angestrebten Bevölkerungszahlen in den "new towns" und durch eine zunehmende Verschärfung bei der Begrenzung der Entwicklungsmöglichkeiten in der Region außerhalb Londons unterstützt wird.

Dieser Wechsel in den politischen Auffassungen ist aus den verschiedenartigen Raumplanungsprogrammen für die Region klar ersichtlich. Auf regionaler Ebene existiert ein Rahmenplan mit empfehlendem Charakter (advisory regional plan), welcher die Grundlage für die vorgeschriebenen verbindlichen Struktur-pläne (statutory structure plans) schafft, die von jeder der insgesamt 13 Kreisbehörden (county authorities) in der Region vorbereitet wurden. Diese Raumordnungspläne sollen flexibel sein, sollen den verschiedenen ökonomischen und sozialen Voraussetzungen Rechnung tragen und einer fortlaufenden Überwachung und Revision unterzogen werden. Sie sind (allerdings) eingeschränkt durch bestehende Verpflichtungen und durch Probleme in bezug auf die Verfügbarkeit der Mittel sowie aufgrund der ungewissen wirtschaftlichen Lage.

Das ursprüngliche Regionalplanungskonzept, der Raumordnungsplan für die Region "Südosten" (The Strategic Plan for the South East, 1970), war in erster Linie ein Flächennutzungsplan, der fünf größere und einige mittelgroße Wachstumsräume in der Region auswies, wodurch andernorts Maßnahmen zur Entwicklungseindämmung möglich wurden. Diesen Plan unterzog man sechs Jahre später einer Revision, um die veränderten wirtschaftlichen und demographischen Trends berücksichtigen und dem aufgetauchten Problem des Londoner Strukturverfalls Rechnung tragen zu können. Obwohl Wahlmöglichkeiten offen gelassen wurden, behielt man in der überarbeiteten Fassung prinzipiell das räumliche Grundgerüst des Planes von 1970 bei.

Die Strukturentwicklungspläne der Kreise können sich an dem weitgefaßten regionalen Raumordnungsprogramm orientieren, während in ihnen gleichzeitig lokale Planungsvorstellungen angenommen werden, die aber möglicherweise, angesichts ihrer starken Betonung auf der Entwicklungsbeschränkung, mit dem vorgenannten weniger restriktiven Regionalprogramm im Widerspruch stehen. Aus diesen Plänen lassen sich drei methodische Ansätze herauskristallisieren: Erstens sind da jene Pläne, die die lokalen Bedürfnisse unterstreichen, indem sie den Beschäftigungs- und Bevölkerungszuwachs auf bestehende Zentren zu lenken versuchen. Zweitens gibt es Pläne, die die Wachstumsräume auf regionaler Ebene miteinbeziehen, wodurch sie andernorts den Einsatz von Beschränkungsmaßnahmen ermöglichen. In einigen Plänen dieser großen Gruppe wird ein positiver Standpunkt gegenüber der Wirtschaftsentwicklung und der Notwendigkeit einer gleichmäßigeren Verteilung der Entwicklungsmöglichkeiten bezogen, während in anderen für eine rigorosere Kontrolle zum Schutz der Umwelt plädiert wird. Die letztere Auffassung ist typisch für die dritte Gruppe von Plänen, die zwei Counties nahe bei London betreffen, die in den Nachkriegsjahren ein schnelles Wachstum erlebt haben und die jetzt ihre Zukunft in einer Konsolidierung durch eine strenge Auflagenpolitik sehen.

Es besteht die Möglichkeit, daß die restriktive Raumordnungspolitik das Wachstumspotential in einigen Teilen der Region beeinträchtigen könnte. Die Pläne gestatten jedoch abweichende Auslegungen, und ihre Resultate hängen zudem von der Durchführung auf der kommunalen Ebene ab, die für mancherlei starke Einflüsse empfänglich ist. Daher ist die Planungsebene in der Raumordnungshierarchie wichtig für das Festsetzen der regionalen Planungsleitziele, aber sie hat keinen Einfluß auf die Ergebnisse.

Notes and references

1. Countryside Review Committee (1976): "The Countryside - Problems and Policies", A Discussion Paper, London, HMSO, p. 5
2. South East Joint Planning Team (1976): "Strategy for the South East: A Review", London, HMSO, p. 51
3. Between 1961 and 1971 the decline of London's population averaged 53,600, from 7.9M. to 7.4M. Between 1971 and 1975 the average rate of decline increased to 82,500 per year and the total population fell to 7.1M. The birth rate has continued to fall and the net outward movement of population has been about 100,000 per year (350,000 moving out and 250,000 moving in).
4. A survey of Gross Domestic Product in 1970 per head of population for the 49 regions of the original 6 EEC countries and the UK, revealed the South East (with £894 per head) as the leading UK region ranking 17th in Europe. (Source: South East Economic Planning Council: "The South East in a European Context", 9 July, 1975).
5. The 'London Factor' is conceived as the absolute disadvantage of being in London which has affected all industries. Among the reasons suggested for disadvantage are inadequate premises, high transport costs, shortage of labour, and failure to secure planning permission. Although government controls on industrial development do not appear to be an important component, industrialists claim that government policy is inhibiting and leads to industry operating in old, overcrowded and poorly serviced plants.
6. The gap between the resident labour force and number of jobs in the capital has been largely filled by commuters from outside whose numbers increased by 104,000 between 1961-71 but have since begun to decline. In 1971 there were an estimated 538,000 travelling into London and 108,000 travelling out.
7. Standing Conference on London and South East Regional Planning (1977): "Strategy for the South East: 1976 Review — a Conference response to Government", SC 700, 17 February, p. 5
8. The Assisted Areas include Development Areas where unemployment rates are high and, within them, Special Development Areas where problems are especially acute. In both these groups no government controls are operated on industry. There are also Intermediate Areas where controls may be operated if industrial development is over 15,000 sq. ft. In all three types of Assisted Area various forms of financial incentive to industry are offered. By the 1970s the whole country, apart from the Midlands, East Anglia, the South East and the South West (excluding Cornwall and Devon) was covered by Assisted Area status in one form or another.
9. ABERCROMBIE, P. (1945): "Greater London Plan", London HMSO; ABERCROMBIE, P. and J.H. FORSHAW (1943): "County of London Plan"

10. Chancellor of the Exchequer and Secretary of State for Industry: "An Approach to Industrial Strategy", November 1975
11. Depts of Environment and Transport (1977): "Local Government and the Industrial Strategy", Circular 71/77, para. 13
12. The most recent comprehensive review of housing policy is: "Housing Policy", A Consultative Document, London, HMSO, June, 1977
13. Greater London Council (1975): "Planned growth outside London", Report to Policy and Resources Committee, 22nd December; also GLC Minutes, 20th July, 1976
14. Dept. of the Environment, and Welsh Office (1974): "New Towns in England and Wales", A consultation document, December, p. 6
15. Speech on Inner Urban Policy made by Secretary of State for the Environment at Manchester, 17th Sept. 1976
16. Dept. of the Environment (1977): "Inner Area Studies, Liverpool, Birmingham and Lambeth", Summaries of consultants' final reports, London, HMSO, p. 8
17. Ibid. p. 46
18. Ibid. p. 63
19. The closure of London's docks has been dramatic. East India docks closed in 1967 followed by St. Katherine and London Docks in 1969, and Surrey Docks in 1970. Millwall and West India Docks will be closed and the Royal Docks system is threatened with closure leaving only Tilbury further down the estuary representing the major port activity of London.
20. Docklands Joint Committee (1976): "London Docklands, A Strategic Plan", A draft for public consultation, March, p. 14
21. Local authority expenditure represents 30% of total public spending in the UK and 13% of gross national product. Central government contributes 61p. for every £1 of local authority expenditure mainly through the Rate Support Grant (RSG). This is composed of three elements; a needs element, (the largest) which attempts to compensate authorities for relative spending needs (using such criteria as numbers of children, declining population, population density, dispersed population); a resources element which is intended to equalise the income from rates among local authorities; and a domestic element which reduces the burden of rates on domestic ratepayers. In its annual settlement of RSG the government can vary the level of grant and alter the criteria by which the individual elements, especially the needs element, are calculated.
22. In 1976/7 London received £740M. as its needs element of RSG whereas full equalisation of its rate rasing ability would have yielded only £470M. London with 15% of the national population receives 21% of total revenue ex-

penditure, a third of the capital expenditure on public housing, 44% of the housing subsidies, and 30% of the Transport Supplementary Grant.
23. HMSO (1977): "Policy for the Inner Cities", Cmnd. 6845, London, June, p. 11
24. After the Assisted Areas priority for industrial development to named occupiers will be given to the inner city partnership areas. In London these include Docklands, Lambeth, Hackney and Islington. These will receive the bulk of aid through the Urban Programme and be granted industrial development certificates if it can be shown that industrialists cannot reasonably go to an Assisted Area. Speculative development will be allowed to firms from the South East region. In addition there are Programme authorities (only Hammersmith in London) which receive some assistance and will undertake their own inner area programme. Finally, there are Construction Package Areas (including six London boroughs) allowed capital expenditure for employment in the construction industry which may be given further assistance and may be granted speculative development to firms from within Greater London. Outside the partnership areas London generally receives low priority for new industrial development and speculative development will only be allowed for those firms displaced within each Borough.
25. Statement by the Secretary of State for the Environment to the House of Commons, 5 April, 1977
26. HMSO (1975): "Food from our own Resources", Cmnd. 6020, London, April, p. 5
27. There are five grades of agricultural land based on physical factors. The highest grades (1 and 2) have few limitations to agricultural use and can support a wide variety of crops, usually cereals and roots. Grade 3 accounted for almost half the total, covers a wide variety and the best land in this category can give high productivity for a limited range of crops. Grades 4 and 5 are below average in productivity the lowest grade appearing mainly in upland areas. The South East has a quarter of its total in the two highest grades (England and Wales 17%) and only 16% in the two lowest (34%).
28. Town and Country Planning Association Policy Statement: "Inner Cities of Tomorrow, Town and Country Planning", May 1977, p. 65
29. There are two regional planning bodies in the South East. One, the South East Economic Planning Council, is appointed by the Secretary of State for the Environment and consists of people drawn from local authorities, industry, trades unions and universities in the region. It advises the minister on all matters of regional significance. The other body, the Standing Conference for London and South East Regional Planning, consists of representatives nominated by the planning authorities in the region. These two bodies, jointly with the government, were responsible for producing the strategic plan for the region. It is an advisory, not a statutory plan.

30. The three plans which had been approved were for Greater London, South Hampshire and East Sussex. By 1978 plans for Oxfordshire, Buckinghamshire, Hertfordshire and Bedfordshire had passed through all stages of participation and examination in public and were awaiting approval. The Kent, Surrey, Berkshire (3 parts), mid and north east Hampshire structure plans were at various stages of participation and that for Essex was due to appear in mid 1978.
31. South East Joint Planning Team (1970): "Strategic Plan for the South East", London, HMSO, p. 4
32. South East Joint Planning Team (1976): "Strategy for the South East: 1976 Review", London, HMSO, p. 2
33. "Built Environment", Editorial, January, 1975
34. South East Joint Planning Team (1976) op. cit. p. 6
35. Ibid. p. 52
36. The actual number of unimplemented permissions is a matter of debate. One estimate of the total commitment in mid 1976 for the South East, excluding London, put the figure as approaching 400,000 dwellings in the private sector. The mid 1975 estimate was 345,000. If this figure were reduced by 50,000 to allow for dwellings under construction and an allowance were made for lapsed permissions it would come closer to the estimate of 229,000 which is based on the returns made to the Department of the Environment of outstanding planning permissions of the counties outside London in mid 1975. Whichever figure is taken it represents 'a considerable preemption of strategic possibilities' (a note to the South East Economic Planning Council, 17 January, 1977). Furthermore, only about half these permissions are within areas where development was to be encouraged under the Strategic Plan, and only between a fifth and one quarter are in the major growth areas.
37. See note 23.
38. Milton Keynes should continue to develop as planned, concentrate on mixed housing development, help to relieve pressure on the surrounding areas, and help the disadvantaged groups from Greater London. South Hampshire should continue to grow under local impetus. There is still considerable potential for development at Crawley but 'further external pressures would not be welcomed in the future'. With the abandonment of Maplin and efforts to revive Docklands, the case for major growth east of London in South Essex is now more doubtful.
39. Bedfordshire County Council (1977): "County Structure Plan" p. 2
40. Oxfordshire County Council (1975): "First Structure Plan for Oxfordshire", p. 52
41. Buckinghamshire County Council (1976): "County Structure Plan", p. 63

42. Ibid. p. 36
43. Letter from South East Economic Planning Council to County Planning Officer, Buckinghamshire, 11 June, 1976
44. Hampshire County Council (1977): "Mid Hampshire Structure Plan: Policies for the Future", and "North East Hampshire Structure Plan: Choice and Policy"
45. Royal County of Berkshire (1977): "East Berkshire Structure Plan", p. 52
46. HMSO (1978): "Airports Policy", Cmnd. 7084, February
47. West Sussex County Council (1977): "West Sussex: the next fifteen years", p. 70
48. East Sussex County Council (1975): "County Structure Plan", p. 15
49. Kent County Council (1977): "Kent Structure Plan", p. 56
50. About 150,000 of Surrey's resident workforce (30%) travel to work in London, and 69,000 travel into the county to work.
51. Hertfordshire County Council (1975): "County Structure Plan", p. 1/5
52. Ibid. p. 2/1
53. Letter from South East Economic Planning Council to Chief Executive, Hertfordshire County Council, 25. Nov. 1975
54. Surrey County Council (1977): "Surrey Structure Plan", p. 48
55. Letter from Surrey Country Planning Office to the South East Economic Planning Council

URBAN RENEWAL AND DISPLACED INDUSTRY

BRIAN CHALKLEY

Urban renewal in Britain has been concerned with social rather than economic goals. Its major objective has been to raise housing standards by clearing or improving the inherited stock of nineteenth century dwellings. Questions of industrial policy have generally played only a minor role in renewal programmes, and planners have given relatively little attention to the inheritance of old industrial premises. The necessity for public intervention to renew outworn residential areas has long been recognized, but with the exception of recently announced industrial improvement schemes (H.M.S.O., 1977), the same principle has not been vigorously applied to industrial areas. In consequence, whereas under the Housing Acts there has been massive clearance of obsolete residential neighbourhoods, there has been no corresponding legislation encouraging the comprehensive redevelopment of the second largest urban land use, industry.

This does not, however, mean that industry has escaped the planners' bulldozer. In some cases demolition has resulted from firms closing down or moving out, thereby allowing the local authority to step in as a ready purchaser for the old properties: these have then been pulled down in order to make way for rebuilding, often for housing and other non-industrial uses. On occasion, local authorities have taken the initiative and negotiated for the purchase of old, outworn properties, grants and loans sometimes being offered to help the firms build new premises elsewhere. More commonly, demolition has followed the imposition of a Compulsory Purchase Order. Some of the firms which have been compulsorily displaced were located in predominantly residential areas and were evicted in the course of housing redevelopment programmes; others stood in the line of road schemes such as urban motorways; and a third group were noxious businesses causing severe damage to the local environment.

Although the displacement of industry has generally, therefore, been subsidiary to the major objectives of urban renewal, it has nevertheless been on a very substantial scale. For example, in the first five phases of Birmingham's post-war redevelopment programme over 1,500 firms had their premises compulsorily acquired by the local authority and then demolished. Local authorities are not required to find alternative accommodation for the firms they displace, and in Birmingham as elsewhere, public assistance in terms of premises and financial aid has not been generous.

The important point to note here is that redevelopment programmes, however large-scale, have not been used as devices for improving the environment of industrial areas or for enhancing firms' economic performance. When renewal schemes have affected industry, they have usually done so for reasons associated with other urban activities. Their impact on industry has been seen as at best secondary or at worst incidental.

Indeed, industry has tended to be the Cinderella of post-war urban planning in Britain. Planners have generally perceived it as in a sense less "respectable" than housing, commercial and recreational uses, and in consequence it has been treated as a "trouble-maker" (causing pollution, noise and traffic problems) rather than as a generator of wealth. In the town plans of the 1950s and 1960s it was often considered as a residual use to be relegated to sites which, on account of their size, shape or location, were unsuitable for anything else.

The contrast between the town planner's approach to the problems of decay in residential and in industrial areas is particularly striking. Major slum clearance programmes have been in operation since the 1930s, improvement grants for houses were introduced in the 1950s, and the idea of rehabilitating whole residential neighbourhoods was given legislative support in the late 1960s. In contrast, there have been no large-scale clearance programmes for outworn industrial areas, no grants for the specific purpose of renovating old industrial buildings and the idea of industrial improvement areas is only now being discussed in Parliament.

Urban planning, in its pre-occupation with housing, has tended to equate the quality of life with the quality of the residential environment. Yet much of peoples' lives is spent working in (and travelling through) industrial districts. To improve the house and to neglect the factory is to have a curiously partial view of what affects the quality of urban life. It is true, of course, that many new industrial estates have been built, mainly on the edge of towns, but nonetheless much of Britain's manufacturing capacity remains in inner-city areas first developed in the nineteenth century. Indeed, within the older parts of many British cities there has been virtually no new industrial building for fifty years or more. The present landscape is a legacy from the Victorian and Edwardian periods. Factories, warehouses, workshops, converted terraced houses, railways, canals and narrow streets form an environment which was once a thriving hive of activity but with the passage of time has deteriorated into what is by modern standards a disordered and decaying industrial slum. Increasingly these areas show signs of serious neglect and dilapidation as economic change shifts them from the mainstreams to the backwaters of the national economy. The investment required to secure the progressive regeneration of buildings and environment has not been forthcoming. The premises are in poor repair; some are lying empty, all are outworn and inefficient.

These areas seem to be incapable of renewing themselves. Many of the constraints which tend to preclude spontaneous private redevelopment of old housing are operative in the industrial context, too. Entrepreneurs and developers are reluctant to build new premises in run-down areas; the size and shape of land ownership plots are often unsuitable for modern buildings; the narrow and irregular street patterns prevent the achievement of good access facilities and are outside the ability of individual firms to modify; above all, many of the local firms (often dependent on low overheads) cannot afford rebuilding, especially in a period of economic recession and rising construction costs. The result is an atmosphere of inertia and gradual decay.

There is a growing recognition that to break out of this downward spiral requires public intervention, and in consequence some local authorities with large obsolete industrial areas have recently begun to formulate programmes for their renewal (see, for example, City of Leeds, 1977, and City of Manchester, 1978). Interestingly, at the national level the government's new interest in these problems has developed more from anxiety about the wider difficulties of inner-city areas than from a specific concern with industrial obsolescence per se. Nonetheless both national and local authorities are now focussing attention on the needs of older manufacturing districts, with two main ends in view. The first is to protect jobs and promote efficiency; the hope is that bringing the industrial fabric up to date will secure the long term future of these older areas by making them suitable for modern industrial activity. The second goal is to improve the quality of the environment so as to make these areas more agreeable places in which to work. This may in turn help to attract new private investment.

In principle, there are two main ways of effecting the necessary modernisation of these run-down areas, namely to demolish and rebuild, or to refurbish and improve the existing fabric. (A similar choice faces the planner when considering the future of decayed residential neighbourhoods.) In practice, for the industrial planner this choice is more notional than real since there is no legislation designed to promote the wholesale clearance of slum industrial areas. Local authorities do, however, have a variety of powers (for example to remove noxious and non-conforming firms) which can allow some public intervention. And together with voluntary acquisition of premises owned by firms willing to sell, it is possible for local authorities to make some inroads into older industrial districts. The major constraint is cost. Both compulsory and voluntary acquisitions involve paying the market prices of the properties concerned, and, for a variety of institutional reasons, land values remain high in those older areas, especially in the inner-cities. In addition, if the land is to be retained in industrial use, the local authority may be burdened with factory construction costs, since it is not always easy to attract private capital into these kinds of areas.

Another deterrent to clearance programmes is the fear of their impact on the firms displaced. There is a widely held view that in the past eviction has often led not to successful relocation in new or existing premises but more commonly to closure and a consequent loss of employment. Compulsory removal, especially for the small firms characteristic of the inner-cities, is thought to be a trauma with which displacees are unable to cope, particularly as they are unlikely to be able to afford any new accommodation offered by the local authority. Indeed, for these reasons a recent government circular has instructed all planning authorities that the displacement of industry "should be avoided if at all possible" (Department of the Environment and Department of Transport, 1977, p. 4). Interestingly, however, such research as exists on the fate of displacees suggests that closure rates are low, that moving often proves a stimulus to enterprise and re-organisation, and that compensation payments, although rarely generous, can provide an assisted passage to improved accommodation and higher profitability (see, for example, McKean, 1975, Thomas, 1976, and Chalkley, 1978). Here is a case of the "conventional wisdom" and the results of academic research being curiously at variance.

Nonetheless, fears about the effects of redevelopment, together with the current economic stringencies mean that the idea of clearance is out of favour, and instead much interest focusses on the possibilities for rehabilitation. This has the great advantage of providing improved accommodation at more modest rentals, low overheads being essential for the survival of many small businesses. A rehabilitation policy also removes the possible spectre of clearance; this is important because fears of demolition can lead to a loss of business confidence in older areas and a resulting neglect of property.

Some local authorities have already been involved in schemes to modernise old factories, mills and warehouses; typically the properties chosen have been sub-divided to provide units for small firms. However, the concept of rehabilitating industrial *areas* as opposed to individual buildings is more recent. As with housing improvement areas, Rochdale in Lancashire has been the pioneer. Its programme, set out in a paper produced by the Rochdale Metropolitan Borough Council (1977), is directed at a predominantly industrial area of 57 hectares just south of the town centre. In practice the scheme has involved not only refurbishing buildings but also re-organising traffic flows, improving access and parking facilities and creating expansion space. Some new factory units are also being built, and a determined attempt is being made to clean up the local environment by a variety of landscaping measures. In addition, some of the most dilapidated premises have been cleared, a certain amount of demolition being necessary even in rehabilitation programmes.

Whether the Rochdale experiment will prove to be merely a cosmetic, patching-up operation, or whether it will succeed in regenerating the economic base is too early to say. Much will depend on the project's ability to evoke a response from private industry. The first signs are that the scheme has at least restored industrialists' confidence in the area's future, and early results have been sufficiently promising for the government to adopt the idea industrial improvement areas in its Inner Urban Areas Bill. The legislative and financial assistance this bill provides will, however, only be available to selected inner-city areas, and hence many authorities facing severe problems of industrial obsolescence will not qualify.

With or without direct government aid, local authorities' funds for industrial renewal are bound to be diminutive in comparison with the scale of obsolescence. Decisions must therefore be taken about which areas to select for action. A full discussion of the criteria to be adopted in making these decisions is beyond the scope of this paper; however it must be said that the degree of obsolescence alone should not be the controlling consideration. The sites selected should have potential for attracting modern industry, since using large sums of public money to fight lost causes could not be justified. For social reasons short-term environmental "holding operations" in decaying areas may on occasion be necessary, but they should not be allowed to prejudice longer-term interests. Similarly, where decayed industrial districts are fulfilling a useful function in accommodating new small businesses dependent on low rents, this "seedbed" should not be disturbed. Public investment should instead be concentrated in areas where it can produce not only substantial environmental improvements, but also a sufficient investment response from industry to justify the injection of government and local-authority resources.

Finally, it needs to be admitted that planning policies alone, however worthwhile, cannot on their own solve the problems of physical decay since these are often merely visual symptoms of a more fundamental economic malaise which lies to a large extent outside the local planner's control. Some of our older industrial areas have lost their former locational advantages as suburban and exurban locations have become more profitable. Many are victims of a lack of enterprise which reflects not only local inertia but economic and political considerations which need to be tackled on a broader basis. National economic recovery is an essential precondition for a really successful attack on obsolescence. The urban planners' contribution to this recovery, as outlined by the government, requires that a higher priority is given to industrial needs (Department of the Environment and Department of Transport, 1977). For if planning is to play its part in improving the quality of life it must recognise that although the good life is more than material success it is impossible without a sound economic base.

Zusammenfassung

Stadterneuerung und die Industrieverlagerung

Bislang beschränkten sich Stadterneuerungsprogramme in England nahezu ausschließlich auf die notwendig gewordene Beseitigung oder Wiederinstandsetzung der Wohnbausubstanz aus dem 19. Jahrhundert. Es hatte sich als unmöglich erwiesen, die älteren Wohngebiete sich unmittelbar selbst durch private Initiativen regenerieren zu lassen, weshalb Stadtplaner die Notwendigkeit eines Eingreifens der öffentlichen Hand erkannten. Eigenartigerweise erhielt jedoch die alte Bausubstanz der Industrie nicht dieselbe Aufmerksamkeit, vielmehr kümmerte sich die Planung überhaupt nicht um die erforderliche Erneuerung oder Verbesserung der Umweltqualität am Arbeitsplatz. Viele alte Industriereviere Englands sind daher in ihrer äußeren Erscheinung ein heruntergekommenes Erbe der Viktorianischen und Edwardianischen Ära. Die Fabrikgebäude sind in üblem Zustand, die Angestellten arbeiten in einer wenig anziehenden Umgebung, und es herrscht allgemein eine Atmosphäre des Verfalls und der Trägheit, die noch verstärkt wird dadurch, daß Firmen schließen oder in gesündere Gegenden umsiedeln.

Es gibt jedoch Anzeichen dafür, daß, wenn auch verspätet, diesen Verfallsproblemen jetzt von offizieller Seite Beachtung zukommt; denn sowohl staatliche als auch kommunale Behörden richten nun zunehmend ihr Augenmerk auf den Bestand an Fabrikgebäuden in diesen älteren Revieren. Im Prinzip gibt es zwei Wege, die notwendige Modernisierung zu bewirken, nämlich entweder Abbruch und Neubau oder Renovierung und Ausbau der bestehenden Bausubstanz. In der Praxis bedingen jedoch die hohen Kosten und die gegenwärtig angespannte Wirtschaftslage, daß ein groß angelegter Wiederaufbau nicht als eine realistische Lösung erscheint, weshalb stattdessen das Interesse nun um eine Wiederinstandsetzung kreist.

Aus diesem Grund legte die Regierung als Teil ihres Programms zur Förderung von Innenstädten einen Plan zur gebietsweisen Industriestrukturverbesserung vor, wonach Zuschüsse für Gebäuderenovierungen, die Neuregulierung von Verkehrsströmen, den Ausbau von Zufahrtswegen und Parkplätzen und für die Verschönerung der örtlichen Umwelt durch diverse landschaftsgestalterische Maßnahmen bereitgestellt werden. Ein Pionierprogramm in Rochdale brachte bereits ermutigende Resultate hervor, aber es ist noch zu früh, um sagen zu können, ob solche Projekte nur kosmetischen Charakter haben oder ob sie helfen werden, die Wirtschaftsgrundlage zu regenerieren. Erfolg oder Mißerfolg, sowohl in Bezug auf die Umwelt als auch in wirtschaftlicher Hinsicht, werden davon abhängen, ob die Projekte zur Strukturverbesserung das Vertrauen der Geschäftswelt wiederherzustellen vermögen und inwieweit die Industrie auch in der Zukunft bereit sein wird, die notwendigen Investitionen in den bislang verfallenden Revieren zu tätigen.

References

CHALKLEY, B.S. (1978): "The relocation decisions of small displaced firms", unpubl. Ph.D. thesis, University of Southampton

City of Leeds (1977): "Leeds policy for industry", Leeds

City of Manchester (1978): "Industrial strategy actions and future programmes. A report of Manchester's director of industrial development", Manchester

Department of the Environment and Department of Transport (1977): "Local government and the industrial strategy"

H.M.S.O. (1977): "Policy for the inner-cities", Cmnd 6845

MCKEAN, R. (1975): "The impact of comprehensive redevelopment area policies an industry in Glasgow", University of Glasgow, Urban and Regional Studies, Discussion Paper 15

Rochdale Metropolitan Borough Council (1977): "Industrial obsolescence. The Rochdale approach", Rochdale.

THOMAS, K. (1976): "The effects of urban redevelopment and renewal on small manufacturing firms in Birmingham", unpubl. M.Phil. thesis, C.N.A.A.

THE ROLE OF THE LOCAL AUTHORITY AND THE INTERACTION OF POLICY DETERMINANTS IN URBAN HOUSING STRATEGY: THE EXAMPLE OF NOTTINGHAM

with 3 figures

M. Sohail Husain

Introduction

A decent shelter is generally acknowledged to be a fundamental human right in western society. Yet in Britain today many families are homeless and thousands more have lived in slums for decades. This unfortunate situation has developed in spite of the policies of successive governments that were designed to solve the 'housing problem' by providing the quantity and quality of dwellings required. This lack of social effectiveness has clearly had a detrimental impact on the 'quality of life' of many people and justifies critical examination of the policies and actions of the decision-making authorities at both national and local levels. Such a comprehensive task obviously cannot be undertaken in this short contribution. However, an attempt is made below to examine the activities of the principal agent responsible for urban housing policy at a local level during the inter- and post-war periods.

The importance of the local authority

Housing is an emotive and political subject. In the past, national election campaigns have been based primarily on the housing issue and central governments, irrespective of political colour, have become deeply involved in the development of successful housing programmes. The nature of such programmes has varied with party dogma, the national economic situation, contemporary housing problems and other factors. However, one common element has been the unwillingness of central governments to assume direct control of the housing system and a consistent preference to work through the existing complex institutional framework. Although central government is able, through legislation, to obtain powers and finance to achieve its objectives, it uses this ability to enable, persuade and oblige individuals and agencies to implement its policy. These bodies include building societies, housing associations, local authorities, landlords, builders and many other interested parties.

This influence has a differential impact on private and public organisations and, in general, local authorities are the most susceptible to government interference. Since 1919 they have been given the duty to assess housing conditions in their areas and prepare plans to satisfy demand. They have been required to tackle the problems of overcrowding and slum clearance and to prepare proposals for redevelopment and improvement where necessary. Moreover, plans for new housing must conform to government-imposed standards before approval and financial assistance from central funds can be given. Nevertheless, it would be quite wrong to visualise the local authority as being totally under the control of central government. On the contrary, within the framework set out above detailed management of the local housing market remains the responsibility of the local authority and, in effect, it is difficult for central government to assess whether local authorities are fulfilling their obligations. It is clear therefore that the local authority is the principal agent of the government for the development of a coherent housing strategy at a local level.[1]

The duties imposed on a local authority enable it either to provide new accommodation itself or arrange for other agencies to do so. The course of action chosen by individual authorities is determined by a variety of national and local influences. However, the combined effect of several factors has resulted in the local authority assuming the dominant role in hous-building in city areas during the inter- and post-war periods to the relative exclusion of the private developer. Of particular significance has been an acceptance that the serious social problems of insufficient and inadequate housing necessitated public authority involvement rather than commercial enterprise. But in addition, the post-war predominance in many urban areas of Labour party councillors who favoured the construction of council homes, and the shortage of open land within existing city boundaries, have severely constrained the activities of the private developer.[2]

The local authority, therefore, has emerged as the primary agency for both policy formulation and implementation at a local level, albeit subject to influence from central government. During this period a series of housing problems has been experienced in British cities which has evoked a variety of responses from local authorities. The following analysis investigates this problem-response relationship and assesses the extent to which the dominant position of the local authority has led to a successful assault on the problems. Such developments have undoubtedly varied in detail according to local circumstances. For this reason a longitudinal profile of developments in one particular city is presented below, which illustrates the interaction of local and other influences. However, a broadly similar sequence of problems and responses has been evident in most large urban areas. Thus, the subsequent critical examination of policy phases draws on experiences from, and has implications for, a much wider range of areas than the individual city considered here in detail. Attention is focused on three main issues: the provision of new housing to meet demand; attempts to improve the quality of the housing stock; and the nature of new residential environments.

Housing problems and policy in Nottingham before 1939

The past housing problems of Nottingham are less notorious than those of larger urban centres. Nevertheless, the problems suffered in this Midland city have been among the most serious and persistent experienced anywhere in Britain.[3] Their origins lie in the eighteenth and early nineteenth centuries when rapid population growth resulted in a shortage of dwellings and severe overcrowding. This situation was largely caused by the unwillingness of burgesses and aristocratic landowners to release land for town expansion. In 1840 town residents were accommodated within the same area as in 1750, even though the population had increased from 10,000 to 50,000 during this period.[4] It was not until the extensive common lands were enclosed in 1845 that outward expansion could continue. The area released (approximately six square kilometers equal to ten times the size of the existing town) was developed rapidly and primarily for residential use. By 1873 most of the freed land had been built upon and the immediate housing shortage had been substantially reduced.

Despite its apparent benefits, the accommodation constructed at that time has provided very serious problems for the local authority in the present century. A high proportion of the new dwellings consisted of working-class terraced housing at a high density and built to low standards. St. Ann's and The Meadows were the two main sites involved, with many buildings in the latter area being below the flood level of the River Trent. Before the end of the century the homes in these areas had been condemned for their unhygienic conditions,[5] but it was not until almost one hundred years later that most were finally demolished. Moreover, in succeeding years the provision of working-class housing again failed to keep pace with population growth. Thus in 1919, when local authorities were given the duty to survey housing conditions in their areas and encouraged to provide accommodation in the form of council housing, serious problems were again evident. Not only was there a severe shortage, which had been intensified by the wartime cessation of building, but in addition much of the existing housing stock was in a very unsatisfactory condition.[6] Nearly 7000 dwellings had been declared unfit for human habitation with the majority of those being in the inner-city area.

Subsequent development of housing policy and house construction have, for the reasons outlined above, been dominated by the actions of Nottingham Corporation. Throughout the period the local authority has tackled its problems largely through the public housing sector, while the private developer has been allowed to play an almost insignificant role. The precise nature of the response has been influenced by a number of local and other factors, such as contemporary trends in house construction, financial incentives from central government and land availability. Thus, while the basic problem has changed little, it will be shown below that the response has varied considerably over time.

In 1919 the response may be seen in the light of two main influences. Firstly, central government had recognised the need for more houses for the working-class to meet post-war shortages and had decided this could be best provided by encouraging public-sector development with fairly generous subsidies.[7] Secondly, the recommendations of the Tudor Walters Report on housing standards had been accepted by the government as minimum requirements for council housing receiving a subsidy.[8] Initially, therefore, Nottingham Corporation attempted to solve its housing problems with the construction of the recommended three-bedroom house on small estates (50-350 dwellings) adjoining existing communities. Wherever possible, land was purchased on the open market, where financial aid from central government enabled the authority to outbid private developers. It was, however, quickly realised that such small estates were having a minimal impact on the housing shortage. In spite of a reduction in government assistance,[9] larger developments began to be undertaken in the late 1920s and compulsory purchase powers were increasingly used to secure remaining land for the public sector. Substantial new estates were constructed on the periphery of the built-up area at Aspley (2838 dwellings), Sherwood (1087 dwellings) and Wollaton Park (1011 dwellings) (figure 1).

The dwellings constructed were scarcely sufficient to accommodate population increase and progress towards a reduction of the housing deficit proved difficult to achieve. It was not until the early 1930s, when growth rates throughout the country had fallen significantly, that clearance of unfit houses could be considered. Such a shift of emphasis was encouraged by the withdrawal of the general subsidy for council house construction and its replacement with one based on the number of people displaced from slum areas and rehoused.[10] By this time the supply of potential building land within the city was almost exhausted and only considerable boundary extensions in the west allowed further construction. With this additional land a total of 17,690 council houses were completed during the inter-war years,[11] a figure which represents a creditable achievement. Indeed BOWLEY has shown that Nottingham was one of only seven County Boroughs in England and Wales which consistently increased its annual capital expenditure on housing under the Chamberlain and Wheatley Acts.[12] Nevertheless, enormous areas of nineteenth-century slum dwellings remained untouched and the magnitude of the housing problem had not been significantly altered.

The housing built during this period was undoubtedly of a very high standard in comparison to earlier working-class accommodation. The geometrical plan of the estates and the design of the dwellings were in marked contrast to the

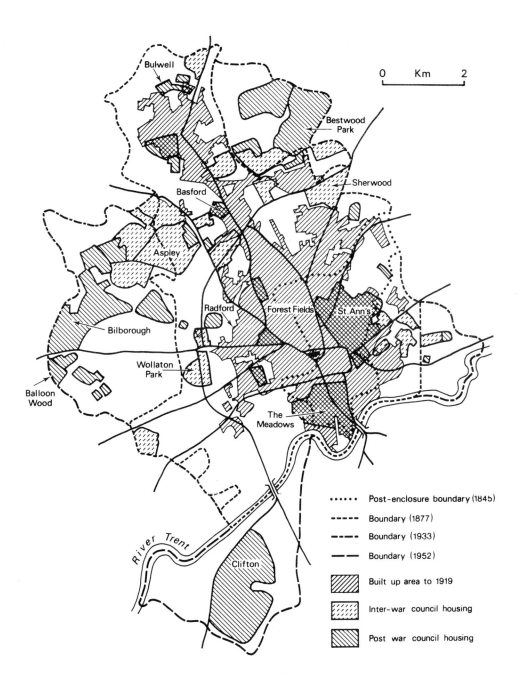

Fig. 1: Development of residential areas during the inter- and post-war periods.

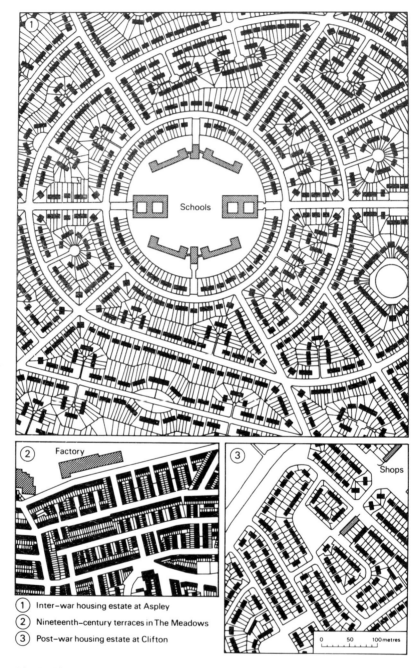

Fig. 2: Characteristic housing layouts of the nineteenth and twentieth centuries.

cramped nineteenth-century terraces (figure 2). Low residential densities (30 persons per hectare), large gardens and a mixture of semidetached and terraced houses were characteristic features. Indeed the standards of architecture and construction on some of the earliest estates (built at a time when subsidies under the Addison Act were particularly generous) were of outstanding quality. Nevertheless, in retrospect one may identify a number of unsatisfactory features in these developments, some of which caused further difficulties for the local authority at a later date.

Although they provided a greatly improved physical environment for the residents, and despite attempts to introduce contrast and variety, the impression created by many of these estates was one of monotonous uniformity. This resulted from the use of similar construction and fencing materials and, occasionally, of a single house design. Their effect was compounded by the sheer size of some developments and the fact that all the dwellings were of almost identical age. A further problem was the absence of services and other amenities in the original plans.[13] Although schools and churches were often present, shopping facilities, recreational areas and social services were either lacking or at a considerable distance from many residents, possibly necessitating expenditure on travel. Experiences elsewhere suggest that such environmental uniformity and lack of adequate neighbourhood services may well have hindered the development of a 'community spirit' and increased the social isolation of the individual.[14] Additionally, it has been argued, the construction of such extensive estates on the city periphery for working-class residents accelerated the process of social segregation and fostered the development of friction between different residential groups.[15] It was also largely responsible for the development of a landscape of extensive suburban sprawl, which has now linked the city to surrounding smaller towns to form an enormous conurbation. Furthermore, the ubiquitous construction of the three-bedroom house for young families created an unbalanced population structure. The young parents initially resident in these houses are now elderly and their children have moved away. The residual aged population exerts pressure on local social services and underoccupation is prevalent.[16] Consequently, the creditable building performance not only had little impact on the slum problem, but had a number of unforeseen and undesirable consequences.

Post-war housing developments in Nottingham

The Second World War interrupted the building programme and by 1945 a national housing shortage had re-emerged. Government encouragement was once again given to house construction for general needs through the Housing (Financial and Miscellaneous Provisions) Act, 1946. Private development was strictly controlled by a licensing system and local authorities were again expected to undertake substantial house-building programmes to meet demand. Moreover, since there had been no radical change in planning attitudes, adherence to the large new suburban estate continued. In Nottingham the most urgent needs were met with the provision of 1000 temporary bungalows and the completion of developments initiated before 1939.[17] By 1947 work had started on the first major post-war estate at Bilborough (2881 dwellings). Shortly before this was completed in 1952 a further boundary extension provided land for the commencement of Clifton estate (6860 dwellings) and this was followed in 1959 by Bestwood Park (3057 dwellings). A total of 12,798 dwellings were constructed in these three areas alone, accounting for a very high proportion of all dwellings built.

It would be wrong, however, to envisage a continuous and regular rate of house construction during these years. On the contrary, variations in the level of incentives offered by central government exerted a powerful effect on local activity. In fact the subsidies provided by the 1946 Act proved inadequate to stimulate major building programmes and few houses were built during the immediate post-war years (figure 3). It was not until the Conservative Government was elected in 1951 that financial assistance was significantly improved.[18] This change was quickly followed by a dramatic rise in house completions at a national and local scale which reached a peak in 1954. By that date the Government believed that post-war shortages had been largely eliminated and that private enterprise could subsequently provide the required additional accommodation. Subsidies on housing for general needs were therefore reduced in 1954, abolished two years later, and not re-introduced until 1961.[19] Figure 3 shows that each of these changes was reflected in the number of local authority house completions. However, despite the encouragement given to private developers at a national level after 1954, it is clear that in Nottingham they continued to play a minor role in house construction.

Although superficially similar to earlier developments, the detailed design of the three new estates was substantially different. Firstly, attempts were made to incorporate recommendations of the Dudley Report,[20] which emphasized the need for service provision and favoured the development of 'neighbourhood units'. Consequently shopping and recreational areas, libraries and other amenities were provided for small communities of about 10,000 people. Secondly, visual uniformity was reduced by using more varied house styles, house sizes and building materials and the adoption of a less formal street pattern. However, to incorporate the additional services, whilst maintaining residential densities, necessitated smaller gardens. Furthermore, even with these modifications it proved extremely difficult to dispel the atmosphere of monotony. Moreover, it was practically impossible to establish the balanced socio-economic population structure that had also been recommended, and residents continued to be drawn mainly from low-income working-class groups.

By the late 1950s two important new factors had already begun to exert an influence on local policy. Firstly, land for housing development within the city boundary was once again in short supply and permission for further extensions

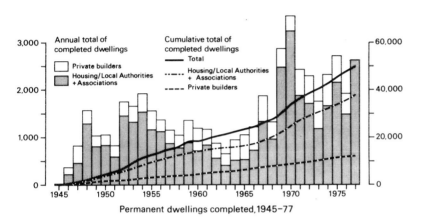
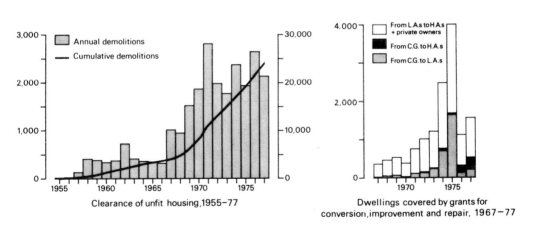

Fig. 3: Post-war dwelling construction, clearance and renovation.

seemed unlikely to be granted. Further, the government, clearly anticipating the development of such a situation nationally, had recommended that council housing densities should be increased.[21] These developments were followed by a gradual movement towards the construction of flatted accommodation. Secondly, the city population had stabilised and subsequently started to fall, and the housing deficit was no longer of such great significance. There was, therefore, no further need to concentrate solely on increasing the housing supply and attention could be turned to improving the quality of the housing stock. The combination of these two trends led to the clearance of some of the worst sites in the late 1950s and the rehousing of residents in small low-rise blocks. In contrast to the extensive peripheral estates, these compact, high-density developments were scattered throughout the city on previously cleared sites or wherever suitable plots were available. These selective small-scale projects, however, made virtually no impact on the enormous expanses of condemned terraces. Over the period 1961-65 the average demolition rate was only 454 houses per annum, at which rate it would have taken 28 years to clear the remaining 12,525 houses which were unfit in 1965.[22] Nottingham Corporation was apparently markedly slow to tackle its slum problem and compared unfavourably with other large cities.

It was not until 1967, when government subsidies were increased,[23] that an additional impetus was given to slum clearance. By this time the residents in the problem areas were in urgent need of help. However, an acceleration in slum clearance also necessitated an increase in new dwellings to rehouse the displaced residents. The situation demanded units which could be constructed quickly and cheaply, whilst making maximum use of the small amount of land available. In response to these requirements a series of prefabricated high- and medium-rise blocks of flats were built on the few remaining vacant plots on the city periphery (for example at Ballon Wood) and on cleared sites closer to the centre (for example at Basford). Irrespective of location these dwellings provided urgently needed accommodation for households from clearance areas. As in other parts of the country, though, such blocks have for various well-documented reasons proved unpopular with the tenants,[24] many of whom quickly applied for alternative accommodation.[25]

The general unfavourable reaction to high-rise living from sociologists, residents and other interest groups curtailed the construction of further blocks for rehousing. However, those already completed began to pose new problems. In one particular multi-storey complex the social problems of the residents, the high incidence of vandalism and the rapid physical deterioration of the buildings have necessitated drastic action by the housing authority. All families with young children have been moved out and a £ 50,000 facelift has been implemented (including renaming of the blocks) to try and create an improved residential and social environment.[26] However, the reputation of most blocks in the city remains unfavourable. Residents from clearance areas seldom wish to be permanently rehoused in them and 'good' tenants (who perhaps maintained their previous dwelling and had no rent arrears) have tended to be 'rewarded' with a conventional estate house. The unfortunate corollary of this policy is that some blocks now house a residue of 'problem families' (in the widest sense of the term), whose problems can only be exacerbated by their unsatisfactory residential environment. Thus, it becomes apparent that while attempting to ease the difficulties in one area, the policy of the local authority had unfortunate repercussions elsewhere.

The construction of the multi-storey blocks marked the beginning of a determined effort by Nottingham Corporation to tackle its slum problem, and this is reflected in the increased number of house demolitions in subsequent years (figure 3). By 1970 plans had finally been completed for the redevelopment of St. Ann's and, in the absence of a suitable alternative strategy, the planners returned to the concept of the large housing estate.[27] The old St. Ann's was demolished stage by stage and rebuilt to a much lower residential density. The comprehensive redevelopment approach involved the complete obliteration of the old street pattern and most pre-existing landmarks. The former terraces have been replaced with semi-detached and linked dwellings of various styles, sizes and materials, each with its own garden. Every house has been connected to a district heating scheme which provides hot water and central heating. A variety of neighbourhood shops, schools, old people's homes and other amenities have also been incorporated in the design and some attempts have been made to reduce visual uniformity.

It is perhaps too early to definitively assess the success of the new St. Ann's but some general observations may be made at this stage. It has been suggested that the redevelopment has totally destroyed an integrated community and there can be no doubt that social networks have been severely disrupted. However, the planners have in various ways attempted to create a physical environment which will encourage social interaction. Moreover, by first offering the new dwellings to the old residents, it may be possible to re-establish a similar social organisation in a new setting. Criticism has also been directed at the poor standard of dwelling construction which undoubtedly reflected need for speed and economy. It seems likely that physical deterioration will be fairly rapid and in a relatively short time the fabric of the dwellings will once again constitute a considerable problem. Some residents are inevitably dissatisfied with service provision, housing costs and other matters. In spite of this, though, many of the defficiencies of earlier estates have been rectified and in general residents are apparently contented with their new homes.

Attitudes to housing in the late 1960s were rapidly changing. The national drive for slum clearance and redevelopment, incorporating the rise and fall in popularity of multi-storey blocks, had by 1969 been replaced by a much greater emphasis on rehabilitation. Grants to private owners in urban areas for home improvements had been available since 1949. Now, with the worst slums cleared from most cities and the cost of comprehensive redevelopment rising rapidly, the government took the opportunity to redirect some of the public investment in housing to dwelling improvement rather than replacement.[28] The Housing Acts of 1969 and 1974 introduced the concepts of the designated General Improvement Area and Housing Action Area, and local authorities became eligible to receive substantial grants to finance area improvements and the purchase of dwellings for renovation. At the same time conditions for grants to private owners from local authorities were greatly relaxed.

In Nottingham the continued progress of major redevelopment schemes maintained completion rates at a high level. There was little possibility of improvement in the worst areas. In other districts, however, where redevelopment was not essential or could not be contemplated immediately, dwelling and area improvements were undertaken on an increasing scale (figure 3). The principal beneficiaries were the occupants of late nineteenth- and early twentieth-century terraces in old industrial villages (such as Bulwell) or close to the city centre (as at Promenade). In some of these areas all the houses have been purchased by the local authority and completely renovated. In General Improvement Areas and Housing Action Areas environmental improvements have included the exclusion of through traffic, the construction of garages and the establishment of recreational areas.[29] Elsewhere owners were encouraged to apply for individual grants from Nottingham Corporation.

In the short term such action had obvious economic and social attractions. Not only was improvement a relatively cheap process, but hardly any additional land was required for new houses. More important, it brought about a rapid improvement in the living conditions for many households without disturbing social networks. In the longer term however, the financial arguments for rehabilitation of homes which, had resources been available, would have been demolished, are much more contentious.[30]

It is apparent, therefore, that during the last decade attempts to improve the city's housing stock have escalated. The combination of a selective clearance programme with a vigorous rehabilitation campaign has improved living conditions for a large number of families. Between 1968 and 1976 17,916 houses were demolished and 3180 were improved by the local authority. Nevertheless, large areas of low-quality housing still remain. Plans for a single policy area covering Basford, Forest Fields and Radford show that in 1974 over 16,000 people were living in properties which, in the opinion of Nottingham Corporation, were unfit for human habitation and for which improvement was not a realistic possibility.[31] The persistence of severe housing stress in the city was also recognised by central government in 1976. At a time of public expenditure restrictions, Nottingham was among 43 areas awarded high priority status for the allocation of government funds because of their housing problems.[32] One may conclude therefore that, although Nottingham Corporation has continued to be very actively involved in the housing market since 1945, and has indeed been responsible for 75% of the 45,000 dwellings built, much remains to be accomplished.

Conclusion

The foregoing account has illustrated several important features of the housing market in Nottingham. It has emphasised the pre-eminence of the local authority, the nature of the housing problems, the interaction of policy determinants and the chronological evolution of a local housing strategy. The importance of this account lies in the fact that in many ways the developments in Nottingham have been characteristic of British cities in general.

It has been shown that, despite the extensive local authority building programmes, long delays in the demolition or improvement of unfit houses have occurred. Indeed the situation throughout Britain has compared unfavourably in this matter with other European neighbours.[33] The reasons for these delays are many and complex. During periods of housing shortages and rapid population growth it was obviously necessary to concentrate resources on increasing the total housing stock. Yet even when growth rates were low and specific grants were available for slum clearance, the work undertaken made only a marginal impact on the total stock of inadequate housing. One must therefore conclude that either individual local authorities failed to perceive the seriousness of the situation and act accordingly or the level of financial support from central funds, on which local authorities were heavily dependent, was inadequate. There is no doubt that certain authorities have shown much greater determination than others to remove its slum housing. But it is also true that, in comparison with other west European countries, British governments have consistently allocated a relatively small amount of national expenditure to housing investment.[34] Moreover, the frequent fluctuations in support levels have made long-term planning by local authorities extremely difficult. This high degree of uncertainty has now been recognised as a major weakness of the present funding system and for this reason Housing Investment Programmes have been recently introduced.[35] These will allow local authorities to draw up more considered and coherent programmes for dealing with their housing problems than has hitherto been possible, although the total funds available will not necessarily be increased.

The long delays had unfortunate social repercussions. Demand accumulated for new housing and this necessitated large-scale projects when resources were finally made available. Critical comment has been levelled at the scale of such developments for esthetic and sociological reasons and at the detailed design of dwellings and neighbourhoods. However, attitudes have evolved in the light of these experiences, even if economic considerations remain an overriding influence on actual policy. The provision of services, a balanced population structure and a stimulating physical setting are now recognised requirements for a successful neighbourhood scheme. Much more consideration is given to the social impact of residential changes than ever before. And public participation in the planning process is widely accepted. These ideas are inevitably affecting the design of new residential environments.

Fundamental changes in approach to urban housing problems have also been outlined above. Of these perhaps the most dramatic has been the shift away from comprehensive clearance and major redevelopment schemes as the main instruments of housing policy to involvement in a much wider range of activities. The new emphasis on selective clearance and rehabilitation has already been discussed. In addition, though, more help is being given by local authorities to housing associations and co-operatives. More attention is being paid to the specialised housing needs of certain minority groups, such as the elderly or handicapped. The sale of council houses to occupants and the purchase of houses on private estates for council tenants have added a new dimension to local authority operations. This considerable diversification may perhaps reduce the previous rigid social and spatial segregation of different tenure groups and should enable authorities to operate a more flexible and effective housing service.

This article has shown that local authorities have a major responsibility to tackle housing problems in urban areas and create a satisfactory residential environment. Their activities, therefore, have a significant influence on the 'quality of life'. The persistence of serious problems suggests that past policies have had only limited success and examination of policy determinants reveals several possible causes for this failure. However, many of the worst problems have now been alleviated and urban populations are no longer rapidly increasing. Moreover, the role of the local authority and its approach to housing problems is changing in response to experience and new ideas. In future, therefore, one may anticipate that local authorities will be in a better position to formulate and implement an effective local housing strategy.

Zusammenfassung

Die Rolle der Kommunalbehörden und die politischen Determinaten städtischer Wohnungsbaupolitik in ihrer Wechselbeziehung: das Beispiel Nottingham

In den Jahren zwischen den Weltkriegen und danach sind die Kommunalbehörden als Hauptträger bei der Ausarbeitung und Durchführung von Wohnungsbaumaßnahmen in städtischen Regionen in England und Wales in Erscheinung getreten. Man hat mit einer Reihe von Wohnproblemen Erfahrungen gemacht, die verschiedenartige Reaktionen dieser Behörden ausgelöst haben. Im Anschluß an eine Analyse der Problem-Reaktion-Beziehung wird die Effektivität der durchgeführten Maßnahmen bewertet. Anhand des Beispiels von Nottingham wird die Aufmerksamkeit auf drei Hauptpunkte gelenkt: die Bereitstellung neuer Wohnungen zur Deckung des Bedarfs, die Bemühungen um die qualitative Verbesserung der Wohnbausubstanz und die Beschaffenheit des Wohnumfelds in

Neubaugebieten. Das Andauern schwerwiegender Probleme läßt vermuten, daß die Maßnahmen in der Vergangenheit nur von begrenztem Erfolg gekrönt waren, besonders wenn man Vergleiche zu den europäischen Nachbarn zieht. Es werden mehrere mögliche Gründe für dieses relative Fehlschlagen aufgedeckt.

Notes and references

1. This has been emphasized recently in Department of the Environment (1977): "Housing policy. A consultative document", Cmnd. 6851, H.M.S.O., 42
2. For further discussion of these influences see BOADEN, N. (1971): "Urban policy making", pp. 59-70, Cambridge, and BOWLEY, M. (1945): "Housing and the state 1919-44, pp. 48-74, London
3. An analysis of the situation in the mid nineteenth century may be found in Royal Commission (1845): "Second report on the state of large towns and populous districts", Appendix - Part II, Parliament Papers XVIII, pp. 249-57; A more recent account is in COATES, K. & R. SILBURN (1971): "Poverty: the forgotten Englishman", Harmondsworth
4. A detailed description is provided in GRAY, D. (1953): "Nottingham: settlement to city", Nottingham
5. SEATON, E. (1873): "A report on the sanitary condition of the Borough of Nottingham", Nottingham
6. THOMAS, C.J. (1971): "The growth of Nottingham's residential area since 1919", East Midland Geographer 5, pp. 119-32
7. Housing, Town Planning, etc. Act, 1919 (Addison Act)
8. Report of the Committee on questions of building construction in connection with the provision of dwellings for the working classes (1918) Cd. 9191, Parliamentary Papers VII (Tudor Walters Report)
9. Subsidies under the Addison Act were curtailed by the Housing Act, 1921. The Housing, etc. Act, 1923 (Chamberlain Act) and Housing (Financial Provisions) Act, 1924 (Wheatley Act) introduced new subsidies. Reductions in the subsidy rate in 1927 and 1928 made house construction an unattractive economic proposition for local authorities; See: BOWLEY, op. cit. pp. 36-134
10. Slum clearance rehousing subsidies were introduced by the Housing Act, 1930 (Greenwood Act). Wheatley subsidies were ended with the Housing (Financial Provisions) Act, 1933
11. THOMAS, C.J., op. cit. p. 120
12. BOWLEY, M., op. cit. p. 104
13. This was contrary to the recommendations of the Tudor Walters Report.
14. For a longer discussion see THORNS, D.C. (1976): "The quest for communi-

ty", pp. 42-63, London
15. WHITE, L.E. (1950): "Community or chaos. New housing estates and their social problems", London
16. Nottingham Corporation has converted some of these houses into flats to solve this problem without severe spatial dislocation of the elderly residents.
17. These temporary dwellings were still occupied in 1978.
18. Housing Act, 1952
19. Housing (Review of Contributions) Order, 1954 and Housing Subsidies Act, 1956
20. Ministry of Health (1944): "Design of dwellings", H.M.S.O. (Dudley Report)
21. Ministry of Housing and Local Government (1952): "The density of residential areas", H.M.S.O.
22. Open University (1977): "The housing situation in Nottingham", Social Science Foundation Course: Making Sense of Society, Summer School Notes, p. 5, Milton Keynes
23. Housing Subsidies Act, 1967
24. JEPHCOTT, P. (1971): "Homes in high flats", Edinburgh
25. Nottingham Evening Post (22 January 1975): "Fear in the sky blocks"
26. Nottingham Evening Post (23 January 1975): "A nick where you do life"
27. Nottingham Corporation (1970): "St. Ann's. Renewal in progress", Nottingham
28. Department of the Environment (1974): "Housing Act 1974: improvement of older housing", Circular 160/74, London; Department of the Environment (1975): "Housing Act 1974: renewal strategies", Circular 13/75, London
29. For a description of the Bulwell G.I.A. see Department of the Environment (1972): "Environmental design in four G.I.A.s.", Area Improvement Note 5, H.M.S.O.
30. ROBERTS, J.T. (1976): "General improvement areas", Farnborough
31. Nottingham City Council (1975): "Basford, Forest Fields, Radford: a report prepared by the Interim District Plan Steering Group", Nottingham
32. Department of the Environment (1976): "Local authority housebuilding: local authority mortgage lending", Circular 80/76, London
33. BERRY, F. (1974): "Housing: the great British failure", pp. 221-31, London
34. United Nations Economic Commission for Europe, Annual Bulletin of Housing and Building Statistics for Europe, 1965-76
35. Department of the Environment (1977): "Housing strategies and investment programmes: arrangements for 1978-79", Circular 63/77 London

PROBLEMS OF URBAN RENEWAL AND REDEVELOPMENT IN A MEDIUM SIZED TOWN

with 2 figures

ALLAN J.R. WADE

Introduction

a) Location and brief description of Hastings and St. Leonards-on-Sea

The Borough of Hastings had an estimated population of 74,400 in 1976 with an administrative area of 2,972 hectares. The town centre was established after 1800 in a valley to the west of the ruins of a Norman Castle on the West Hill. The historic "Old Town" which formed the nucleus of one of the ancient Cinque Ports, as well as a 210 ha. Country Park are both to the east of the town centre and the ancient Castle.

The so called 19th Century new town of St. Leonards-on-Sea and a designated 429 ha. town expansion area are both to the west of the central area. To the north, one of the Wealden ridges forms the limit of the built-up area and rises to about 170 metres above sea level.

b) Regional context and policies for the area

Hastings forms a sub-regional centre for shopping and employment purposes. It was selected in the Strategic Plan for South East England as part or a "medium growth area".[1] A Town Expansion Scheme area was officially designated in 1971 for some 18,000 persons under the Town Development Act, involving the transfer of homes and jobs from Greater London. The Government and the East Sussex County Council are both intending to secure the improvement of road and rail facilities to the town. The town's peripheral position in the South East Region is partly responsible for the fact that it is not as prosperous as some parts of London and the outer metropolitan area.

c) Inter-related local problems - tourism, town expansion and unemployment

Concern in Hastings with retirement and unemployment problems, can be observed from the town's Development Plans of 1955[2] and from its reviews in

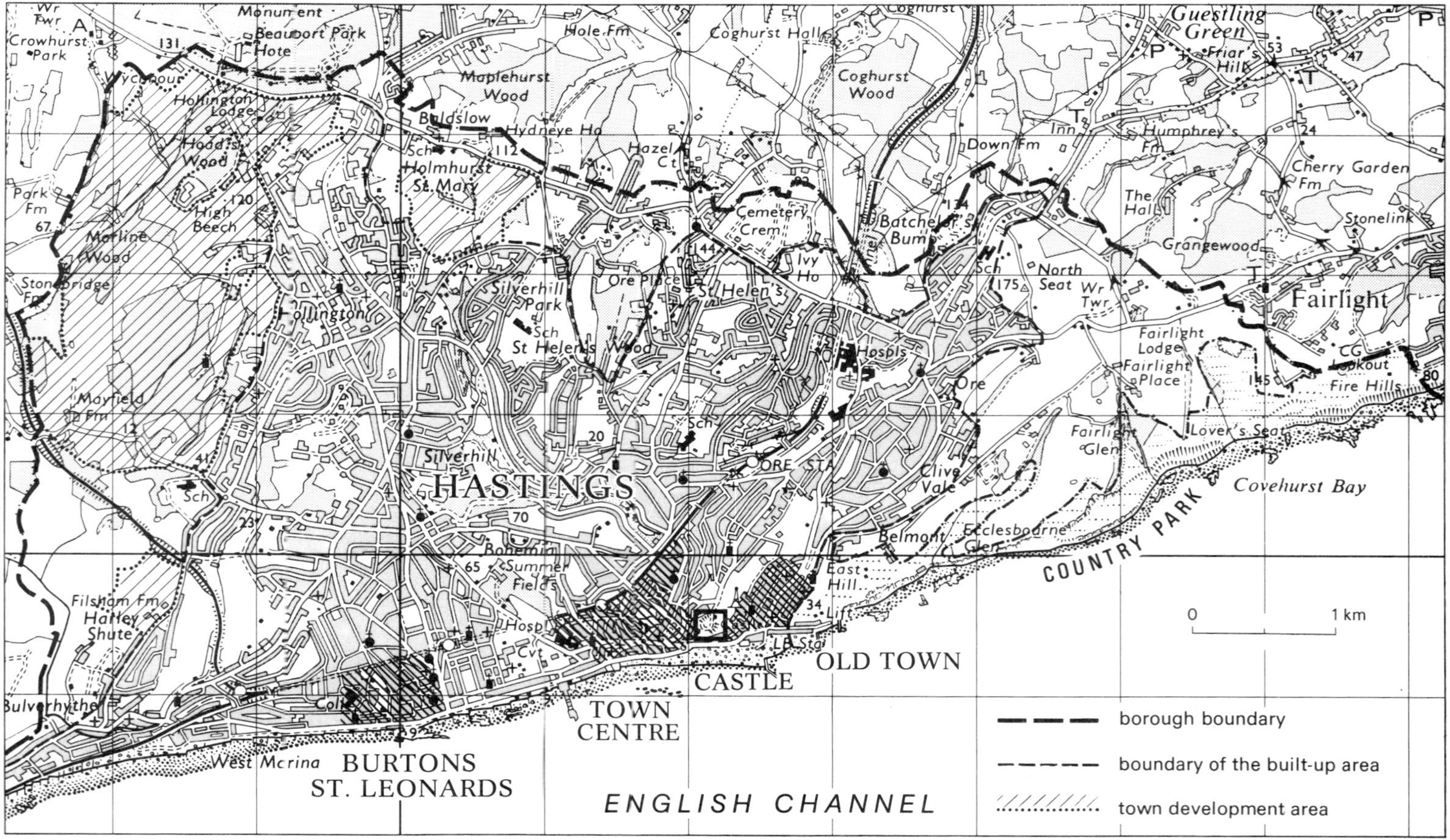

Abb. 1: Town development area

1965 and 1971 as well as an article published by the Town Planning Institute in 1966.[3] The Hastings Council has aimed at the protection and enhancement of the town as a holiday resort and residential town. It took positive steps in the early sixties to secure additional employment by encouraging new employment to move to its own industrial estate as well as supporting the transfer of the Accounts Division of what is now the Department of the Environment to the town. These changes do not appear to have, so far, had any direct effect on the tourist industry.

The amended Development Plan for Hastings as approved by the Secretary of State for the Environment in 1971[4] stated that "The problem of social imbalance in the town of Hastings due to the high proportion of elderly people and the relative lack of suitable employment for young people has been the concern of the Local Planning Authority for many years." This lack of balance had its effect not only on the resources available for the provision of adequate social services but also upon the resources for the further development of the town as a holiday resort.

These problems may well have been accentuated by over-reliance on the seasonal tourist industry (as both an economic and employment base for the town) in the first half of this century. Relatively poor communications by road and rail to London during the period from 1900 to 1950 - together with limited alternative employment opportunities led to both a drift from the area and comparative stagnation which was reflected in an nearly static total population and a deteriorating age structure up to 1950.

These issues which bear a clear relationship to both geographical position of the town within the region and journey times and cost to London. The broadening of the town's employment base and the introduction of young families and new employment from London and elsewhere in the South East Region has both attendant risks and potential advantages for the local tourist industry.

On the one hand the additional 15-20,000 population of the town expansion scheme will generate more traffic and congestion. On the other hand there should be better all year round support for local entertainment and amenities which visiting summer tourists can also enjoy. A planned expansion scheme (with well distributed open spaces, sports complexes, protected woodlands and the retention of other natural features) is also a better proposition for visiting tourists than mundane urban sprawl with a bare minimum of amenities.

The level of male unemployment in January 1978 was about 11%. Young men tend to leave the town because of the lack of job opportunities and old ladies retire to the area, attracted by the sea and suitable accommodation. The amount of Guest House Accommodation which is available has been substantially reduced in the last twenty years although there has been a considerable growth in self-catering accommodation, particularly in relation to Caravan Sites on the periphery of the town. The economic issues are such that the climate for urban renewal and redevelopment is not always favourable.

The problem of urban decay in a medium sized town

Causes:

a) Obsolescence

Some of the problems associated with inner cities have been reviewed in several papers recently published in volume 3 of the I.B.G.'s "Transactions".

Urban decay in smaller towns is generally less extensive, but the investment and rate resources of a medium sized town are limited. The problems of obsolescence in the older small towns, where a large number of dwellings were built in the last century can be proportionately as difficult as those of the larger metropolitan areas. (For instance about 50 per cent of the 31,000 residential properties in Hastings and St. Leonards were built before 1900).

We could indulge in a learned discussion of the meaning of the term obsolescence. The word is used in relation to areas and properties which are old and passing into disuse. The local authority is often asked to solve the problems which are caused by neglect. Some problems date back to the days before the introduction of building bye-laws. The lack of basic facilities such as internal lavatories and bathrooms and the absence of sufficient rear open space for public health purposes are especially difficult to solve if the properties in question are cramped or in multiple occupation. Once roofs begin to leak, walls crumble and dry rot sets in; properties inevitably tend to become disused and the Public Health Authority is likely to impose closing orders. If sufficient obsolete or unfit properties exist in a given area then a Clearance Order may well be published.

The Planning Authority may have misgivings concerning the boundaries of the clearance areas which emerge from this process. Some additional properties are often needed to provide satisfactory sites for redevelopment purposes. A second category of "blighted" properties can be identified while proposals for compulsory purchase are examined by the appropriate Government Department. 672 houses have been demolished in Hastings since 1955 in connection with clearance procedures by the Public Health Authority. A further 447 additional properties were officially described as coming within areas of "obsolete development" by the local planning authority.[5]

The description "obsolete development" was in effect revealed in every land charge search when a property changed hands. It has, on occasions, led to potential purchasers looking elsewhere. It may well have depressed property values in these areas and it has certainly affected the availability of mortgages and to some extent grants for housing improvements. The "quality of life" inevitably tends to deteriorate over a long period before redevelopment begins.

The location of these areas does not conform to any consistent pattern. They are not confined to a declining ring around the town centre. Their distribution is related to the older areas of the town, but the town's growth had no coherent pattern in the last two centuries — apart from linear development along the coast before the advent of modern planning legislation.

b) Physical damage (war/accidental damage)

The town incurred some war damage between 1939-45. The number of properties which were demolished amounted to some 463 buildings. The explosion of a Gas Main during roadworks and other accidental damage mainly due to fire in recent years has resulted in the destruction of perhaps a dozen properties. The town is not highly prosperous and a number of cleared sites remain with plans approved but no development in progress. Advertisement signs and car parks are perhaps better than nothing but they in no way replace the homes, shops and hotels which were there before properties were seriously damaged or destroyed.

c) Blight due to road schemes etc.

Although the local authority cannot be blamed for accidental damage road schemes are a different matter. Hastings was a County Borough until 1974 but its right to approve major road proposals was removed with the re-organisation of local government. The new East Sussex County Council defined a "band of interest" in 1975 for a Town Centre Relief Road which directly affected some 314 properties. The County Council were accepting purchase notices within this "band of interest". The Borough Council questioned the extent of the road scheme and it was agreed in December last that the northern section of the road could not be justified on environmental grounds. The designation and consequential blight was removed and the Council's Estates Officer is now able to recommend approval to mortgages in appropriate cases.

d) Lack of investment in redevelopment

If the private investor or developer does not come forward to deal with the redevelopment of the older privately owned properties in a town, then the quality of life may suffer despite all the efforts of a local authority to improve properties through housing improvement schemes. Problems are more likely to arise in a town with extensive areas of old properties and considerable areas of undeveloped sites which are allocated for building purposes in the Approved Town Map.

The more densely populated areas are less attractive to the entrepreneur. The older properties with large gardens may be replaced by blocks of flats at higher densities which are often let for retirement, but I am not certain that the visual and architectural quality of the new buildings always matches the planner's hopes when dealing with applications for sites of this kind in urban areas.

The case for and against restoration in relation to:

a) Ancient Monuments

The term "Ancient Monuments" in English legislation[6] is a special category which excludes churches, caves and excavations. These ancient monuments are sometimes owned by the Department of the Environment. Those which are in local authority or private ownership are subject to special statutory protection but Government grants are not necessarily available for their repair and maintenance. Hastings contains seven scheduled ancient monuments of which four are wholly or partly in the Borough Council's ownership.

It may be thought that the case for the restoration of ancient monuments is not a matter for argument. The relevant issues can be highly complex. I have only time to deal with one example in relation to Hastings. Hastings Castle was built on a headland in the 11th Century.[7] Part of the Castle subsequently collapsed into the sea in the 13th century and although there is now no threat from the sea, the ruins are causing problems at the present time. While schemes for restoration of ancient monuments must be considered on their merits, the need to spend £18,000 this year in connection with the protection of Hastings Castle illustrates the scale of the problems which can arise. Complete restoration of the original structure would be both physically and financially impossible and would in any case only produce a picturesque sham from the remaining area of Castle ruins.

b) Individual buildings of special architectural interest

The distribution of buildings of architectural and historic interest has a clear relationship to the historic growth and development of the town which can be demonstrated from cartographic sources. Alterations to individual listed buildings require planning permission in Britain. These applications are examined by Conservation Officers and are generally handled with care and sensitivity. A town with 634 listed buildings of all types and a high proportion of occupied dwellings of special interest will inevitably possess some buildings which are at times neglected, although only 18 have been demolished since 1969.

c) Designated conservation areas

The term "conservation" was first used by Lord Holford in relation to areas of architectural and historic interest in the context of the Old Town at Hastings. He produced a skilled appreciation of the townscape and natural setting of the area some twelve years ago.[8] He stated in relation to "Preservation Policy" that:

"Every means should be pursued to ensure that this town, as a living community, is just as capable of adjusting itself to outside change, as in the past. The way in which we meet the challenge of new shopping techniques, of the motor car, and of the increasing demands of the holiday"season", will determine whether the Old Town becomes an untouchable antique, a decayed area, or a community that goes on growing into the twentieth century".

A second nationally outstanding conservation area is embodied in Burtons' St. Leonards which was designed by John and Decimus Burton in the last century.

d) The improvement and conversion of residential properties

A detailed paper on housing policy areas has been recently produced by Norman Dennis and published in the "I.B.G. Transactions". This paper covers the main criteria and issues concerning the clearance and improvement of residential areas.[9]

Urban renewal and redevelopment in the last twenty years:

a) Private sector — extent and rate of redevelopment

Local statistics for the period from 1966 to 1976 show considerable fluctuations in the rate of residential development:

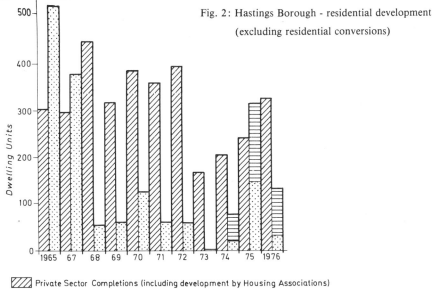

Fig. 2: Hastings Borough - residential development (excluding residential conversions)

▨ Private Sector Completions (including development by Housing Associations)
☰ Public Sector Completions by Greater London Council
⋯ Public Sector Completions by Hastings Borough Council

215

Private sector conversions which have transformed large properties into smaller units more suitable for the family size of today represent less than 10% of residential completions in the last few years.

A large number of the private sector completions have taken place on green field sites. Redevelopment and infilling accounts for roughly half the total of new private sector dwellings. Demolition of privately owned properties for private sector redevelopment represents a very small proportion of the town's 31,000 residential hereditaments which means that the process of renewal is not keeping pace with the ageing process which inevitably affects many of the older properties which were built in the last century.

b) Public sector intervention

The redevelopment of slum clearance areas

672 houses have been demolished by the local authority following clearance order procedures since 1955. The pace of local authority housing completions has reflected the need to both re-house the occupiers of many of the unfit properties as well as the need to make the best use of the 25 slum clearance areas which were left over from the clearance process. The financial implications of town's housing and investment programme in 1978[10] indicate that £ 800,000 of the allocation of new public sector housing schemes is devoted to green field sites. The town's slum clearance reaches its conclusion by 1981 while the municipal improvement of older properties is paralleled by homes loans and improvement grants at about £ 700,000 a year. The total housing investment programme allocation proposed in the Borough Council's Budget for the next four years varies from £ 2.42 million to £ 2.93 million.

Government and civic development schemes

The new Telephone Exchange in the town centre and an office block for the Property Services Agency replaced a cinema which was closed some years ago. Local Crown offices occupy the site of an old slaughter house which has perceptibly improved the quality of life around the site in question. Other schemes which are being studied include the redevelopment of cleared sites which had to be acquired by the local authority for shopping and hotel purposes while Civic offices have been established in the grounds of a former preparatory school. The possibility of using current powers under the Community Land Act are being actively explored by the local authority and redundant or obsolete premises which are in the hands of the Gas Board and the National Bus Company are being actively examined with a view to redevelopment of a fringe area on the edge of the town centre for some 9,290 sq. metres of new shopping development. Although these redevelopment schemes are significant, they do not provide a complete solution to the problems of urban renewal.

c) Environmental and functional implications

So far as townscape is concerned, the Borough Council has produced policies in relation to the height of new buildings which could otherwise be completely out of scale with sensitive areas containing older low rise buildings. The pressure for tall blocks of flats for Council housing such as were contained in the four 17 storey blocks which were built in St. Leonards in the 60's appears to have receded. The quality of life within tall blocks of flats has been considered elsewhere but their visual impact on the townscape varies from place to place and generalisations may be unwise.

Some urban geographers may be concerned with the uniformity that tends to arise with modern shopping development. The rectangular lines of so many schemes which are put before the local planning authorities must give rise to some misgivings and doubts that change is not always for the best.

Redevelopment of the older areas of the town clearly needs to be dealt with great care and sensitivity if the street scene is not to deteriorate. On the other hand, there are many modern buildings which represent a considerable advance on the decaying edifices which they have replaced. It is clearly easier to control the situation where the rate of change is gradual. If a local authority is faced with a flood of private sector applications, then less office time will be available for each application.

Conclusions

It is my view that the rate of renewal and the improvement in the quality of the environment depends on there being a sufficient level of economic activity within the sub-region and that the well being of peripheral areas and older towns in an otherwise prosperous region is often dependent on both the support of the local authority and the availability of investment from other areas.

Zusammenfassung

Probleme der Stadterneuerung und des Wiederaufbaus in mittelgroßen Städten

In dieser Arbeit wird sowohl Bezug auf die historische als auch die gegenwärtige Verflechtung des Seebades Hastings mit der umgebenden Region genommen. Es wird das Ausmaß betrachtet, in dem der gegenwärtige örtliche Beschäftigungsgrad abhängig ist (a) von Strukturveränderungen im Fremdenverkehr und (b) von der Schaffung neuer Arbeitsplätze durch neu in die Stadt ziehende Firmen. Die Entfernung von Hastings nach London ist ein Faktor, der zum wirtschaftlichen Klima der Stadt, die an und für sich nicht typisch für Südost-England ist, beiträgt.

Die städtischen Verfallserscheinungen und Überalterungsprobleme von Hastings, wo die Hälfte aller Grundstücke vor 1900 bebaut wurden, werden kurz abgehandelt. Den Abbrucharbeiten, die im Zuge örtlich begrenzter Sanierungen von Slumgebieten, bei der Beseitigung von Kriegsschäden und bei Straßenprojekten notwendig geworden waren, standen nicht in vollem Umfang Investitionen zum Wiederaufbau gegenüber, mit dem Ergebnis, daß es nun eine Anzahl geräumter Baugrundstücke gibt. Und dies hat dazu geführt, daß das Stadtbild als Ganzes beeinträchtigt wird. Das Ausmaß des von privater und öffentlicher Seite unternommenen Wiederaufbaus und der Beseitigung von Baulücken während der letzten zwanzig Jahre wird untersucht. Die Möglichkeit für neue Entwicklungen in den Randbereichen des Stadtzentrums werden beschrieben.

Die Altstadt von Hastings ist historisch bedeutsam. Die Restauration alter Baudenkmäler wie z.B. der Festung und der Schutz der Gebäude von besonderem architektonischen und historischen Interesse erhalten Priorität. Der Ausdruck "Denkmalschutz", der zuerst von Lord Holford im Zusammenhang mit der Altstadt von Hastings gebraucht wurde, wird inzwischen auf drei entsprechend gekennzeichnete Denkmalschutzgebiete angewendet — zwei von ihnen haben sogar außerordentliche nationale Bedeutung. Besondere Sorgfalt lassen daher die Kommunalbehörden bei der Prüfung von Planungsvorhaben zur Füllung von Baulücken und zur Substanzerneuerung hinsichtlich ihrer Tragweite für solche Stadtteile walten, die ausgesprochen attraktiv sowohl für die Besucher als auch die Anwohner sind.

Die Notwendigkeit zur Erhaltung der Lebensqualität des städtischen Wohnumfeldes wird als vorrangig angesehen, wenn die älteren Stadtviertel angemessen geschützt werden sollen. Die Stadterneuerung und die qualitative Verbesserung des Wohnumfeldes hängen davon ab, ob es sowohl ein ausreichendes Wirtschaftsleben als auch genügend praktische Unterstützung seitens der Kommunalbehörden am Rande der allgemein als wohlhabend geltenden Südostregion Englands gibt.

References

1. South East Joint Planning Team (1970): "Strategic plan for the South East", Appendix D
2. WADE, A.J.R. (1977-8): "A geographical analysis of the tourist industry of the Eastbourne, Hastings and Folkestone area", M. Phil. thesis, University of London, pp. 119-21
3. BAXTER, E.O. (1966): "Town Planning Institute Conference Handbook - Article, p. 95-100
4. Hastings Borough Council (1971): "Written statement" and "Explanatory Report", Development Plan Amendment 9
5. Hastings Borough Council (1965): "Written statement", Development Plan Amendment no. 6
6. Ancient Monument Act (1931), 21 and 22, Geo 5 c 16, Section 15
7. MANWARING BAINES, J. (1963): "Historic Hastings", pp. 3-4
8. Lord HOLFORD and HASKELL, R.A. (1966): "The old town, Hastings", A report on its conservation and development, publ. by Hastings Borough Council
9. DENNIS, N. (1978): "Housing policy areas: criteria and indicators in principle and practice", I.B.G. Transactions, New Series 3, 1, pp. 2-22
10. CARRIER, R. (1978): "Hastings budget 1978-79", pp. 163-64

Note: This paper does not necessarily represent the views of the Hastings Borough Council

LEISURE AS A TOOL FOR SOCIAL DEVELOPMENT IN OIL-AFFECTED AREAS OF THE HIGHLANDS AND ISLANDS OF SCOTLAND

with 3 figures and 2 tables

BRIAN DUFFIELD

The discovery of oil and gas under the North Sea has proved to be the most important single event in Scotland's post-war economic history and its profound effects upon the economic life of the nation were topics of discussion and debate long before oil began to flow. Assessments of the implications for the national economy and for the communities affected by all stages of the cycle of North Sea oil developments, viz., exploration, manufacturing, construction and production are continuing, but for those communities in the Highlands and Islands that have long been isolated from the mainstream of national economic development, the impact of oil-related developments has proved to be profound, not only for the local and regional economies but also for the very fabric of social, cultural and community life.

It was concern for these factors and others which led the HIDB and the Commission of the European Communities (EEC) to commission a research project in 1975 to 'provide information and ideas on provision for recreation in the Highlands and Islands ... as a basis for urgent action in oil-affected areas'. This paper attempts to describe briefly the framework of this research and the conclusions of the study as to the contribution leisure planners and providers can make to social and community development.

The areas covered in the study were those where oil-related developments had been accompanied by substantial immigration. Six such areas were defined:

a) Shetland
b) Orkney
c) Lewis
d) Lochcarron
e) Moray Firth
f) South Argyll

This paper draws from experience in the Moray Firth to illustrate the work undertaken and the major conclusions of the study. The main elements of the methodology adopted are described briefly, but a more detailed presentation of the research, and the findings for the indicidual study areas are set out in the various research reports relating to the study.[1)]

A schema for leisure planning

A simplistic approach to the problems of leisure planning, particularly in areas affected by oil-related developments, would be inappropriate and, in defining alternative policies, it must be explicitly recognised that the communities are very diverse, not only in their historical and cultural development and geographical setting, but also in their ability to accommodate change and in the nature of the economic developments that affect them.

Leisure is but one facet of these problems of change and cannot be isolated from the general process. Accordingly, a procedure for evaluation was adopted that allowed the changing patterns of need for leisure and recreation to be analysed as part of the social and economic development of the study areas.

While each study area is unique in its culture, geography and economic history and in respect of the character of oil-related development, it is possible to isolate certain key factors that are likely to condition the processes of change in each locality and so permit a consistent evaluation to be made. A schema was therefore devised for this purpose, having as its objective the definition of key areas and issues relating to provision for leisure and recreation.

This schema is no more than a general methodology for approaching the problems of formulating plans for leisure provision in areas affected by oil-related industry. It is presented, not as a mechanistic device, but as a guide to a thought process of evaluation and analysis, to be modified where individual circumstances and conditions demand and to be subject at all times to the discipline of personal knowledge and field experience.

The schema has four key axes and is presented in figure 1.

A. 'The nature of the area' is concerned with the various elements in the economic and social development of the study areas, such as traditional patterns of work, that condition responses to leisure and recreational provision.

B. 'The impact of oil-related industry' deals with the general characteristics of oil-related developments and their effect on the local communities in the study areas. The oil-related industries are characterised by distinct phases, each with its own impact. The expected duration of industrial development itself will similarly condition the response of employers and employees in their choice of policies for recruitment, accommodation and assimilation within the wider community.

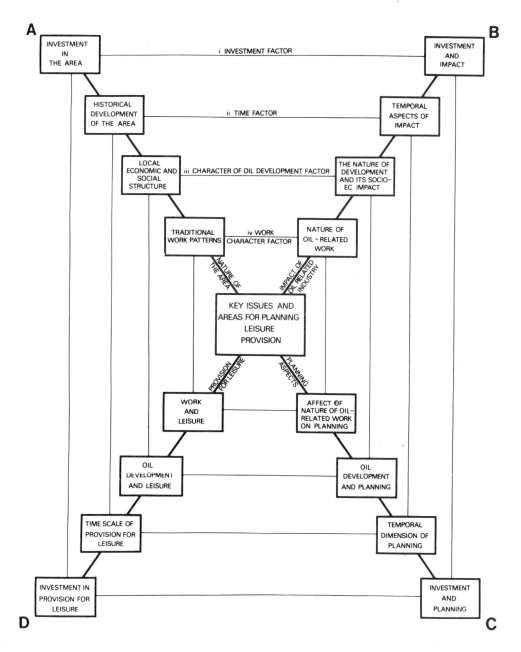

Fig. 1: Oil affected areas -
A schema for defining key areas and issues for leisure and recreation provision

C. 'Aspects of planning' related to the local area are concerned with the framework of decision-making at an international, national, regional and district scale, by examining the relationship between planning and oil-related development. The time factor in planning can also be of fundamental importance for leisure provision, with the scheduling of development not only affecting the timetabling of the construction of social and recreational facilities but also being responsible for related human problems that often occur when provision of such social facilities lags behind industrial and residential development. Such difficulties are particularly acute in times of economic stringency and rapid industrial development, both of which are occurring simultaneously in the study areas. In these circumstances the timing of provision can be as important as the nature of the facilities themselves.

D. 'Provision for leisure' is concerned with the contrasting perceptions of leisure in the different communities and deals with the investment and timescales involved in provision and the relationships between oil developments, work and leisure.

Each of the key axes is evaluated against four factors that will themselves affect the resolution of the forces being studied:

i) An investment factor.
ii) A time factor.
iii) A character of oil development factor.
iV) A character of work factor.

The fact that the areas of enquiry along all the axes are interdependent is the key to the whole framework of evaluation, which was intended to emphasise the impossibility of abstracting questions relating to recreation and leisure from the physical, spatial, social, economic and cultural environment within which they are set.

What is required is an understanding of the 'leisure system' which characterises community life within a specific area. Such a system will not only contain the sum of the individual characteristics of the inhabitants of the area studied, but will also reflect the institutional framework, social institutions and collective values that predominate within it, as well as the external pressures to which the society will be subject. Such an approach is particularly desirable for oil-affected areas where externally-induced processes of rapid social and economic change are under way.

The relevance of this holistic framework is best illustrated with respect to a particular area, and the rest of this paper largely relates to one of the six areas studied, namely, the Moray Firth.

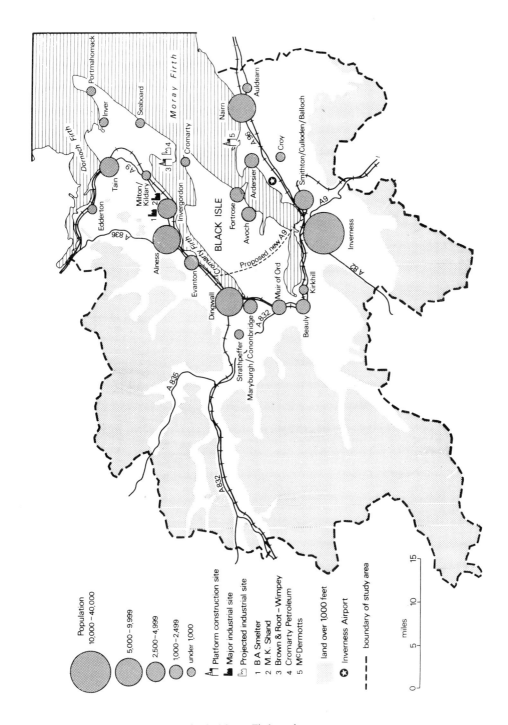

Fig. 2: Moray Firth study area

The Moray Firth

The Moray Firth study area covers an extensive zone around the oil-related developments on the Cromarty and Moray firths (figure 2). This area includes the coastal fringe of the Highlands, a rich coastal plain where efficient arable farming is practised and where most of the industrial developments have taken place, while to the west lies a mountainous and sparsely-populated area, where livestock rearing and forestry are the most important activities. The urban settlements are dominated by Inverness, which, by virtue of its position as the natural centre of the region, has also become the administrative and commercial capital. The other major settlements are Dingwall, Nairn, Tain, Invergordon and Alness. One noteworthy feature of the area has been the strong sense of community that exists within the small urban settlements, in contrast to the area as a whole, which still lacks a developed sense of regional identity.

The industrialisation of the Moray Firth area began with the growth of estate industry which drew from the new pool of labour made available by the Clearances, while the coming of the Highland Railway provided the most dramatic impetus to the development of the emerging urban structure. Inverness' period of most rapid expansion was between 1861 and 1881 after the arrival of the railway, and in the later years of the 19th century heavy industry developed in the town, further confirming its economic importance and contributing to its growth. Inverness and the other developing urban centres became the foci for migration from the rural areas, where unemployment was persistent and chronic; others moved further afield and emigration to the south or abroad persisted throughout the 19th century and has continued almost to the present day.

Industrialisation continued in the 20th century, although at a faltering pace, and the fortunes of the individual settlements varied.

As a whole, the area continued to be characterised by unemployment and emigration, and plagued by the economic uncertainties brought about by a semi-industrialised regional economy, with a relatively incoherent mix of urban and rural communities. Individual settlements retained a strong local character and identity without the clear development of an urban hierarchy and, while some towns benefitted from the emergence of service functions, there remained a strong contrast between an urban and increasingly industrialised society and the community-oriented pattern of life in the rural areas.

The late 1960s, however, saw the deliberate injection into the region of a new dynamic of industial development. Since the establishment of the Highlands & Islands Development Board in 1965 the Moray Firth region has been promoted as a 'growth area'. The plan was based on the theory that the eventual growth of the region would centre around large-scale, capital-intensive, industrial development in the vicinity of Invergordon, and it foresaw an eventual future population of between 250,000 and 300,000 centred at the industrial development at Invergordon and with further regional development at Inverness. The strategy depended on the construction of a fast route, following approximately the line of the present A9 trunk road, with all new industrial developments related to this route and major growth in the service sector continuing to be concentrated in Inverness itself.

A partial realisation of this policy came in 1967 with the decision by British Aluminium to site their new smelter at Invergordon. Construction of the smelter began quickly and in the same year that it was opened (1971) planning permission was granted for a rig construction yard at Nigg. Since then, the growth of the Moray Firth area has been closely connected with that of oil-related industry.

The economic situation in the area changed virtually overnight. Emigration came to a halt and immigration of workers for the new industries took its place. Problems associated with the uncertain transition to an industrial society that had prevailed in the region up until the 1960s were now replaced by new challenges and problems associated with rapid industrialisation, the new marked growth of urban settlements and accompanying social change.

The impact of oil-related industry in the early 1970s has played its part in the acceleration of population growth, particularly in the North Moray Firth (table 1). Over this period (1971-76) the population in the Moray Firth was among the fastest growing in the United Kingdom. Immigration was the major factor in growth, notably in the North Moray Firth which has received the greater number of oil-related firms and where the original base population was smaller. In absolute terms, growth resulting from immigration has been greater in the South Moray Firth where influences other than oil-related development have been at work in a more diversified economy.

Table 1: The development of the Moray Firth area's population

	1971	1976	1981	Net Change	Net Migration
Ross & Cromarty District	35,120	45,400	47,600	+2,370	+10,110
Inverness District	49,330	55,050	57,500	+2,080	+ 6,090
Nairn District	8,330	9,700	9,750	+ 95	+ 1,325
Highland Region	171,800	190,000	195,350	+5,510	+17,960

Source: Highland Regional Council, 1976

At present there is a variety of oil-related firms in the region, employing a total of about 6,000 people, most of whom work in manufacturing activities, although the figure fluctuates with the demand for labour in the platform construction and pipe coating yards.

The changes resulting from these developments have, however, not merely been quantitative and their implications for leisure and society in the Moray Firth are discussed below.

Oil, leisure, and society

Patterns of social life and the associated character of leisure and recreation have been subject to rapid change which in many ways was directly related to the economic stimulus of industrial development associated with both oil and other industry. An assessment of the contemporary needs of the inhabitants of the Moray Firth area for recreation and leisure can no more be divorced from an appreciation of the processes of change resulting from the economic and social development in the area than can the long-term economic prospects of the area themselves be divorced from the national pattern of oil-related developments.

An understanding of the process of change is as crucial as an understanding of the character of the communities themselves.

There have been considerable social developments in the Moray Firth area in the recent past, arising from the rapid industrialisation of the area. Any period of economic development inevitably brings deep social change, some advantageous in the improved material conditions of sections of the population and in the revitalisation of the area and some disadvantageous in the social dislocation of both local residents and newcomers.

The improved material conditions of sections of the population are evident from improvement of housing conditions, increased car ownership and the acquisition of a range of consumer goods which characterise many of the households in the Moray Firth area. For many people, the growing industrialisation of the area will mean increased disposable income, capable of supporting a growing interest in the range of urban-based leisure activities.

The polarisation of the local social structure which has occurred accentuates the differences between those groups being disadvantaged by, and those benefitting from the economic developments. Along with the farmers, the land-owners have tended to be the most disadvantaged by the developments and have provided the impetus for two pressure groups: 'The Easter Ross Land Use Committee' and the 'Cromarty Refinery Opposition Workers', who have opposed 'indiscriminate and unsuitable development' of industry, particularly on good quality arable land.

In this changing situation middle-class professional and business groups have emerged as leaders at the local community level. There has also been the emergence of a stronger working-class interest in support of development, expressed most recently in the pro-development group: 'Support Cromarty Oil Terminal'.

The growth of trade unionism in the area and the establishment of local trades councils bear witness to the emergence of social strata that reflect the industrial and economic development in the area.

The social dislocation experienced by both locals and newcomers alike derive from the long working day on the new sites, the lack of infrastructure and the simple social pressures that result from rapid social change. Social dislocation occurs under a number of heads, including welfare problems, disruption of local services, and bureaucratic and other forms of alienation; there is, for example, evidence that welfare problems are on the increase, while reports from the local police indicate an increase in crime.

The scale of social change in the Moray Firth area is thus greater than in the more traditional study areas where oil developments are taking place on a major scale. Stylised Highland folklore is replacing the vestiges of traditional culture and, in the circumstances, those committed to a more traditional life-style are inevitably isolated. What would have been in the past regular traditional dances are now reserved for more organised fetes and the local identity of some of the villages has been swamped by rapid change.

Patterns of leisure and recreation have not been unaffected by these changes and it is appropriate to consider the changing character of leisure in the Moray Firth as a consequence of the economic growth and industrialisation now taking place.

The mix of pre-industrial and industrial society is very complex and no simple characterisation can be made by reference to either complete industrial communities, such as exist in Central Scotland, nor to complete pre-industrial communities such as are found in the more remote parts of the Highlands and Islands. In a period of stability these contrasting social forces co-exist, as they have done in the Moray Firth area protected by an incoherent regional structure. However, when the processes of change are accelerated, as they have been during the past decade by a deliberate policy of encouraging economic growth, it is inevitable that society will slowly but inextricably reflect the nature of the dominant social force. In the Moray Firth in the 1970s that dominant social force has become industrialisation, and it is not therefore surprising to find that the features of pre-industrial society are increasingly identifiable as survivals of a past age, continually being modified by the dominant pattern of present-day life.

The leisure of industrialised societies is, first of all, something quite separate from work and it was the very nature of industrialisation that established this character of leisure. As T. BURNS has noted 'it is only when work came to be done in a special place, at a special time and under special conditions that leisure came to be demanded as a right'.[2] The leisure of communities in industrialised societies inevitably reflects the organisation of work, and leisure itself becomes subject to a whole range of constraints. This situation contrasts with the pattern prevailing in pre-industrial society where work and leisure were integrated and where the maintenance of face-to-face relationships in communities was essential to a social organisation that was related to the subsistence of individuals and families. In such societies the segregation of leisure from other aspects of social and economic life had no meaning, as all these factors were intertwined in the patterns of culture of a society whose very existence depended upon these inter-relationships and on inter-personal co-existence. In an industrial society, these motive forces disappear and, almost as a mirror image, leisure emerges, subject to the same rigid constraints as the work place. Leisure often seems a 'vacuum', to be filled by leisure and recreational activity, which is often opposed to and seen as compensation for the rigours of working life — a pattern which is accompanied by the decline of community social inter-relationships based on a common economic and community experience.

A further aspect is the changing nature of work that has taken place in the area. Not only has there been the growing dominance of industrial work patterns but these have often been those associated with 'boom' industrial developments where extreme cyclical patterns of employment, coupled with extended working hours, contrast with periods of lay-off and the periodic recession associated with oil-related industry, particularly in the North Moray Firth. Shift work and non-working hours have an inevitable effect on social life in general and on leisure life in particular and, throughout the field work undertaken in the area, the constant comment was that there was greater prosperity but less leisure time available.

Evidence confirms the growing dominance of compensatory leisure activities in the Moray Firth region. The survivals of leisure patterns of the 'pre-industrial' type are found outwith the major settlements and owe their preservation to the small scale of communities, both urban and rural, and their relative isolation, compounded by the lack of infrastructural development. While the situation varies from area to area and no grand generalisation can be made that would be relevant to all the communities in the region, it is clear that the processes of industrialisation and urbanisation will tend to accelerate these trends. The future will inevitably see the emergence of both old and newly-created urban communities which will become increasingly industrial in social character, if not in the provision of leisure facilities.

However, although the importance of the changes in individual settlements in the Moray Firth area must be recognised, it must also be acknowledged that the oil-related developments and other economic changes are likely to have an effect on the overall settlement structure.

Although in the past the functioning of settlements was hindered by infrastructural weaknesses in the Moray Firth area, a long-established hierarchical structure of settlements was evident. The area was dominated by three settlements. Inverness, the regional 'capital', had in 1971 some 40,000 people living within 8 kilometres of the town, and no other urban centre challenged its dominance within the area as a whole. Dingwall and Nairn, the 'district' capitals of the North and South Moray Firth areas respectively, had some 10,700 and 10,600 people within the same radius and exercised a similar dominance in their respective districts. A series of third-order settlements commanded populations of between 4,000 and 6,000 people within the 8 kilometre range (table 2). It seems likely, however, that the building of the smelter and the coming of the oil-related developments and associated economic changes will not only lead to a significant increase in population over the decade 1971-81 but also disturb the existing relationships between the settlements in the urban hierarchy. Some of these changes are quantified in table 2, but figure 3 allows a more rapid assimilation of the structural changes that could occur.

Table 2: Moray Firth - population pressure on oil-affected communities, 1971-81

	Resident population within specific distance					
	8 km			16 km		
	1971	Projected 1981	% Change	1971	Projected 1981	% Change
Inverness	40,220	44,770	11.3	52,380	57,250	9.3
Dingwall	10,740	10,990	2.3	21,700	21,950	1.2
Tain	4,360	6,360	45.9	9,980	13,730	37.6
Invergordon	5,520	9,970	80.6	17,880	24,630	37.8
Alness	6,380	9,980	56.4	17,830	22,820	25.0
Evanton	6,370	9,370	47.1	19,320	23,620	22.3
Milton/Kildary	2,810	4,260	51.6	16,830	23,580	40.1
Seaboard villages	2,420	2,720	12.4	7,530	10,680	41.8
Nairn	10,590	11,340	7.1	23,500	24,970	6.2
Culloden/Smithton/Balloch	34,610	39,300	13.6	49,820	54,690	9.8
Ardersier	5,520	6,520	18.1	48,360	53,480	10.6

Source: Office of Population Censuses and Surveys and TRRU estimates.

Fig. 3: Moray Firth - population distribution 1971-81

Coping with the impact

Faced with this process of industrialisation that has severely challenged their ability to respond effectively, the local authorities have inevitably concentrated their attention on coping with this development and on providing the necessary housing. When a growth strategy for the Moray Firth was first being formulated, it was fair to say that both local and national government were moving towards dustries, the local authorities had to deal with a population explosion. The industrial expansion, more rapid than had been initially envisaged, and the resulting the aluminium smelter at Invergordon and the rapid growth of the oil-related industries, the local authorities had to deal with a population explosion. The industrial expansion, more rapid than had been initially envisaged, and the resulting housing crisis monopolised their attention. The scale of this development is indicated by the fact that the housing stock in the Inner Moray Firth area increased by 25 per cent between 1971 and 1976. Provision for leisure and community needs inevitably played a very small part in the authorities' response to this crisis. The rapidly expanding communities have thus found themselves with an inadequate social infra-structure.

As the pace of development now slackens and anxious assessments are made of prospects for further economic development and the consolidation of existing industrial investments, it is clear that the Regional and District authorities are faced with a situation of both qualitative and quantitative changes in the leisure needs of the population, particularly in the expanding communities.

The processes of industrialisation and urbanisation impinge on the social as well as the economic life of the affected communities. The 'Leisure System' in the Moray Firth area reflects these changes, with the traditional pattern of informally-organised and community-based recreation being replaced by the more formal patterns of leisure and recreation that characterise modern industrialised societies. Such changes would have been inevitable in any evolving urban society, but they have been accelerated in the Moray Firth area not only by the rapidity of the growth of the communities, but also by the immigration of incomers with interest and aspirations that are attuned to the industrial societies from which they come. This process has been further exacerbated by the fact that these migrants have been drawn largely from the younger age groups which, as the survey evidence has demonstrated, have the most strongly-developed levels of interest in recreational activities, particularly those of a formal kind. It is this mismatch of these newly emerging needs and the historical legacy of pre-existing leisure facilities that constitutes the challenge to leisure planners in the area. Such deficiencies may seem to be simply an inevitable, if undesirable, consequence of rapid change, particularly in a period of general economic stringency; but it can be asserted that 'it is precisely in periods of rapid change that leisure planning must be accepted as a development tool'. Such a view is all the more relevant in the Moray Firth where the future prospects are so uncertain.

However geographically, economically and socially isolated the Moray Firth and other oil-affected areas in the Highlands and Islands may have been in the past, they are now at the frontier of economic development. As a result, these peripheral and generally underprivileged societies, with distinctive cultures that have long been challenged at a distance by the forces of a modern industrialised economy, have suddenly experienced rapid social change that has been imposed from outside; for these changes are the result of decisions by government and by large, often multi-national corporations. At the same time, there is no uncertainty that any benefits that they might bring to offset the obvious disruptions of existing community life will last sufficiently long to compensate for the disruption.

In these circumstances, provision for leisure and recreation would not merely serve as a means of improving the 'quality of life' of both new and long-established residents (desirable though that general objective might be), but would also help secure a range of social objectives that is essential to the healthy development of the emerging communities and a necessary adjunct to economic change. Leisure and recreation are effective tools for easing the transition from one social system to another that results from industrial development; they can aid the assimilation and integration of incomers into the existing communities and help them to adjust to the prevailing patterns of social life; they can sustain the needs of old-established residents who depend upon a more traditional 'pattern' of life; and they can fulfil the newly-generated aspirations of communities that are undergoing urbanisation.

Thus it becomes clear that provision for leisure ceases to be merely another 'supportive' social service and becomes a 'developmental' tool, helping to form, extend and develop communities through the processes of social activity, just as, in the same way, it satisfies these needs for the individual himself. The role of social provision in the context of rapidly-expanding communities is clearly identified in the Cullingworth Report[3] which states that' ...the scale and pace of development in expanding towns, coupled with the abnormal age structure, make it far less easy for deficiencies to be accepted there than in communities which are growing more slowly. *The desirable, in fact, becomes the necessary'*. (Author's emphasis).

The same report (p. 52) cogently expresses the dilemma facing leisure planners and providers in observing that: 'social issues rarely raise the same articulate expression of views as lack of sufficient houses or a temporary glut of empty houses. Few social standards are as clear as the worker's need for a job and a family's need for a house'.

Such an awareness is all the more acute in a period when public expenditure throughout the United Kingdom is being severely restrained and when, as recently as June 1976, the Scottish Office has identified expenditure on leisure and recreation as a prime target for cutbacks in local authority spending.[4] This paper again turns to the Cullingworth Report and accepts its conclusion (p. 89): 'that to build houses without parallel provision of community facilities and amenities will result in the unnecessary creation of social problems. This short-term saving in local authority expenditure may well turn out to be a false economy. What is saved, and more, may have to be spent by the personal social services in the rescue of families in distress'.

Subject Plans in particular can be used to ensure a more effective consideration of the social needs of communities in general and of leisure needs in particular. Adopting a proposal first outlined in the Cullingworth Report relating to social provision in the context of rapidly-expanding communities, it can be concluded that, alongside any physical plan for the development of oil-affected communities, there should be a Social Development Plan and an accompanying programme of provision relating to the physical expansion of the settlements concerned.

Such a Plan would not, of course, be confined to an identification of recreational needs but would embrace other aspects of social provision, particularly programmes for education, health and social welfare. The aim would be to ensure that, even under the pressure of rapid change, community facilities, (particularly those for leisure provision) would keep in step with the physical expansion, and hence the growing needs, of oil-affected communities.

Such Social Development Plans and other more particular policies related to leisure and recreation would begin to provide practical validation of KAPLAN's dictum that '...ultimately a theory of leisure can be little less than a theory of man and a theory of the emerging culture'.[5]

Zusammenfassung

Freizeit als ein Mittel zur Verbesserung der Sozialstruktur in den von der Erdölförderung betroffenen Gebieten des Hochlandes und der Inseln Schottlands

Der Verfasser untersucht die Ergebnisse und Schlußfolgerungen einer Studie zur Sozialstruktur nach Entstehen der von der Erdölförderung abhängigen Industrien auf dem Hochland und den Inseln Schottlands, gestützt auf Erfahrungen im Moray Firth Gebiet.

Ein Schema zur Freizeitplanung

Es wird ein Schema zur Freizeitplanung entwickelt, das der Vielgestaltigkeit der Gemeinden auf dem Hochland und den Inseln Schottlands Rechnung trägt. Diese Vielgestaltigkeit der Gemeinden ist in ihrer historischen und kulturellen Entwicklung, ihrer geographischen Lage und ihrer Aufgeschlossenheit Strukturveränderungen gegenüber begründet. Das Schema wurde entworfen, um bestimmte Schlüsselfaktoren zu isolieren, von denen man mit großer Wahrscheinlichkeit annahm, daß sie die Umwandlungsprozesse an jedem Ort mitbedingen würden.

Das Schema unfaßt vier Ausgangsachsen:

    a) die Gebietsstruktur
    b) der Einfluß der vom Erdölgeschäft abhängigen Industrien
    c) Planungsaspekte
    d) Versorgung mit Freizeitmöglichkeiten

Jede Ausgangsachse wurde einer Bewertung nach vier Faktoren unterworfen, die selbst die Auflösung der hier untersuchten Kräfte beeinflussen:

    1. ein Investitionsfaktor
    2. ein Zeitfaktor
    3. ein Faktor zur spezifischen Kennzeichnung der Entwicklung der Erdölindustrie
    4. ein Faktor der Arbeitsverhältnisse

Die Tatsache, daß die Untersuchungsbereiche entlang aller Achsen wechselseitig abhängig sind, ist der Schlüssel zum gesamten Bewertungsrahmen, der die Unmöglichkeit der Abstraktion von Erholung und Freizeit betreffenden Fragen aus der physischen, räumlichen, sozialen, wirtschaftlichen und kulturellen Umgebung betonen soll. Was gefordert wird, ist das Verständnis für das "Freizeitsystem", das das Gemeinschaftsleben innerhalb eines spezifischen Gebietes charakterisiert. Ein solches System enthält nicht nur die Summe der individuellen Eigenschaften der Einwohner im Untersuchungsgebiet, sondern spiegelt auch das institutionelle Grundgerüst, die sozialen Institutionen und kollektiven Werte wider, die in ihm vorherrschen, sowie die äußerlichen Zwänge, denen diese Gesellschaft unterworfen ist. Ein solcher Ansatz ist besonders wünschenswert für die vom Erdölgeschäft betroffenen Gebiete, wo extern angeregte Prozesse eines beschleunigten sozialen und wirtschaftlichen Wandels schon angelaufen sind.

Die Relevanz dieses holistischen Schemas wurde am Beispiel des Moray Firth veranschaulicht.

Der Moray Firth

Das Moray Firth-Untersuchungsgebiet umfaßt eine weitgestreckte Zone auf dem östlichen schottischen Festland rund um die Moray und Cromarty Firths. Das Gebiet schließt die "Hauptstadt der Inseln", Inverness, mit einer Bevölkerung von 40.000 und einer Reihe anderer kleiner städtischer Zentren mit ein, z.B. Dingwall, Nairn, Tain, Invergordon und Alness, deren jedes durch einen stark ausgeprägten eigenen Gemeinschaftsgeist ausgezeichnet ist, im Gegensatz zum Gesamtraum, der noch immer ein wohlentwickeltes Gefühl für eine regionale Identität vermissen läßt.

In kultureller Hinsicht ist der Moray Firth eine Übergangszone, die eine verwirrende Mischung von Merkmalen des Hochlandes und des Tieflandes aufweist. Seit der Einsetzung der Kommission für die Strukturentwicklung der Hochlande und Inseln (Highlands & Islands Development Board) 1965 wurde der Moray Firth als ein Industrieentwicklungsgebiet gefördert, und als sich in den frühen siebziger Jahren im Zuge der Erdölexploration davon abhängige Industrieunternehmen entwickelten, wurde der Industrialisierungs- und Verstädterungsprozeß dramatisch beschleunigt. Die Abwanderung hörte auf und wurde von einer Zuwanderung von Arbeitskräften für die neuen Industrien abgelöst.

Zur Zeit der Untersuchung (1976) gab es in der Region eine bunte Zusammenwürfelung von Firmen, die vom Erdölgeschäft abhingen und die insgesamt ungefähr 6 000 Leute beschäftigten. Von diesen arbeiteten die meisten in Betrieben des Sekundären Sektors, obwohl die Zahlen je nach Arbeitslage bei der Bohrplattformkonstruktion und in den Röhrenwerken schwanken. Trotz gewisser Vorschläge zur Errichtung einer Ölraffinerie, die im Gebiet um Nigg gebaut werden soll, bleiben die Aussichten für die Region ungewiß.

Der Stellenwert der Freizeit

Die rasche Bevölkerungszunahme in der Region während des Zeitraumes 1971 - 1975 hat eine erhöhte Nachfrage nach Freizeitangeboten aus einer breitgefächerten Palette von Freizeitinteressen verursacht; aber dieser Bedarf scheint zu großen Teilen nicht befriedigt worden zu sein. Es wurde die Schlußfolgerung gezogen, daß eine effektive Politik der Industrie- und Wohnbereichsentwicklung von einem angemessenen Programm zur Freizeitgestaltung begleitet sein muß. Unter diesen Umständen hört die Freizeit auf, nur irgendeine ergänzende soziale Dienstleistung unter vielen zu sein. Sie wird vielmehr ein Instrument zur Strukturentwicklung, das unter Einsatz sozialer Aktivitäten in ganz derselben Weise, Gemeinschaften zu gründen, auszuweiten und zu entwickeln hilft, wie es die Bedürfnisse eines jeden Menschen befriedigt.

References

1. Tourism & Recreation Research Unit (1976): "A research study into provision for recreation in the Highlands and Islands, Phase I - Areas affected by oil-related developments
   — Vol. A: Oil, leisure & society
   — Vol. B: Area studies & recommendations
   — Directory of leisure activities
   — Inventories provided for each of the six areas under study: Shetland, Orkney, Lewis, Moray Firth, Lochcarron and South Argyll
   — Summary report
2. SMITH, M.A., S.R. PARKER & C.S. SMITH, eds. (1973): "Leisure & society in Britain", London
3. Ministry of Housing & Local Government, Welsh Office (1967): "The needs of new communities (Cullingworth Report)", H.M.S.O. London
4. Scottish Development Department (1976): "Finance Circular no. 27, Scottish Office, 17th June
5. KAPLAN, M. (1975): "Leisure: theory & policy", London

PLANUNGSAUFGABEN UND DIE VERBESSERUNG
DER LEBENSQUALITÄT

— Zum Exkursionsprogramm des Symposiums "Planen und Lebensqualität" —

Mit 10 Bildern und 5 Karten, teilweise als Beilagen

GERHARD AYMANS, HANNS J. BUCHHOLZ und GÜNTER THIEME

Die für die Landesentwicklung zuständigen Behörden in Großbritannien wie in der Bundesrepublik Deutschland gehen bei der Erfassung räumlicher Lebensbedingungen insofern gleichartig vor, als sie sich trotz vieler Unterschiede im einzelnen beide eines Verfahrens bedienen, dessen Grundlagen im voraus festgelegte, untereinander nicht austauschbare, normierende Meßwerte (Arbeitslosenquote, Wanderungssalden usw.) sind. Dieses Verfahren folgt rechtlich aus dem Gleichheitsgrundsatz, kann man doch nur dann — wenn überhaupt — allen Regionen eines Landes gleiche E n t w i c k l u n g s m ö g l i c h k e i t e n bieten, wenn man zuvor ihre Entwicklungsz u s t ä n d e vergleichbar erfaßt und wenigstens insoweit vergleichbar gemacht hat. Dennoch wird häufig und mit guten Gründen bezweifelt, daß man die Wirklichkeit räumlicher Lebensbedingungen auf die angesprochene Art und Weise tatsächlich erfassen kann. Selbst die Verfasser des Raumordnungsberichts, die in der Bundesrepublik "die bei der räumlichen Entwicklung des Bundesgebietes zugrunde zu legenden Tatsachen"[1] darzulegen haben und hierbei auf die normierenden Meßwerte des Raumordnungsprogramms zurückgreifen, sind sich der Tatsache bewußt, daß mit ihrem Vorgehen zahlreiche Probleme inhaltlicher und methodischer Art verbunden sind.[2]

Eine Reihe der erwähnten Probleme sind in den Vorträgen und Erörterungen des Symposiums zur Sprache gekommen, so daß sie hier nicht erneut aufgegriffen werden müssen. Im Zusammenhang mit dem Exkursionsprogramm und dieses begründend sind jedoch noch einmal die geographischen Aspekte räumlicher Lebensbedingungen anzusprechen. Unter diesen Aspekten ergibt sich, daß man alle Verfahren, die räumliche Lebensbedingungen nur durch eine vergleichende Erhebung von Notwendigkeiten (ausreichende Zahl von Arbeitsplätzen, hinreichender Wohnraum, befriedigende Versorgungseinrichtungen usw.) zu erfassen suchen, als unzureichend ansehen muß, da allein schon fragwürdige Gebietszuschnitte die tatsächlichen Lebensbedingungen in einem Gebiet nach oben wie nach unten verfälschen können. Hinzu kommen die Verzerrungen, die sich aus der räumlichen Zuordnung der erhobenen Tatbestände zueinander ergeben können. Es ist durchaus denkbar und vielerorts auch festzustellen, daß bestimmte Mängel, etwa ein unterdurchschnittliches Pro-Kopf-Einkommen, durch andere Tatbestände, etwa durch einen hohen Anteil an privatem Wohneigentum und ein niedriges Mietpreisniveau, praktisch ausgeglichen werden. Im Falle der Bundesrepublik Deutschland erlauben die Rechtsvorschriften zur Erfassung räumlicher Lebensbedingungen es zwar nicht, positive und negative Erhebungsergebnisse der oben genannten Art gegeneinander abzuwägen, doch ändert das nichts an deren realer Existenz. Das bedeutet, daß man r a u m b e d i n g t e Mängel an Lebensqualität nur erkennen kann, wenn man sich mit konkreten Räumen auseinandersetzt und die Information über diese nicht auf ein halbes Dutzend vergleichbarer, durchweg ökonomischer Meßwerte zusammenschrumpfen läßt. Was weiß man beispielsweise schon von einem Versorgungszentrum, wenn man nur — und sei es noch so detailliert — die Zahl und die Branchengliederung seiner Geschäfte und Dienstleistungseinrichtungen kennt? Weiß man nicht, gerade im Hinblick auf die Lebensqualität eines derartigen Versorgungszentrums, wesentlich mehr, wenn man die räumliche Ordnung seiner Straßen, Plätze und Passagen begriffen hat, wenn man um die Gestaltung seiner Gebäude und Fassaden weiß sowie seine Grünanlagen, Brunnen und Ruhebänke kennt?

Diese und ähnliche Fragen stellen bedeutet nicht, daß eine auch meßbar bessere Versorgung in einer Stadt nicht zur Hebung der Lebensqualität in dieser Stadt beitragen kann. Diese und ähnliche Fragen stellen bedeutet vielmehr, daß die Lebensqualität beispielsweise einer Stadt oder eines alten Stadtkerns nicht nur wirtschaftliche, sondern auch außerwirtschaftliche, ästhetische, soziale und andere Dimensionen hat, die sich positiv oder negativ, jedenfalls aber konkret auf die Lebensqualität aller Räume auswirken. Diese Auffassung hat hinter den Exkursionen gestanden, die im zweiten Teil des Symposiums ins R u h r g e b i e t, ins M ä r k i s c h e S a u e r l a n d und an den N i e d e r r h e i n geführt haben. Die folgenden Ausführungen fassen unter Verzicht auf Einzelheiten wesentlich erscheinende, auf den Exkursionen angesprochene Merkmale der besuchten Regionen noch einmal kurz zusammen.

Anmerkungen

1) Der Bundesminister des Innern: Raumordnungsbericht 1972 der Bundesregierung. Bonn 1973, S. 11
2) ebenda, S. 12 ff.

Hanns J. Buchholz: Das Ruhrgebiet

Das R u h r g e b i e t ist seit 150 Jahren auf der Basis des Steinkohlenbergbaus und der zu Beginn des 19. Jahrhunderts in Deutschland einsetzenden Industrialisierung entstanden. Seine Strukturen sind geprägt
— von der Schnelligkeit der Gesamtentwicklung
— von den Ansprüchen der Großindustrie
— vom Mangel an vorausschauender Planung für den Gesamtraum und das Detail
— vom Fehlen bedeutsamer Zentren, die zu Kristallisationskernen der Entwicklung werden können und
— von der Großflächigkeit des intensiv-städtisch genutzten Raumes.

Als Ergebnis der Entwicklung gibt es heute
— ein ungeordnetes Flächennutzungsgefüge mit vielfältigen gegenseitigen negativen Beeinflussungen
— hohe ausgedehnte bauliche Verdichtung und entsprechend fehlende Freiräume
— komplexhafte Wohnbebauung mit größerer Orientierung auf Industrieanlagen als auf Stadtkerne im Sinne traditioneller innerstädtischer Systeme
— mangelnde Selbstdarstellung und Repräsentation des Bürgers und seiner Stadt im baulichen Gefüge und Aufriß besonders auch der Zentren.

H e r n e ist ein charakteristisches Beispiel dieser Entwicklung: In einem ländlich, von kleinen Bauernschaften geprägten Gebiet waren seit der Mitte des 19. Jahrhunderts (1856: Zeche Shamrock) mehrere Schachtanlagen abgeteuft worden. Sie bildeten eigene Wachstumskerne in bezug auf die Wohnbebauung (Zechenkolonien) und das Straßennetz; die Lage und Zuordnung der Bauernschaften blieb ohne Belang.

1847 wurde die erste Ferneisenbahnlinie (Köln — Minden) im Ruhrgebiet eröffnet. Um schwierige Geländeformen (besonders Steigungen) zu vermeiden und damit die Baukosten niedrig zu halten, hatte man eine Linienführung nördlich der Mittelgebirgsausläufer über Duisburg — Frintrop (Essen) — Gelsenkirchen — Wanne — Herne — Castrop — Dortmund gewählt. Daß Herne einen Bahnhof erhielt, ergab sich aus der Absicht, die Stadt Bochum an die Eisenbahnlinie anzuschließen. Insofern nannte man den Bahnhof "Herne-Bochum".

Aus der Verkehrsbeziehung zwischen Bochum und diesem (seinem) Bahnhof[1] erwuchs die Bedeutung der gegenwärtigen Hauptgeschäftsstraße (Bahnhofstraße) in Herne, die zugleich "Sammlerschiene"[2] für die seitlich abseits gelegenen Zechenstandorte und Bergarbeitersiedlungen wurde (Siehe Karte 1, Beilage). Die Bedeutung der Bauernschaft Herne als Gegenpol der Verbindungsachse zum Bahnhof "Herne-Bochum" dürfte außerordentlich gering gewesen sein.

Es entstand bis zur Jahrhundertwende eine — privat mit Wohn-Geschäftshäusern bebaute — schlauchartige, ca. 1.200 m lange Einkaufs- und Wohnstraße, die gleichzeitig auch Hauptverkehrsstraße von Bochum über Herne nach Recklinghausen (B 51) wurde.

Im Grunde handelte es sich um eine durchaus attraktive Straße; denn Herne war eine rasch wachsende Bergbaustadt, die in vielen Teilen die insgesamt doch recht kräftige wirtschaftliche Prosperität des Steinkohlenbergbaus erkennen ließ. Viele Geschäftsleute investierten in repräsentable Wohn-Geschäftshäuser, die im Stil der Gründerzeit bis hin zum Jugendstil reich dekoriert waren (Bild 1). Sieben Meter breite Bürgersteige auf jeder Seite und die Baumreihen am Straßenrand lassen ebenfalls eine gewisse Großzügigkeit dieser Stadt deutlich werden, die in ihrer Aufstiegsphase bis zum ersten Weltkrieg durchaus großstädtisch anmutende öffentliche Gebäude (Rathaus, Post, Amtsgericht) errichtete.

Die Zeit nach dem 1. Weltkrieg brachte Stagnation und Bedeutungsschwund nach Herne: Auch wenn man — u.a. im Rahmen von Arbeitsbeschaffungsprogrammen und aufgrund von Eingemeindungen von 1926/29 — am Ende der 20er Jahre noch weitere große Behördenbauten (Polizeiamt, Sparkasse) erstellte und bis 1931 die Fahrbahn der Bahnhofstraße auf 12 m verbreiterte (auf Kosten der Bürgersteige und Baumreihen), so machte sich doch nun die monostrukturelle Abhängigkeit dieser Stadt vom Steinkohlenbergbau (1928: 55,3 % aller Erwerbstätigen im Bergbau) negativ bemerkbar. Anders als in gemischtwirtschaftlichen Gemeinden ergaben sich beim konjunkturbedingten Rückgang der Beschäftigungszahlen des Bergbaus keine alternativen Erwerbsmöglichkeiten: im Mai 1932 lebten 44,9 % der Herner Bevölkerung von öffentlichen (staatlichen oder gemeindlichen) Unterstützungszahlungen! Öffentliche Investitionen zur Verbesserung der Stadtstruktur waren in dieser Situation nicht verfügbar, so daß Herne gegenüber der Zeit vor dem 1. Weltkrieg weithin unverändert blieb. Auch der 2. Weltkrieg hat das Zentrum von Herne nicht wesentlich beeinträchtigt. Die Tatsache, daß der Bereich der Bahnhofstraße in Herne unzerstört blieb, führte nach 1945 sogar zu einem kurzfristigen Anstieg der zentralörtlichen Bedeutung Hernes, weil die größeren Nachbarzentren Dortmund, Bochum, Essen und Gelsenkirchen sehr stark unter Bombardierungen gelitten hatten.

Der Wiederaufbau der genannten Nachbarstädte schuf relativ moderne, sowohl den wachsenden Verkehrsbedürfnissen als auch veränderten Kaufgewohnheiten entsprechende Kernbereiche, so daß Herne auch infolge dieser Entwicklung an Bedeutung verlor. Hinzu kam, daß die Hauptgeschäftsstraße in Herne aufgrund der enormen Motorisierung in den 50er Jahren am Individualverkehr förmlich erstickte: Orts- und Fernverkehr (es gab noch keine Autobahn A 43 Wuppertal — Recklinghausen), Straßenbahnen und Omnibusse brachten den

Bild 1: Die Bahnhofstraße in Herne vor dem Ersten Weltkrieg: Haupt- und Repräsentationsstraße

Bild 2: Die Bahnhofstraße in Herne um 1970: Hauptgeschäfts- und Hauptverkehrsstraße

Bild 3: Die Bahnhofstraße in Herne um 1978: Einkaufsstraße als Fußgängerbereich

Verkehrsfluß immer wieder zum Erliegen, für die Fußgänger ergaben sich häufig gefährliche Situationen, und die Anwohner waren ständig dem Verkehrslärm und den Abgasen ausgesetzt (Bild 2).

Tabelle 1: Beschäftigte in der Stadt Herne 1938 - 1970 im Bergbau

Jahr	Zahl der Beschäftigten	
1938	11.650	
1945	10.521	
1950	15.691	
1953	16.916	(Höchststand)
1955	15.994	
1960	9.390	
1965	4.667	
1970	3.127	

Quelle: Nach Unterlagen der Stadtverwaltung der Stadt Herne

Als dann seit dem Ende der 50er Jahre die Bergbaukrise im Ruhrgebiet erkannt wurde, die sich in besonders unangenehmer Weise in der Bergbaustadt Herne (1955 = 5 Zechen mit 25 Schächten; 4 % der Kohlenförderung des Ruhr-

Tabelle 2: Einwohner der Stadt Herne (Alt-Herne) 1939 - 1979

Jahr	Einwohner	Jahr	Einwohner
1939	94.649	1970	105.566
1946	97.324	1975	102.602
1950	111.591	1976	101.971
1955	116.477	1977	101.501
1960	115.304	1978	100.629
1965	109.148	1979	100.056

Quelle: Nach Unterlagen der Stadtverwaltung der Stadt Herne

gebietes) z.B. durch hohe Wanderungsverluste bemerkbar machte, sah man die Notwendigkeit zu grundsätzlichen Strukturwandlungen der Stadt.

Im Rahmen der Aufstellung eines Flächennutzungsplanes (1962) wurde ein 'Entwicklungsplan Stadtkern' erarbeitet und 1964 verabschiedet, der ganz besonders auf vier Ziele ausgerichtet war:

(1) Entfernung des Fahrverkehrs aus der Hauptgeschäftsstraße
(2) Brechung der Längsstruktur der Hauptgeschäftsstraße

(3) Bau eines Kulturzentrums mit Kulturhalle, Volkshochschule und Bibliothek
(4) Sanierung der Altwohnbebauung und der unzureichenden Gewerberäume und -flächen

Zur Realisierung dieser Ziele bedurfte man eines entsprechenden Bebauungsplanes (der ab 1965 von privaten Architekten erstellt wurde), der Finanzierungshilfe durch das Land Nordrhein-Westfalen (1969 Bewilligung der Förderungsmittel) und der Kooperation der betroffenen Bürger; denn man hatte sich das Prinzip gesetzt, keine Zwangsmaßnahmen (z.B. Enteignungen) anzuwenden.

Die Organisation der Durchführung wurde dreigeteilt:
— Die P l a n u n g liegt in den Händen der Gemeinde.
— Die B o d e n o r d n u n g (also Erwerb der Immobilien, Regulierung der Entschädigung, Neuordnung der Gesamtfläche und Vorbereitung zur Wiederbebauung) übernimmt als Treuhänderin die "Landesentwicklungsgesellschaft Nordrhein-Westfalen für Städtebau, Wohnungswesen und Agrarordnung" (LEG). Sie kann als nicht-behördliches Unternehmen nach wirtschaftlichen Gesichtspunkten — aber ohne wirtschaftliche Eigeninteressen — flexibler auf Probleme reagieren als eine Stadtverwaltung.
— D i e W i e d e r b e b a u u n g erfolgt durch private Bauherren bzw. Anlagegesellschaften.

Die Alteigentümer werden entweder direkt im sanierten Gebiet entschädigt (teilweise unmittelbar, z.T. über Immobilienfonds, durch die kapitalschwächere Betroffene zu Miteigentümern an Neubauten werden), oder sie erhalten Ersatz in anderen Stadtteilen; denn die Stadt Herne hat ihren gesamten Althausbesitz in das "Vermögen" der Treuhänderin eingebracht.

Die Möglichkeit, über Immobilienfonds Anteile am sanierten Stadtzentrum zu erhalten, steht auch allen betroffenen Nicht-Eigentümern offen.

Das Gesamtverfahren ist noch keineswegs abgeschlossen, doch wesentliche Planungsziele hat man z.T. schon realisiert: Die Bahnhofstraße in Herne ist zu einer Fußgängerzone geworden (Bild 3). Der Kraftfahrzeugverkehr wird tangential am Kernbereich vorbeigeleitet, wobei rückwärtige Stichstraßen die Belieferung besonders der Gewerbebetriebe ermöglichen (Karte 2). Die bisher noch ebenfalls seitlich umgeleitete Straßenbahn wird ab 1984 als U-Bahn (Stadtbahn) unter der Bahnhofstraße verkehren.

Die Brechung der linienhaften Längsstruktur des Hauptgeschäftszentrums in Herne ist wohl nur teilweise erreicht worden (Bild 4, Beilage). Im Bereich der Einmündung der Bebelstraße in die Bahnhofstraße ist ein kleiner Platz entstanden, der auch durchaus vom Publikum als sog. "Verweilplatz" angenommen wird. An der Bonifatiuskirche (alter Turm als Mahnmal) wurde ein seitlicher Appendix mit Geschäften geschaffen. Am Südende der Bahnhofstraße entstand das sog. "City Center" mit 37 Geschäften und Dienstleistungsbetrieben und 800 m Schaufensterfront in zwei Ebenen, darüber Wohnungen, Praxen und Parkplätze.

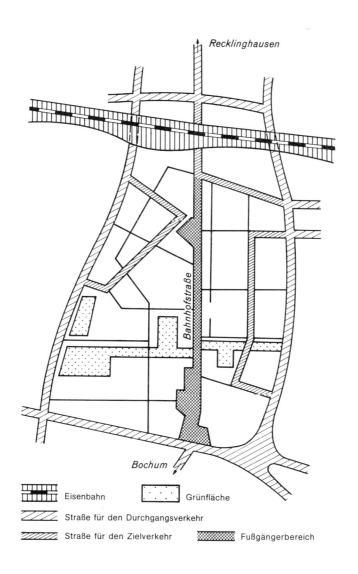

Karte 2: Schema des Entwicklungsplanes "Herne Stadtkern"

Und zu den positiven Ergebnissen der Umstrukturierung des vormals völlig linear ausgedehnten Zentrums ist auch der Bau des Kulturzentrums (Planungsziel 3) zu zählen. Seine Lage westlich des Südendes der Hauptgeschäftsstraße sorgt hier für eine flächenhafte Verbreiterung des Zentrenbereiches.

Aber die übrige Erschließung von Seiten- und Parallelstraßen wurde bisher nicht erreicht. Trotzdem: die Plattierung der Einkaufsstraße, ihre Ausstattung mit Bänken und Blumenkübeln sowie ihre Unterbrechung durch feste Verkaufsstände oder gastronomische Betriebe in der Straßenmitte schaffen schon jetzt eine Atmosphäre, die sich wesentlich und positiv von der Situation v o r der Sanierung unterscheidet. Erheblich trägt dazu auch bei, daß die anfangs durchaus diskutierte Flächensanierung nicht stattgefunden hat. Ganz erheblich hat die seit den 70er Jahren schwieriger gewordene wirtschaftliche Gesamtsituation dazu geführt, daß Veränderungen von Altbaugebieten vorsichtiger betrieben wurden. So sind Wohngeschäftsneubauten im unmittelbaren Zentrenbereich in größerer Konzentration nur am Nordende der Bebelstraße und im neuen City-Center entstanden. Im übrigen hat man aber im Rahmen von Objektsanierungen zahlreiche Wohnungen modernisiert, gewerbliche Räume nach gegenwärtigen Anforderungen umgestaltet und die Fassaden aus der Zeit der Jahrhundertwende (Bilder 5 und 6) renoviert. Ein Farbgestaltungsplan dient den Besitzern als Anregung.

Zusammenfassend kann man feststellen, daß selbstverständlich funktionale Notwendigkeiten bei der Sanierung des Stadtkerns Herne einen hohen Stellenwert haben:
— Beschleunigung des Durchgangsverkehrs
— Minderung der Gefährdung der Passanten
— technische Verbesserung der Wohnungen
— zeitgemäße Gestaltung gewerblich genutzter Räume und Flächen

Aber darüber hinaus sind große Investitionen in Projekte geflossen, die noch vor einiger Zeit in den nüchternen, zumeist traditionslosen Städten des Ruhrgebietes als unnötig und überflüssig angesehen wurden, nämlich in — wenn auch oft bescheidene — Projekte zur Hebung der Lebensqualität. Erst die starke Abwanderungstendenz der heute mobilen Bevölkerung und insbesondere die mangelnde Zuwanderung haben gezeigt, daß — in bezug auf den Stadtkern — gar nicht so sehr eine quantitative Erweiterung (von 59 auf 68 Geschäftseinheiten im ersten fertiggestellten Bauabschnitt) des Angebotes, sondern eine qualitative **Verbesserung des Milieus** von entscheidender Bedeutung sein kann.

Bild 5: Renovierte Fassaden aus der Zeit der Jahrhundertwende an der Bahnhofstraße in Herne

Bild 6: Renovierte Fassaden aus der Zeit der Jahrhundertwende an der Bahnhofstraße in Herne

Hanns J. Buchholz: Das Märkische Sauerland

Das M ä r k i s c h e S a u e r l a n d hat vielfach das Image eines naturbestimmten Erholungsgebietes. Dem Ortsfremden ist oft unbekannt, daß es sich um eines der wichtigsten Industriegebiete Deutschlands handelt. 1978 gab es 218 Industriebeschäftigte pro 1000 Einwohner im Märkischen Kreis; Nordrhein-Westfalen wies zum Vergleich nur 155 Industriebeschäftigte pro 1000 Einwohner auf.

Die gegenwärtige Wirtschaftsstruktur des Märkischen Sauerlandes entstand im Mittelalter auf der Basis von
— Eisenerz, das in Form von Gangerzen vielfach an der Oberfläche ausstreicht,
— Holzkohle, die in den weit verbreiteten Waldgebieten gewonnen werden konnte,
— Wasserkraft, die von zahlreichen Bächen günstiger Größenordnung angeboten wurde, und
— verfügbarer Arbeitskraft: die flachgründigen, nährstoffarmen Böden sowie die relativ hohen Niederschläge und niedrigen Durchschnittstemperaturen in dem durchweg stark reliefierten Gebiet zwangen große Teile der landwirtschaftlich tätigen Bevölkerung zum Nebenerwerb.

Während die eigene Erzförderung und -verhüttung schon seit dem späten Mittelalter immer mehr an Bedeutung verloren hat, entwickelte sich eine hoch qualifizierte Verarbeitungsindustrie, die
— auf Eisen basierte
— sich auf Nicht-Eisen-Metalle erweiterte und
— schließlich eine Fülle weiterer Verarbeitungs- und Fertigungsprozesse hinzunahm.

Generell hat sich im Westen des Bergisch-Märkischen Industriegebietes (Remscheid-Solingen) eine Spezialisierung auf Schneidwaren ergeben, während der Osten (heute: Märkischer Kreis) ganz überwiegend von der Drahtindustrie geprägt ist. Aus gewerblicher Tradition und verstärkt durch Absprachen der handwerklichen Zünfte im 17. und 18. Jahrhundert bildeten sich Schwerpunkte der Produktionsausrichtung:
— im Bereich Lüdenscheid: grober Draht,
— im Bereich Altena: mittlerer Draht,
— im Bereich Iserlohn: feiner Draht.

Die heutige Produktionspalette ist allerdings in allen Bereichen wesentlich differenzierter.

Daß hier nicht, wie im Ruhrgebiet, ein weitflächig verdichtetes industrielles Ballungsgebiet entstanden ist, liegt an der starken Reliefierung besonders des

Märkischen Sauerlandes. Die orographische Gesamtstruktur ist charakterisiert durch tief zertalte Hochflächen, so daß sich unmittelbar benachbart ganz wesentliche Unterschiede von Bebauungs- und sonstigen Nutzungsmöglichkeiten ergeben. Das dominante Raumordnungsproblem des Märkischen Kreises besteht in der Auseinandersetzung zwischen Industriestadt und Mittelgebirgs-Naturlandschaft[3]) (Karte 3, Beilage). Auf diese Problematik soll hier im wesentlichen eingegangen werden.

Die frühe städtisch-gewerbliche Entwicklung des Märkischen Sauerlandes hat ihren Ausgang von den Hochflächen genommen. Die Hochflächen waren verkehrsmäßig begünstigt, da die Bach- und Flußtäler wegen ihrer Enge und der unregulierten Wasserläufe von Überschwemmungen bedroht und darum nur schwer bebaubar und passierbar waren. Die ersten Städte (z.B. Lüdenscheid, Neuenrade) lagen daher auf der Hochfläche.

Mit dem Übergang zur Nutzung der Wasserkraft siedelte sich das metallbe- und -verarbeitende Gewerbe in den Tälern an — und zwar nicht in den großen Tälern (z.B. Lenne), deren Wassermassen bei der damaligen Technologie nicht beherrschbar waren, sondern in den kleineren Bachtälern (z.B. Nettetal, Rahmedetal), deren Wassermengen mit Hilfe kleinerer Stauanlagen zum Antrieb der Wasserräder ausreichen.

Im Zeitalter der Industrialisierung und des Eisenbahnbaus wuchsen die Industriestädte in den größeren Flußtälern (z.B. Altena, Werdohl), da nun geeignete Maßnahmen gegen die Flußüberschwemmungen ergriffen werden konnten, da die Dampfmaschine an die Stelle des Wasserrades trat und somit die Standortbindung an die kleineren Bachläufe entfiel und da die Eisenbahn Taltrassen bevorzugte. Unser Zeitalter des Kraftwagenverkehrs begünstigt nun wieder die Hochflächenstädte: Die Erreichbarkeit z.B. der Stadt Lüdenscheid war bis in die 60er Jahre vergleichsweise gering; denn nur eine Stichbahn verband Lüdenscheid (seit 1880) mit der Volmetalbahn bei Brügge. Hinzu kam eine Kleinbahnverbindung nach Altena. Seit der Anbindung an die Autobahn "Sauerlandlinie" (Dortmund-Frankfurt), die über die Hochflächen geführt wird, hat sich die Situation der Stadt Lüdenscheid z.B. gegenüber Altena völlig gewandelt.

Noch mehr aber beeinflußt das Flächenpotential die Entwicklung der Städte: A l t e n a hat in seinem Bereich das Lennetal einschließlich der einmündenden Seitentäler nicht nur auf dem Talboden, sondern auch an den steilen Talhängen (bis 45°) quasi vollständig baulich ausgefüllt (Bild 7). Expansionsflächen werden aber dringend benötigt, denn
— die Wohnansprüche der derzeitigen Einwohner Altenas wachsen und tendieren zu einer günstigeren Relation der Wohnfläche je Einwohner;
— eventuelle Zuwanderer müßten untergebracht werden können;
— die Verkehrsdichte steigt und drängt nach einer Verbreiterung des Straßenraumes;

Bild 7: Die Talstadt Altena

— Gewerbebetriebe, die modernisieren oder expandieren wollen, benötigen ausgedehnte Grundflächen;
— für neue Gewerbebetriebe müßten Flächen bereitgestellt werden können;
— zur Entflechtung der stark gemischten Flächennutzung bedarf es der Aussiedlung von emittierenden sowie Lärm oder Lastverkehr erzeugenden Industrie- und Gewerbebetrieben aus dem Innenstadtbereich.

Bisher werden nur 12 % der Gemeindefläche Altenas städtebaulich genutzt — und das ist auch weiterhin die maximal zur Verfügung stehende bebaubare Fläche. Als ein Ergebnis dieser Situation hat Altena seit 1964 ständig Wanderungsverluste zu verzeichnen, so daß die Wohnbevölkerung, bezogen auf den Gebietsstand zum 1.1.1975 erheblich abgenommen hat:

Tabelle 3: Entwicklung der Einwohnerzahl der Stadt Altena 1961 - 1978

Jahr	Zahl der Einwohner	Abnahme in v.H.
1961	32.587	
1970	30.299	-7,2
1974	28.100	-7,0
1976	25.945	-7,7
1978	25.240	-2,7

Quelle: Erläuterungsbericht zum Flächennutzungsplan der Stadt Altena. Altena 1978, S. 3

Der neueste Flächennutzungsplan von Altena aus dem Jahr 1978 weist zwar Ausweich- und Erweiterungsflächen aus (insbesondere Gewerbegebiet Stortel = 22,5 ha; Wohngebiet Nettenscheid = 17,7 ha) (Karte 3, Beilage). Jedoch das Gewerbegebiet Stortel deckt nicht einmal die Hälfte des Bedarfs, und die übrigen vorgesehenen Gewerbegebiete stehen bestenfalls mittelfristig zur Verfügung, da sie größtenteils gegenwärtig anderweitig genutzt werden. Das Wohngebiet Nettenscheid, bisher teilweise bebaut, liegt 6 km entfernt von der Innenstadt Altenas, völlig separat auf der Hochfläche ca. 200 m über dem Nettetal und ca. 250 m über dem Lennetal. Seine Erreichbarkeit ist sehr problematisch mit allen Konsequenzen versorgungstechnischer, sozialer und finanzieller Art.

Die sichtbaren Grenzen der Entwicklung Altenas haben ganz wesentlich dazu beigetragen, daß bei der zum 1.1.1975 rechtskräftig gewordenen Kommunal- und Kreisreform die Stadt Altena den Kreissitz an Lüdenscheid verloren hat. Die Zuweisung des Kreiskulturamtes kann nicht darüber hinwegtäuschen, daß Altena um einen ganz bedeutenden zentralörtlichen und strukturellen Sektor ärmer geworden ist. Die Lagegunst neigt sich in der Gegenwart wieder den Hochflächenstädten zu.

Entsprechend befindet sich die Stadt L ü d e n s c h e i d in einer weitgehend besseren Situation. Auf der Hochfläche gelegen, verfügt sie über ein durchaus befriedigendes Flächenreservoir. Zum Erreichen von neuen Wohn- oder Gewerbegebieten sind keine schwierigen Höhenunterschiede oder Distanzen zu überwinden. Fast 250 ha Gewerbegebiete sind im gegenwärtig geltenden Flächennutzungsplan enthalten. Im gesamten Stadtgebiet werden aber z.Z. nur ca. 80 ha von Gewerbe- oder Industriebetrieben genutzt. Insofern besteht hier keine Mangelsituation. Entsprechendes gilt für den Bedarf und das Angebot an Wohnbauland (Karte 4, Beilage).

Jedoch stellt sich grundsätzlich ein ähnliches Problem in bezug auf die Auseinandersetzung zwischen Industriestadt und Naturlandschaft: Die meisten neuen Ausbaugebiete liegen auf der Hochfläche und somit an exponierter Stelle.

Hochgebaute Wohntürme oder Fabriken und Lagergebäude ragen aus den Waldgebieten heraus (Bild 8) und sind weithin sichtbar.

Bild 8: Die Höhenstadt Lüdenscheid

Die Talstädte des Märkischen Sauerlandes wachsen über die Talränder auf die Hochflächen — und die Hochflächenstädte erweitern ihren städtisch bebauten Raum. Das bedeutet: Die Täler sind schon bisher im Laufe der historischen Entwicklung industriell-städtisch bebaut worden. Jedoch die gewerbliche und die Wohnbebauung lagen "versteckt" in schmalen Siedlungsgassen. Auch die Hochflächenstädte wie Lüdenscheid und Neuenrade hatten sich in Mulden angesetzt, die in die Hochflächen eingesenkt sind. Nun aber werden auch die höher gelegenen Bereiche bebaut — und eine ganze Landschaft beginnt, ihre Physiognomie zu verändern.

Allerdings befinden sich die Städte in einem echten Dilemma: Auf der einen Seite entsprechen die Wohnungen der Altbaugebiete sowohl von ihrer Größe und Ausstattung als auch von ihrer unmittelbaren Nachbarschaft zu Gewerbe- und Industriebetrieben her immer weniger den modernen Ansprüchen. Auf der anderen Seite bedeutet der Aufbau größerer Wohnanlagen auf den Hochflächen oder die Aussiedlung von Industriebetrieben auf die Hochflächen eine außerordentlich störende, da weithin sichtbare Beeinträchtigung der Waldgebirgslandschaft des Sauerlandes. Der Konflikt ist kaum lösbar; er kann nur gemildert werden, wenn Baustil, Material und Mikrostandort der Neubauten zu gleichgewichtigen Faktoren neben solchen wie Verkehrsanschluß, Bodenpreis und Flächenangebot werden. Die bisherigen Entwicklungen sind nicht ermutigend.

Die Betonung scheinbar nicht notwendiger Faktoren bei Planungs- und Entwicklungsmaßnahmen, zum Beispiel
— Baustil, Gebäudeformen und -farben, Baumaterial,
— bauliche Ensemblebildung in Stadtkernen, Einheitlichkeit ohne Uniformität, Zentrenorientierung der Bebauung anstelle agglomerativer Siedlungssysteme,
— Fußgängerbereiche, Parks, Blumen, Springbrunnen gerade in den Zentren von Industrieballungen,
— Erhaltung von relativ natürlichen Landschaftsteilen, von Bergsilhouetten,
— aber auch: zwangsfreie, auf Überzeugung basierende Planungs- und Sanierungsverfahren, die Einverständnis und Zufriedenheit in der Bevölkerung schaffen,

ist der Kritik ausgesetzt, realitätsfern und ignorant gegenüber Rentabilitäts- und Effizienzansprüchen zu sein. Sicherlich — die Versorgung der Bewohner von Herne war auch ohne Sanierungsmaßnahmen und ohne Zentrenaufbau gewährleistet, und das ökologische Gleichgewicht wird durch die Aussiedlung von Wohnanlagen und Fabriken auf die Hochflächen des Märkischen Sauerlandes nicht nennenswert beeinträchtigt. Aber die Suche nach mehr "Lebensqualität", die erreicht werden kann sowohl durch Bewahrung überkommener Strukturen als auch durch die Gestaltung gegenwärtiger Entwicklungen, ist eine sehr verständliche Reaktion auf den ganz außerordentlichen Industrialisierungs- und Verstädterungsprozeß, der das gesamte Rheinisch-Westfälische Industriegebiet geprägt hat und weiterhin formt. Dabei sind die rein funktionalen Notwendigkeiten der Wirtschaft und der Bevölkerung eigentlich immer, wenn man die zeitbedingten Maßstäbe anlegt, ausreichend berücksichtigt worden. Nur haben die Städte des Ruhrgebietes nie eine außerökonomische Attraktivität erreicht, und im Märkischen Sauerland besteht eine gewisse Gefahr, daß die landschaftliche Attraktivität beeinträchtigt wird. Die Auswirkungen dieser Situation auf zunehmende Abwanderungen sowie auf mangelnde Ansiedlungsbereitschaft von Erwerbspersonen, besonders auch von Unternehmern und Unternehmen, sind im Ruhrgebiet deutlich erkennbar. Im Märkischen Sauerland sollte es gar nicht erst zu einer derartigen Situation kommen. Insofern haben die oft kostspieligen, vordergründig unrentierlichen Maßnahmen zur Verbesserung der Lebensqualität durchaus ihre ökonomische Relevanz.

Anmerkungen

1) Der Hauptbahnhof "Bochum" an der Bergisch-Märkischen Bahn wurde erst 1862 eröffnet.
2) Vgl. P. BUSCH über Wanne-Eickel in seinem Aufsatz: "Zur Siedlungsstruktur der Stadt Wanne-Eickel" in: "Bochum und das mittlere Ruhrgebiet", Festschrift zum 35. Deutschen Geographentag in Bochum. Paderborn 1965, S. 177-186
3) Verkürzt mag in dieser Gegenüberstellung der Begriff "Naturlandschaft" verwendet werden, obwohl sich die nicht-städtisch oder -industriell genutzten Flächen nicht in einem "natürlichen" Urzustand befinden, sondern land- und forstwirtschaftlich genutzt werden.

Literatur

BEUTIN, L.: Geschichte der Südwestfälischen Industrie- und Handelskammer zu Hagen und ihrer Wirtschaftslandschaft. Hagen 1956.

BUCHHOLZ, H.J.: Darstellungen und Analysen des Strukturwandels an der Ruhr. In: Westfälische Forschungen, 24. Bd., 1972, S. 195-210.

BUCHHOLZ, H.J.: Das polyzentrische Ballungsgebiet Ruhr und seine kommunale Neugliederung. In: Geographische Rundschau, Jg. 25, H. 8, 1973, S. 297-307.

BUCHHOLZ, H.J.: The Influence of Industries on Urban Structure of the Ruhr. In: Case Studies in Industrial Geography. Ed. by K. Hottes and F.E.I. Hamilton. Paderborn 1980, S. 136-140. (= Bochumer Geographische Arbeiten, H. 39)

HOTTES, K.: Das Ruhrgebiet im Strukturwandel. Eine wirtschaftsgeographische Zwischenbilanz. In: Berichte zur deutschen Landeskunde, Bd. 38, 1967, S. 251-274.

LEYH, M. und L. ROTHENBERG, K.-H. SMITS: Das Herner Modell. Stadtkernerneuerung als Maßnahme zur Strukturverbesserung einer Gemeinde. O.O.u.J.

MÖLLER, W.: Stagnation und Fortschritt im märkischen Wirtschaftsraum. In: Südwestfälische Wirtschaft, 1967, H.2.

SCHÖLLER, P.: Städte als Mobilitätszentren westdeutscher Landschaften. In: Tagungsbericht und wissenschaftliche Abhandlungen. Deutscher Geographentag Berlin 1959, S. 158-167.

Die Bilder wurden freundlicherweise von den Stadtverwaltungen Herne, Altena und Lüdenscheid zur Verfügung gestellt.

Gerhard Aymans und Günter Thieme: Die Unteren Niederrheinlande

Die Unteren Niederrheinlande (Karte 5, Beilage) berühren im Südosten und Süden zwar eine der größten städtisch-industriellen Agglomerationen der Welt, doch sind sie selbst eher ländlich geprägt. Ihre jüngere Entwicklung und auch ihre Entwicklungsmöglichkeiten sind sehr wesentlich bestimmt
— durch das Vorherrschen kleinstädtischer und dörflicher Wohnplätze sowie einer Vielzahl ehemaliger und derzeitiger landwirtschaftlicher Hofstellen in Streulage
— durch das Fehlen eines Oberzentrums im Gebiet selbst
— durch die Nähe zum Ruhrgebiet und zum Krefelder Industriegebiet
— durch die unmittelbare Nachbarschaft zu den Niederlanden und deren Oberzentren Nimwegen und Arnheim.

Durch die Nähe zum Ruhrgebiet sind große Teile der Unteren Niederrheinlande, nämlich die ehemaligen Landkreise Moers und Geldern, planerisch schon recht früh (1923) dem Siedlungsverband Ruhrkohlenbezirk zugewiesen worden. Da dieser sich seiner Hauptaufgabe entsprechend jedoch vor allem für das Ruhrgebiet selbst verantwortlich gefühlt hat, ist seinem ländlichen, insbesondere seinem linksrheinischen Verbandsgebiet, vorwiegend nur die Stelle eines E r g ä n z u n g s r a u m e s zugefallen. Die räumliche Zuständigkeit des Siedlungsverbandes Ruhrkohlenbezirk für den südlichen Teil der Unteren Niederrheinlande hat sich aber auch auf den nördlichen Teil des Gebietes ausgewirkt. Da sie sich nämlich im Westen bis an die deutsch-niederländische Staatsgrenze erstreckte, war der nördliche Teil des Gebietes, der ehemalige Kreis Kleve und Stücke des ehemaligen Kreises Rees, planerisch vom Rumpf der Rheinlande abgeschnitten. Man kann diesen nördlichen Teil der Unteren Niederrheinlande daher als einen R e s t r a u m bezeichnen. Er ist in der Tat noch zu Beginn der 70er Jahre das einzige Gebiet Norddeutschlands gewesen, für das weder nach Landesrecht rechtswirksame Pläne und Programme noch Pläne und Programme in Aufstellung oder in Ausarbeitung vorgelegen haben[1].

Auf eine kurze Formel gebracht könnte man die Unteren Niederrheinlande bis zur Neuordnung der Planungszuständigkeiten im Jahre 1975 planerisch als einen E r g ä n z u n g s r a u m   u n d   R e s t r a u m   i n   g r e n z n a h e r   R a n d l a g e bezeichnen. Die Bezeichnungen Ergänzungsraum und Restraum müssen aus heutiger Sicht nicht unbedingt negative Tatbestände beinhalten. Als ausgesprochen positiv ist u.a. die Tatsache zu werten, daß planerisch über keinen der beiden (ehemaligen) Teilräume gleichsam unwiderruflich verfügt worden ist: Der südliche Teilraum ist als Ergänzungsraum jahrzehntelang nur als Reserve für zukünftige Entwicklungen bereitgehalten worden, während der nördliche Teilraum als Restraum, nicht zuletzt wegen seiner flußabwärtigen Insellage, in noch höherem Maße von der Übernahme überregionaler Funktionen verschont geblieben ist. Allerdings umschreiben die stichwortartigen Kurzbegriffe Ergänzungsraum und Restraum auch die Tatsache, daß die Unteren Niederrhinlande nicht zuletzt aufgrund der früheren Planungszuständigkeiten daran gehindert worden sind, sich selbst zu entwickeln. Wesentlich hierzu wäre u.a. eine Stärkung der bestehenden Nord-Süd-Verbindungen entlang der B 9 und der Eisenbahnstrecke Krefeld-Geldern-Kleve sowie entlang der B 57 und der Eisenbahnstrecke Krefeld-Xanten-Kleve gewesen, doch sind diese in den letzten Jahrzehnten nicht nur ungenügend weiterentwickelt, sondern sogar zurückgebildet worden. Ja es zeigt sich sogar, daß die Planungsstrukturen den Raumstrukturen entgegenlaufen. Während die Raumstrukturen sich nämlich im wesentlichen in nord-südlicher Richtung erstrecken, verlaufen die regional wirksamen Planungsstrukturen im wesentlichen in west-östlicher Richtung.

Die starke Abnahme der Zahl der in der Landwirtschaft beschäftigten Personen seit dem Zweiten Weltkrieg hat auch hier nicht dazu geführt, daß die Bevölkerung heute sehr viel stärker konzentriert in den Hauptorten des Gebietes lebt. Da Nordrhein-Westfalen wie die übrige Bundesrepublik erst seit den 60er Jahren eine umfassende Landesplanungsgesetzgebung kennt und für die Unteren Niederrhinlande bis 1975 alle drei der früheren Landesplanungsgemeinschaften zuständig gewesen sind, ist die räumliche Planung des Gebietes bis vor kurzer Zeit von kleinräumigen Einzelplänen bestimmt gewesen, die häufig nicht das Ziel einer möglichst hohen S i e d l u n g s v e r d i c h t u n g, sondern das einer S i e d l u n g s s t r e u u n g verfolgt und planerisch verfochten haben. So ging etwa MACHTEMES in seinem Gutachten zum Kreisordnungsplan Kleve von der Vorstellung aus, daß Siedlungen von 3.000, 12.000 bis 15.000 und 25.000 Einwohnern ideale Gemeindegrößen seien, darüber hinaus aber erst wieder Großstädte mit weit über 100.000 Einwohnern. Da letzteres für Kleve unerreichbar schien, empfahl er die schnelle Entwicklung dieser Stadt zu dämpfen und das Wachstum des Kreises möglichst auf die Schwerpunkte Goch, Kalkar, Kranenburg und Uedem zu konzentrieren (Gruppe Hardtberg: Kreisentwicklungsplan Kleve. Bonn 1973. S. 34). Aber selbst diese bescheidene Siedlungsverdichtung auf die Hauptorte des Gebietes hat sich nicht erreichen lassen. In den 70er Jahren zeigt sich vielmehr, daß die Wohnbevölkerung vieler Nebenorte in ihrer Summe rascher wächst als die der Hauptorte (vgl. AYMANS und ENZEL, 1980, S. 80).

Die Bevölkerungszunahme in den Unteren Niederrhinlanden wird seit Beginn der 70er Jahre nicht mehr von Geburtenüberschüssen, sondern von Wanderungsüberschüssen — vor allem im Bevölkerungsaustausch mit dem Ruhrgebiet — getragen. Das Gebiet ist also vor allem als Wohngebiet stark nachgefragt. Die Arbeitsplatzentwicklung zeigt demgegenüber stark negative Tendenzen. Wenn sich unter den gegenwärtigen konjunkturellen Bedingungen der Prozeß der Abwanderung von Erwerbstätigen aus dem primären Sektor auch deutlich verlangsamt, werden in der Landwirtschaft noch auf Jahre hinaus Arbeitsplätze aufgegeben werden. Das gilt im Exkursionsgebiet insbesondere dort, wo adelige Großgrundbesitzer ihre früher nur passiv betriebene Landwirtschaft nunmehr aktiv betreiben, d.h. die früher praktisch ausnahmslos verpachteten Flächen in wachsendem Maße selbst in Bewirtschaftung nehmen und darüber hinaus, aus Gründen der Verwaltungsvereinfachung, die Zahl der Hof- und Parzellenpächter rasch verringern. Demgegenüber gibt es nur wenige Orte, in denen die Zahl der in der Landwirtschaft beschäftigten Personen nicht oder nur sehr langsam abnimmt. Das gilt in erster Linie von den Bauernschaften in der Stadt Straelen und ihrer näheren Umgebung, wo in den letzten Jahrzehnten auf ärmlichen Böden eine intensive Gartenbauwirtschaft entwickelt worden ist, deren Schwerpunkt zunächst der Gemüseanbau im Freiland, dann der Gemüsebau unter Glas und schließlich der Schnittblumenanbau unter Glas gewesen ist. Insgesamt ist in den Unteren Niederrheinlanden jedoch auch weiterhin mit einem spürbaren Rückgang der Beschäftigten in der Landwirtschaft und in den von ihr abhängigen ländlichen Gewerben zu rechnen.

Auch im produzierenden Gewerbe ist nicht mit einem spürbaren Wachsen der Zahl der Beschäftigten zu rechnen. Es mag hier oder dort eine Betriebsneugründung geben, die das örtliche Arbeitsplatzangebot qualitativ und quantitativ verbessert, doch wird das Arbeitsplatzangebot im produzierenden Gewerbe insgesamt noch stärker zurückgehen als im Landesdurchschnitt. Der Grund für diese pessimistische Beurteilung der Arbeitsplatzentwicklung im sekundären Wirtschaftsbereich liegt in der traditionellen gewerblichen Struktur des Gebietes. Diese ist nämlich nicht nur durch ein Vorherrschen schrumpfender Branchen (Lebensmittel, Textil, Leder usw. gekennzeichnet) sondern auch — teilweise über Aufkäufe — durch einen hohen Anteil an Zweigbetrieben, deren Hauptbetriebe außerhalb des Gebietes liegen. Krisen wirken sich in derartigen Unternehmensstrukturen fast immer zunächst auf die Zweigbetriebe aus, deren Arbeitsplätze fast zwangsläufig stärker gefährdet sind als die der Hauptbetriebe. Die Unteren Niederrheinlande weisen nicht zuletzt deshalb in jüngerer Zeit örtlich hohe Arbeitslosenquoten auf. Nennenswerte Zuwächse an Arbeitsplätzen sind auch im tertiären Sektor nicht zu erwarten, da das Gebiet innerhalb seiner Grenzen kein Oberzentrum besitzt, sondern auf Krefeld und Duisburg ausgerichtet bleibt, ja teilweise sogar die benachbarten niederländischen Oberzentren Nimwegen und Arnheim in Anspruch nimmt. Hinzukommt, daß in den Unteren Niederrheinlanden im letzten Jahrzehnt Gebietsreformen sowohl auf Gemeindeebene als auch auf Kreisebene durchgeführt worden sind und daß in deren Folge zumindest Arbeitsplatzverlagerungen in die beiden neuen — und alten — Kreisstädte Kleve und Wesel haben hingenommen werden müssen. Weiterhin haben auch zahlreiche, von den Trägern öffentlicher Belange durchgeführte Rationalisierungsmaßnahmen — ungeachtet ihrer allgemeinen Notwendigkeit — das lokale Arbeitsplatzangebot bei der Bundesbahn, im Gerichtswesen, im Krankenhauswesen usw. weiter vermindert. Dieser schon in den 60er Jahren einsetzende Prozeß wird sich vorerst weiter fortsetzen, keinesfalls aber umkehren lassen.

Die Beschäftigtenrate wird voraussichtlich noch auf Jahre hinaus sinken und hinter den durchschnittlichen Verhältnissen im Lande zurückbleiben. Allerdings wird diese Entwicklung von zwei sehr verschiedenartigen Ursachen bestimmt sein: Zum einen wird der regionale Arbeitsmarkt, vor allem im primären und sekundären Sektor, weiter schrumpfen und die Zahl der a u t o c h t h o n e n Auspendler weiter wachsen, zum anderen werden aber auch die Zuwanderungen aus den benachbarten großstädtisch-industriellen Gebieten anhalten und damit die Zahl der a l l o c h t h o n e n Auspendler weiter wachsen. Die voraussichtlich auch weiterhin sinkende Beschäftigungsrate zeigt also nicht nur ein unzulängliches Arbeitsplatzangebot in der Region an, sondern umgekehrt auch ein offenbar stark nachgefragtes Wohnplatzangebot.

Es mag viele Gründe geben, die inzwischen nicht mehr unbedeutenden Wanderungsgewinne im Bevölkerungsaustausch mit dem Ruhrgebiet und dem Krefelder Industriegebiet als nicht wünschenswert anzusehen, wenn sie nicht mit einem entsprechenden Zuwachs an Arbeitsplätzen verbunden sind, doch ist es müßig, diese Entwicklung zu beklagen, da sie nicht verhindert, sondern nur gestaltet werden kann. Jedenfalls müssen die Städte und Gemeinden der Unteren Niederrheinlande sich der Tatsache bewußt werden, daß ihre Region dabei ist, sich inselhaft, an den bestehenden Siedlungen anknüpfend, zu einem ausgedehnten Wohnvorort des Rheinisch-Westfälischen Industriegebietes zu entwickeln. Die Verantwortlichen werden zwar hier wie in jeder anderen Region auch weiterhin bemüht sein, industrielle und gewerbliche Unternehmen zur Ansiedlung zu bewegen, um die Lebensqualität der Region durch ein weiter gefächertes Arbeitsplatzangebot zu verbessern, doch sind derartigen Bemühungen sehr enge Grenzen gesetzt, die nicht zuletzt auf die Setzungen der Landesplanung und auf die räumlichen Prioritäten zurückgehen, die das Land und das Land zusammen mit dem Bund gesetzt haben. Hier ist der Gestaltungsspielraum der einzelnen Städte und Gemeinden außerordentlich eng.

Vergleichsweise groß hingegen ist der Gestaltungsspielraum der Städte und Gemeinden bei der Entwicklung ihrer Gebiete zu Wohnvororten der Rheinisch-Westfälischen Industrieagglomeration. Hier ist der Gestaltungsspielraum nicht nur rechtlich, sondern auch tatsächlich groß, da der Zuwanderungsstrom über die Jahre gewachsen ist und inzwischen jede Gemeinde des Gebietes erreicht hat. Er trifft hier jedoch auf Städte und Gemeinden, deren Wohnplätze nur im Ausnahmefall der Kreisstädte über die Größe kleiner Mittelstädte hinausreichen. Man würde diese daher in ihrem gewachsenen Zuschnitt zerstören, wollte man den Zuwanderungsüberschuß aus den Großstädten auf sie allein konzentrieren. Um welche Probleme es hierbei im einzelnen geht, ist im Rahmen der Exkursion zunächst am Beispiel der Stadt Xanten aufgezeigt worden.

Die Stadt Xanten

Die heutige Stadt Xanten mit ihren rund 17.000 Einwohnern auf einer Fläche von 72 qkm ist erst im Zuge der Gebietsreform von 1969 aus einer Reihe bis dahin selbständiger Gemeinden entstanden, deren funktionaler Mittelpunkt das alte Xanten (8 qkm) allerdings schon länger gewesen ist. Die einst blühende, aber schon im ausgehenden Mittelalter wirtschaftlich in den Schatten der regionalen Entwicklung geratende, ursprünglich kurkölnische, später klevische Stadt, hatte noch um 1500 rund 5.000 Einwohner, doch sank deren Zahl bis um 1750 auf weniger als 2.000 ab (vgl. G. KNOPP, 1975). Auch in den beiden folgenden Jahrhunderten, in denen die Bevölkerung der Rheinlande zunächst langsam, allmählich aber immer schneller wuchs, blieb die Bevölkerungsentwicklung in Xanten weit hinter der im Lande zurück. Um 1950 hatte die alte Stadt erst 3.400 Einwohner. Erst seither, im Zuge ihrer Entwicklung zu einem der vielen Wohnvororte des Rheinisch-Westfälischen Industriegebietes hat Xanten jene Einwohnerzahl wieder erreichen und übertreffen können, die sie schon im Mittelalter gehabt hatte.

Die Entwicklungsmöglichkeiten dieser kleinen Stadt sind zwar nicht notwendigerweise auf einen weiteren Ausbau als Wohnstadt sowie als Freizeit- und Erholungsschwerpunkt beschränkt, doch scheinen keine anderen Entwicklungsmöglichkeiten so sinnvoll zu sein wie gerade diese (vgl. H. TRAUTEN, 1975). Dafür sprechen insbesondere die Lage der Stadt an einer sehr abwechslungsreichen, reizvollen Stelle der niederrheinischen Tieflande und vor allem ihr großer Reichtum an Kulturdenkmälern der allerersten Ordnung. Zu diesen gehört das nordöstlich des mittelalterlichen Stadtkerns gelegene Gebiet der römischen Stadt Colonia Ulpia Traiana, die schon seit Jahrzehnten archäologisch bearbeitet und jetzt, im Zuge der Maßnahmen zur Stadtentwicklung, zu einem archäologischen Park von überregionaler Bedeutung gestaltet wird. Die Aufbauten der römischen Stadt sind zwar schon im Mittelalter restlos abgetragen worden, doch hat der Jahrhunderte währende Wachstumsstillstand Xantens dazu geführt, daß alle Grundmauern der römischen Stadtsiedlung und ihre unterirdischen Versorgungs- und Entsorgungssysteme praktisch unversehrt und unüberbaut geblieben sind. Das ist in Deutschland nur hier der Fall.

Zu den Kulturdenkmälern der allerersten Ordnung gehört auch der Dom und seine Immunität. Der Entstehung der rheinischen Städte mit römischer Wurzel entsprechend ist auch Xanten nicht über der römischen Stadt selbst, sondern über deren Gräberfeldern entstanden. Schon im 4. Jahrhundert stand an der Stelle des heutigen Doms eine erste Gedächtniskapelle, der eine Reihe kirchlicher Bauten folgte, ehe im 8. Jahrhundert hier auch das Stift entstand, an deren Wehrmauern sich schon bald eine bedeutende Marktsiedlung anlehnte. Der Grundstein zum heutigen Dom, der seinem kirchlichen Rang nach und als Bauwerk zu den bedeutendsten Sakralbauten der Rheinlande ihrer Zeit zählte, wurde im Jahre 1236 gelegt, wenige Jahre nach der Verleihung der Stadtrechte an den

Bild 9: Xanten: Schrägluftaufnahme von Süden mit der Stiftsimmunität im Zentrum der ehemals ummauerten Stadt (Mittelgrund) sowie dem Gelände des archäologischen Parks (Hintergrund links). Freigegeben Reg. Präsident Düsseldorf Nr. 16/52/9894.

Markt Xanten. Als der Dom 1517 vollendet war, hatte der allmähliche Niedergang der Stadt aber schon begonnen und die Verlagerung des Rheinstroms nach Osten (über 2 km) im Jahre 1535 schnitt dann auch den Handel von der leistungsfähigsten Verkehrsachse des gesamten Raumes weitgehend ab. Das Stift bleib unter diesen Umständen bis zu seiner Auflösung im Jahre 1802 auch wirtschaftlich die bedeutendste Einrichtung der kleinen Stadt, die bis in das 20. Jahrhundert hinein kaum über ihre mittelalterlichen Mauern hinauswuchs.

In Anbetracht der landesplanerischen Zielvorgabe, Xanten in erster Linie als Wohn-, Freizeit- und Erholungsort zu entwickeln (vgl. P. MOELLE, 1975), sind die Altstadt, der von ihr umschlossene Dom mit der Immunität und die — teilweise — zu einem archäologischen Park zu gestaltenden Überreste der Colonia Ulpia Traiana die wichtigsten räumlichen Elemente, die bei der Stadterneuerung und -entwicklung zu berücksichtigen sind. Deshalb sollen alle Neubauten im mittelalterlichen Kern an den überkommenen räumlichen Maßstäben ausgerichtet sein, doch soll die Stadt kein Museum ihrerselbst werden. Sie soll vielmehr Wohn- und Wohngeschäftshäuser erhalten, die allen Anforderungen auch in den vorgegebenen Dimensionen gerecht werden. Hierbei auftretende Schwierigkeiten, etwa beim Einzelhandel, der Beschäftigte immer mehr durch vergrößerte Verkaufsflächen ersetzt, sollen durch die Einbeziehung häufig funktionslos gewordener rückwärtiger Grundstücksteile aufgehoben werden.

Aber auch außerhalb der mittelalterlichen Grenzen ist der Dimension der alten Stadt und der Existenz der Kulturdenkmäler Dom und Römerstadt Rechnung zu tragen. Sie sollen nicht verdeckt, sondern herausgehoben werden. Das bedeutet, daß neues Baugelände auf den noch offenen Flächen nicht in der unmittelbaren Nachbarschaft der Altstadt, sondern deutlich von ihr getrennt erschlossen werden sollte. Dem tragen die bestehenden Pläne zur Stadtentwicklung weitgehend Rechnung. Die Möglichkeiten Xantens, Zuwanderer in seinem Hauptwohnplatz aufzunehmen, bleiben nach diesen Vorstellungen jedoch auf wenige Tausend Menschen beschränkt. Sollte Xanten dem großen Zuwanderungsdruck, insbesondere aus dem Ruhrgebiet, erliegen und Wohnplatz für Zehntausende von Zuwanderern werden wollen, müßte wohl ein völlig neues Entwicklungskonzept erarbeitet werden.

Da schon seit geraumer Zeit zahlreiche Industriebetriebe aus dem Ballungskern des Rheinisch-Westfälischen Industriegebietes in dessen Randzone verlagert werden, könnte vielleicht auch Xanten das eine oder andere Unternehmen zur Niederlassung bewegen, doch sollte man von dieser Möglichkeit auch weiterhin nur Gebrauch machen, wenn dies den außerordentlich hohen Wohn-, Freizeit-und Erholungswert der Stadt nicht beeinträchtigt. In Anbetracht der Dimensionen des mittelalterlichen Stadtkerns und des offenen Geländes des archäologischen Parks, der im Zuge eines großen, etwa 300 ha umfassenden Auskiesungsvorhabens in einen ausgedehnten Freizeitpark mit großen Wasserflächen übergehen soll, dürften große Flächen und große Gebäude beanspruchende Industrieanlagen ebenso störend wirken wie alle umweltbelastenden Einrichtungen.

Es ist nicht damit zu rechnen, daß die geplante Entwicklung Xantens in absehbarer Zeit zu einem wesentlich vermehrten Arbeitsplatzangebot im tertiären Bereich führen wird, da viele Arbeitnehmer, insbesondere im Einzelhandel und im Gaststättengewerbe, unterbeschäftigt sind, doch ist hier durch Zuwanderer, Ausflügler und Feriengäste zumindest mit einer besseren Auslastung der Einrichtungen zu rechnen, die unter den gegebenen Verhältnissen nur wenig gegen den nicht unerheblichen Kaufkraftabfluß in die Zentren der Ballungsrandzone (u.a. Wesel und Moers) ausrichten können. Es ist also vorerst weniger mit einer Vermehrung als vielmehr mit einer Verbesserung der Arbeitsplätze zu rechnen, die sich auch in besseren Verdienstmöglichkeiten niederschlagen dürfte.

In Anbetracht der besonderen Qualitäten Xantens, die auf seine Lage zum benachbarten Industrierevier, auf seine Lage im Naturraum und nicht zuletzt auf sein reiches Erbe aus römischer, kurkölnischer und klevischer Zeit zurückgehen, scheinen die bestehenden Entwicklungspläne die bestmögliche Antwort auf die Frage nach der Verbesserung der Lebensqualität zu sein. Dem entspricht auch die Tatsache, daß dem Arbeitswert eines Standortes immer weniger Bedeutung im Vergleich zu seinen Wohn-, Freizeit- und Erholungswert zukommt. Xanten wird wohl im wachsenden Maße das vergleichsweise gute Arbeitsplatzangebot des nahegelegenen Ballungsrandes in Anspruch nehmen und seinerseits dem größeren Raum beachtenswerte Freizeit- und Erholungsmöglichkeiten bieten.

Die Niederrheinische Landwirtschaft

Das Gebiet am linken Niederrhein ist — wenigstens physiognomisch — noch immer weitgehend ländlich-agrarisch geprägt. Dieser äußere Eindruck wird zwar durch den Anteil der Erwerbstätigen im primären Sektor nicht bestätigt, der zum Zeitpunkt der letzten Volkszählung 1970 bei 17,8 % im ehemaligen Kreis Geldern und bei 11,1 % im ehemaligen Kreis Kleve lag und somit weit hinter dem Beschäftigtenanteil im sekundären und tertiären Wirtschaftssektor zurückblieb.

Dennoch erscheint eine kurze Behandlung von Struktur, Entwicklung und Problemen der Landwirtschaft im Rahmen einer Niederrheinexkursion durchaus gerechtfertigt, stellt sich doch — durchaus im Sinne des Rahmenthemas unseres Symposiums — die Frage, ob die Agrarwirtschaft am Niederrhein weiter entwickelt und gefördert werden soll, oder ob eine Verbesserung der Lebensbedingungen in dieser Region vielmehr durch den Versuch einer verstärkten industriellen Entwicklung bewirkt werden kann.

Die Landwirtschaft am linken Niederrhein zeichnet sich generell sowohl durch günstige natürliche Produktionsbedingungen als auch insbesondere durch eine für deutsche Verhältnisse überdurchschnittlich gute Betriebsstruktur aus.

Die vergleichsweise hohe Produktivität der niederrheinischen Landwirtschaft geht recht eindrucksvoll aus der Gegenüberstellung des Anteils der landwirtschaftlichen Erwerbstätigen zu dem Anteil der Landwirtschaft an der gesamten Wertschöpfung hervor: Während im Bundesdurchschnitt der Anteil der Landwirtschaft am Bruttoinlandsprodukt um mehr als 50 % hinter ihrem Beschäftigtenanteil zurückbleibt, klaffen diese Werte am Niederrhein erheblich weniger weit auseinander (vgl. Landwirtschaft am Niederrhein 1976, S. 33).

Eine Reihe weiterer Faktoren verdeutlicht die bevorzugte Stellung der niederrheinischen Landwirtschaft (ebenda, S. 45 ff.). Der hohe Anteil von Vollerwerbsbetrieben mit generell ausreichender Landausstattung, das relativ niedrige Durchschnittsalter der Betriebsinhaber, die zudem ganz überwiegend eine landwirtschaftliche Fachausbildung absolviert haben, sowie ein unter Berücksichtigung des jeweiligen Betriebsziels adequater Mechanisierungsgrad, all das führt zu einem der höchsten Betriebserträge pro Arbeitskraft unter den Agrarregionen der Bundesrepublik Deutschland (vgl. Agrarbericht 1980, Materialband, S. 232).

Diese durchaus günstige Agrarstruktur ist nicht zuletzt das Ergebnis der historisch gewachsenen Siedlungsverteilung und Agrarverfassung. Zum einen verhinderte das im Exkursionsgebiet seit jeher praktizierte Anerbenrecht weitgehend eine Aufteilung der Betriebe in unrentable Wirtschaftseinheiten, zum anderen sicherte die am Niederrhein außerhalb der Städte und größeren Gemeinden weit verbreitete Streusiedlungsstruktur mit einer Vielzahl kleiner Bauernschaften den Betrieben eine überdurchschnittlich gute innere und äußere Verkehrslage. Auch bei einer angestrebten Erweiterung der Wirtschafts- oder auch Wohngebäude war dieser Streusiedlungscharakter zweifellos vorteilhaft.

Neben diese historisch bedingten Gunstfaktoren treten jedoch Entwicklungen, die in jüngster Zeit eine durchgreifende Veränderung der Betriebsverhältnisse der Landwirtschaft bewirkt haben. Zum einen sind dies die verbreiteten Substitutionsvorgänge der Produktionsfaktoren. Der Faktor Arbeit wird zunehmend durch Kapital ersetzt, was zu einer umfassenden Mechanisierung der Landwirtschaft geführt hat. Schon vorher war innerhalb der Gesamtzahl der landwirtschaftlich Beschäftigten der Anteil familienfremder Arbeitskräfte fast bis zur Bedeutungslosigkeit reduziert worden. Ein weiterer, besonders in jüngster Zeit wirksamer Substitutionsprozess ist die Ersetzung des Produktionsfaktors Arbeit durch Boden mit dem Ergebnis einer beträchtlichen Vergrößerung der landwirtschaftlichen Betriebe.

Von ähnlich großer Bedeutung wie die erwähnten, im Grunde für alle Betriebe in gleicher Weise zutreffenden Entwicklungen ist für die Agrarwirtschaft am Niederrhein eine Art betriebsinterner Spezialisierung der Produktion: Handelte es sich früher durchweg um Gemischtbetriebe mit erheblicher Bedeutung der Selbstversorgung, so dominieren — zumindest unter den Vollerwerbslandwirten — heute Betriebe, die sich auf wenige, im Extremfall sogar nur einen einzigen, hochspezialisierten Produktionszweig wie etwa Geflügelzucht, Schweinemast oder Milchwirtschaft beschränken.

Bei dieser Spezialisierung, die nicht zuletzt durch die oft sehr hohen Investitionsbelastungen bei der Entwicklung eines Betriebszweiges auf einen modernen betriebswirtschaftlichen und produktionstechnischen Stand geradezu erzwungen wird und die selbstverständlich auch eine ganze Reihe von Problemen aufwirft, entsteht keineswegs ein einheitliches regionales Muster der Agrarproduktion. Charakteristisch ist vielmehr ein recht vielfältiges Bild auf unterschiedliche Produktionsrichtungen spezialisierter Betriebe in ein und derselben Gemeinde.

Die bislang geschilderten Entwicklungen lassen sich exemplarisch in der Gemeinde Weeze/Kreis Kleve aufzeigen. 1978 gab es hier noch 238 landwirtschaftliche Betriebe mit etwa 4.700 ha landwirtschaftlicher Nutzfläche. Ungefähr 60 % der gesamten landwirtschaftlich genutzten Fläche sind im Besitz einer Vielzahl bäuerlicher Familienbetriebe, ca. 40 % befinden sich in der Hand zweier adeliger Großgrundbesitzer (Zahlenangaben nach unveröffentlichtem Material der Gemeindeverwaltung Weeze), die den kleineren Teil dieser Fläche als Gutsbetrieb selbst nutzen, den Rest an ortsansässige Landwirte weiterverpachtet haben.

Für die Gutshöfe, die jeweils über eine beträchtliche Betriebsfläche verfügen und für ihre Bewirtschaftung auf Lohnarbeitskräfte angewiesen sind, kann ein sinnvoller Strukturwandel nur durch arbeitsextensive Produktion, d.h. durch Reduzierung der Zahl der Arbeitskräfte oder Vergrößerung des Betriebes bei Beibehaltung der Beschäftigtenzahlen erreicht werden. Konsequenterweise sind auf dem Gutshof von Schloß Wissen die Haltung von Robustrindern, die während der gesamten Vegetationsperiode auf der Weide bleiben können sowie eine sehr arbeitsextensive Variante der Schweinemast mit automatischer Fütterung und Tränkung der Tiere wichtige Betriebszweige.

Die Anpassung bäuerlicher Betriebe an die Erfordernisse rentablen Wirtschaftens sieht notwendigerweise anders aus. Als Beispiel mag der von uns besuchte Laxhof im Südosten der Gemeinde Weeze dienen. Der Hof, bis 1974 einer der für die Region typischen Gemischtbetriebe, hat sich seither ausschließlich auf die Schweinehaltung spezialisiert, betreibt hierbei allerdings sowohl Aufzucht als auch Mast und die Vermarktung an einen festen Kreis von Metzgern. Die Landausstattung des Betriebes (26 ha, ausschließlich Pachtland) reicht als Futterbasis für den Viehbestand (etwa 50 bis 60 Sauen, 150 - 200 Ferkel und 400 Mastschweine) nicht aus, so daß in beträchtlichem Umfang Grund- und Spezialfuttermittel zugekauft werden müssen. Die hier beschriebene, durchaus arbeits- und kapitalaufwendige Intensivierung der Produktion in Form der inneren Aufstockung durch Veredlungswirtschaft bildet gleichsam das andere Extrem des agrarischen Strukturwandels gegenüber dem extensiv wirtschaftenden Großbetrieb. Zweifellos wird der bäuerliche Familienbetrieb in der Bundesrepublik auf absehbare Zeit die dominierende Betriebsform darstellen. Die Forderung nach Anpassung der

Landwirtschaft an die Bedürfnisse des Binnen- bzw. EG-Marktes — und dies kann nichts anderes als Stagnation, wenn nicht Reduzierung der Agrarproduktion bedeuten — wie auch landschaftsgestalterische Gesichtspunkte lassen jedoch zum Beispiel eine extensiv betriebene, naturnahe und somit auch unbedenklich ökonomische Weidewirtschaft in Großbetrieben als denkbare Alternative erscheinen, mag auch das agrarische Gunstgebiet des Niederrheins hierfür nicht der geeignete Standort sein.

Die Stadt Goch

Die Stadt Goch (1978: 28.593 Einwohner, davon 60% in der Kernstadt) verfügt nicht in gleicher Weise wie Xanten über ein sich in bedeutenden Bauwerken manifestierendes historisches Erbe. Dennoch überflügelte Goch als lokaler und zentraler Ort unter zunächst geldrischer, später klevischer und brandenburgischer Herrschaft spätestens im 18. Jahrhundert die berühmtere südöstliche Nachbarstadt an Einwohnern. Eine erste wirtschaftliche Blüte der Stadt, deren einstmals ummauertes halbmondförmiges Zentrum sich südwestlich der Niers erstreckte und im Mittelgrund der Schrägluftbildaufnahme noch sehr gut erkennbar ist, brachte die Entwicklung des Textilgewerbes, besonders der Woll- und Leinenweberei, mit sich. Nach dem Niedergang dieser mittelalterlichen und frühneuzeitlichen Gewerbezweige folgte erst im 19. Jahrhundert, besonders nach dem Anschluß an das Eisenbahnnetz im Jahre 1863, ein erneuter Aufschwung. Auch die Gewerbebetriebe dieser Zeit, mit dem Bereich der ehemaligen Stadtbefestigungen und zum anderen der nördlichen Stadterweiterung in Nähe der Bahnlinie nach Kleve (Bildhintergrund rechts) als wichtigsten Standorten zeigten die enge Verbindung der Stadt mit ihrem agrarischen Hinterland: Neben Getreide- und Ölmühlen, Plüschweberei, Leder- und Schuhfabrikation sowie einer Pinselfabrik wiesen lediglich die Tabakindustrie und die bedeutenden Margarinewerke auf überlokale wirtschaftliche Verflechtungen, insbesondere mit den Niederlanden, hin. Auch heute noch bestimmen keineswegs Wachstumsbranchen die gewerbliche Struktur Gochs, so daß das Angebot an nichtlandwirtschaftlichen Arbeitsplätzen in jüngster Zeit sogar leicht zurückgegangen ist (vgl. WEISSE et.al.1972, S. 67 ff.). Zum Zeitpunkt der letzten Volks- und Arbeitsstättenzählung übertraf die Zahl der erwerbstätigen Einwohner diejenigen der zur Verfügung stehenden Arbeitsplätze erheblich, so daß ein negativer Pendlersaldo von 1.248 Personen entstand.

Trotz dieses unzureichenden Arbeitsplatzangebotes weist die Stadt Goch auch in den 70er Jahren noch ein Bevölkerungswachstum auf, das nur anfänglich primär auf Geburtenüberschüsse, ab Mitte der Dekade jedoch ausschließlich auf Wanderungsgewinne zurückzuführen ist.

An dieser Stelle kann nicht im einzelnen auf Struktur und Entwicklung der

Bild 10: Goch: Schrägluftaufnahme von Süden mit dem Stadtkern im Bildmittelgrund und dem Industriebereich an der Ausfallstraße nach Kleve im Bildhintergrund recht. Freigegeben durch den Reg. Präsidenten Düsseldorf Nr. 20 B 96.

Migration im Bereich der Stadt Goch eingegangen werden (vgl. hierzu AYMANS und ENZEL, 1980). Es erscheint jedoch bemerkenswert, daß einige der 1969 eingemeindeten ländlichen Vororte Gochs, bezogen auf das gesamte Wanderungsvolumen, erheblich kräftigere Außenwanderungsgewinne verzeichnen als die Kernstadt und daß auch bei der Binnenwanderung (Umzüge innerhalb der Gemeinde) einige Vororte günstigere Wanderungssalden aufweisen als das Zentrum (ebenda, S. 76).

Bei einem Blick auf die Alters- und Haushaltsstruktur der Wandernden zeigt sich sehr deutlich die selektive Wirkung der Migration: Während die Kernstadt Goch Wanderungsgewinne vor allem bei jüngeren Erwerbstätigen (Altersgruppe 15-24 Jahre) und ältere Personen (über 45-jährige) aufweist, sind es, komplementär hierzu, die Kinder bis 14 Jahre sowie die 25- bis 44-jährigen, die in die Vororte, beispielsweise den während der Exkursion besuchten Ort Kessel, ziehen. Eine Erklärung dieses Sachverhaltes ist mit Hilfe des sogenannten Lebenszyklusmodells möglich, das bekanntlich davon ausgeht, daß junge Familien aufgrund ihrer Ansprüche an Wohnung und Wohnumfeld zu einem Umzug an den Stadtrand oder sogar ins ländliche Umland tendieren, während junge Einpersonenhaushalte sowie ein Teil der schrumpfenden Haushalte ihren Wohnstandort eher in der Innenstadt oder im innenstadtnahen Bereich suchen. Die charakteristische Randwanderung wachsender oder stagnierender Haushalte führt zu erheblichen Veränderungen der Siedlungs-, Wirtschafts- und Sozialstruktur in den Zuzugsgemeinden, so z.B. im Wohnplatz Kessel, 6 km nordwestlich von Goch gelegen, an dessen Ortseingang ein beachtliches Neubauviertel mit überwiegender Einfamilienhaus-Bebauung entstanden ist und sich offenbar weiter ausdehnt. Der bis in die 60er Jahre ländlich-agrarisch geprägte Ort hat seinen Charakter nicht zuletzt durch den Zuzug zahlreicher, vor allem junger Familien, besonders aus Goch und Kleve, erheblich verändert. Die neu Zugezogenen behalten durchweg ihren Arbeitsplatz in der Stadt bei, so daß Kessel nicht nur politisch-administrativ ein Ortsteil von Goch geworden ist, sondern auch durch den Prozeß der Wohnvorortbildung funktional eng mit Goch und abgeschwächt mit Kleve verflochten ist.

Zusammenschau

Der Raum am linken Niederrhein galt lange Zeit als eine Region, die gegenüber den benachbarten Verdichtungsräumen an Rhein und Ruhr einen beträchtlichen Entwicklungsrückstand aufwies. In der Tat bleiben die meisten ökonomischen Kennziffern, so z.B. Industriebesatz, Arbeitsplatzangebot, Einkommensniveau, Versorgung mit infrastrukturellen Einrichtungen sowie — als klassischer Indikator der wirtschaftlichen Entwicklung — das Bruttoinlandsprodukt pro Kopf der Bevölkerung mehr oder minder deutlich hinter den Vergleichswerten der Nachbarregionen zurück, wenn auch bezeichnenderweise der Niederrhein nie zu den Notstandsgebieten, Bundesausbaugebieten und Gebieten regionaler Aktionsprogramme der 50er, 60er und frühen 70er Jahre gehörte[2]. Andererseits zählt der Kreis Kleve, sowohl was die Gesamtwanderung als auch was die Binnenwanderung angeht, mit einem positiven Saldo zu den bevorzugten Regionen der Bundesrepublik (vgl. Raumordnungsbericht 1978, S. 119 ff.). Offensichtlich sind diese Wanderungsströme, die zweifellos als wichtiger Indikator für subjektiv empfundene Lebensqualität anzusehen sind, nicht arbeits- sondern wohnorientiert. Dies macht bereits deutlich, daß zur Einschätzung des Begriffs "Lebensqualität", so diffus und schwer operationalisierbar dieser auch sein mag, ökonomische Variable allein keinesfalls ausreichen, sondern vor allem um soziale und ökologische Dimensionen erweitert werden müssen (vgl. z.B. OECD 1976, S. 21 ff.).

Welche Konsequenzen sind hieraus für eine sinnvolle regionale Strukturpolitik zu ziehen? Die wichtigsten alternativen Raumordnungskonzepte — ausgeglichene Funktionsräume bzw. großräumige Vorranggebiete (vgl. ERNST und THOSS 1977, HÜBLER et.al. 1980) — können in ihrer idealtypischen Fassung keine Lösung bieten. Bei der Realisierung des Leitbildes großräumiger Vorranggebiete wären die ländlichen Gebiete — und dazu zählen weite Teile der Region linker Niederrhein — im wesentlichen als Agrar- und Erholungsräume anzusehen und hätten eine Art ökologischer Ausgleichsfunktion zu erfüllen, eine industrielle und infrastrukturelle Förderung würde sich erübrigen. Etwas überspitzt formuliert ergäbe sich aus dieser These, daß derartige Regionen weniger einen Wert für sich selbst, sondern lediglich als Ergänzungsgebiet der Verdichtungsräume hätten. Diese Auffassung widerspricht zum einen jeder seriösen Interpretation des Raumordnungsgrundsatzes der Herstellung gleichwertiger Lebensbedingungen. Zum anderen wird nicht genügend beachtet, daß die Teildimensionen der Lebensqualität nicht substituierbar sind, sich also beispielsweise eine hohe Arbeitslosenquote nicht gegen eine überdurchschnittlich gute Umweltqualität aufrechnen läßt.

Auch eine starre Anwendung des Konzeptes der ausgeglichenen Funktionsräume erscheint wenig überzeugend, denn weder eine Angleichung der ländlichen Region des linken Niederrheins an die Verhältnisse der benachbarten Ballungsgebiete noch die Orientierung an einem imaginären Bundesdurchschnitt kann ein erstrebenswertes Planungsziel sein. Erforderlich ist vielmehr eine regional differenzierte Raumordnungspolitik, die im Falle des Niederrheins sowohl das agrarische Potential bewahrt und fördert sowie die Erschließung geeigneter Standorte für die verschiedenen Arten der Freizeitnutzung betreibt, aber auch die im Raum vorhandenen Wachstumskräfte des gewerblichen Bereichs nutzt. Ein Bestand an qualifizierten Arbeitskräften, geringe Fluktuation der Belegschaft oder die Möglichkeit flexibler Anpassung kleinerer Betriebe an gewandelte Nachfragestruktur (vgl. DEITERS 1980, S. 58) — all dies sind Argumente dafür, daß auch eine den jeweiligen regionalen Gegebenheiten angepaßte Politik der Industrialisierung nicht ohne Chance ist.

Anmerkungen

1) Der Bundesminister des Inneren: Raumordnungsbericht 1972 der Bundesregierung. Bonn 1973, S. 69. Dieser Quelle zufolge sind am 1.9.1972 neben dem nördlichen Teil der Unteren Niederrheinlande nur große Teile Bayerns und einige Gebiete in Baden-Württemberg ohne bereits rechtswirksame bzw. in der Aufstellung oder Ausarbeitung befindliche Programme und Pläne gewesen.

2) Erst in jüngster Zeit — und wohl nicht zuletzt aufgrund der räumlichen Zusammenfassung mit dem westlichen Ruhrgebiet — taucht das Niederrheingebiet als ein "Schwerpunktraum mit Schwächen der Erwerbsstruktur" unter den Gebietseinheiten des Bundesraumordnungsprogramms auf (Raumordnungsbericht 1978, S. 77).

Literatur

AYMANS, G. und E. ENZEL: Bevölkerungswanderungen am unteren Niederrhein — Die Stadt Goch in den Jahren 1970-78 als Beispiel. In: Niederrheinische Studien. Hrsg.: Gerhard AYMANS, Bonn 1980, S. 73-89. (= Arbeiten zur Rheinischen Landeskunde, Heft 46).

DEITERS, J.: Industrialisierung ländlicher Räume gescheitert? In: Geographie heute, Bd. 1/1980, S. 57-58.

Der Bundesminister des Inneren: Raumordnungsbericht 1972 der Bundesregierung. Bonn 1973.

Bundesminister für Raumordnung, Bauwesen und Städtebau (Hrsg.): Raumordnungsbericht 1978 und Materialien. Schr.reihe "Raumordnung" des Bundesmin. f. Raumordn., Bauw. und Städtebau, Nr. 06.040. Bonn 1979

ERNST, W. und R. THOSS (Hrsg.): Beiträge zum Konzept der ausgeglichenen Funktionsräume. Mater. z. Siedl.- und Wohn.wesen und z. Raumpl., Bd. 15, 1977.

Gruppe Hardtberg: Kreisentwicklungsplan Kleve. Bonn 1973.

HÜBLER, K.-H. et al.: Zur Problematik der Herstellung gleichwertiger Lebensverhältnisse. Abh. d. Akad. f. Raumf. und Landesplanung, Bd. 80, 1980.

KNOPP, G.: Entstehung, Entwicklung und Sozialstrukturen. In: Xanten, Europäische Beispielstadt. Hrsg.: Landeskonservator Rheinland. Köln 1975. S. 32-34.

MOELLE, P.: Landesentwicklung — Nordrhein-Westfalen — Programm. In: Xanten, Europäische Beispielstadt. Hrsg.: Landeskonservator Rheinland. Köln 1975. S. 37-38.

OECD (Hrsg.): Measuring Social Well-Being. A Progress Report on the Development of Social Indicators. Paris 1976.

TRAUTEN, H.: Entwicklungsplanung. In: Xanten, Europäische Beispielstadt. Hrsg.: Landeskonservator Rheinland. Köln 1975. S. 38-39.

WEISSE, R.D. et al. (Bearb.): Stadt Goch. Stadtentwicklungsplan und Flächennutzungsplan. Teil 2. Berlin 1972.